PRAISE FOR BEST PRACTICES IN TALENT MANAGEMENT

"Many times when one reads about best practices from other organizations, the writing misses a critical and necessary foundation required for the content to be meaningful and relevant. In this book, Carter and Goldsmith bring a valuable contribution and that is to ask their readers to step back and consider their own context first and then determine how any of these outstanding talent management actions can make a difference in their particular organization. By culling for the principles behind the choices made, the stories revealed in these outstanding cases, the reader gains insight and practical advice."

-Teresa Roche, vice president and chief learning officer
Agilent Technologies

"This century, talent management will contribute to shareholder value creation more than any other organizational discipline. However, it remains an elusive concept. This book brings value to any CEO or HR leader by providing specific examples of effective talent management."

-Geoff Smart, CEO of ghSMART, and co-author of the
New York Times bestseller *Who: The A Method for Hiring.*

"Good story-telling is part art and part science. Louis Carter knows that and he shows this knowledge by his ability to gather an array of critical stories about organizations who have heeded the wake-up call to take action in the critical arena of talent management. My hat is off to the Best Practice Institute—this book lives up to its name!"

-Beverly Kaye, Founder/CEO: Career Systems International,
co-author, *Love 'Em or Lose 'Em: Getting Good People to Stay*

"As a long-standing business philosopher, I look for depth, foundations, root causes, and lasting answers; for that, facts, information, experiences and testing—and a solid data base—are essential. The compendium I needed I found here—and so will you!"

-Peter Koestenbaum

About This Book

The purpose of this best practices handbook is to provide you with the most current and necessary elements and practical "how-to" advice on how to implement a best practice talent management program within your organization. The handbook was created to provide you with a current 21st century snapshot of the world of talent management today. It serves as a learning ground for organization and social systems of all sizes and types to begin attracting, retaining, and motivating top talent through more employee- and customer-centered programs that emphasize consensus building; self-, group, organizational, and one-on-one awareness and effective communication; clear connections to overall business objectives; and quantifiable business results. Contributing organizations in this book are widely recognized as among the best in organization change and leadership development today. They provide invaluable lessons in succeeding during crisis or growth modes and economies. As best practice organizational champions, they share many similar attributes, including openness to learning and collaboration, humility, innovation and creativity, integrity, a high regard for people's needs and perspectives, and a passion for change. Most of all, these are the organizations that have invested in human capital, the most important asset inside of organizations today. And these are the organizations that have spent on average $1M on talent management, an average of $2M over the course of their programs, with an average rate of return on investment of over $5M.

Within the forthcoming chapters, you will learn from our world's best organizations in various industries and sizes:

> Key elements of leading successful, results-driven talent management;
> Tools, models, instruments, and strategies for leading talent management;
> Practical "how-to" approaches to diagnosing, assessing, designing, implementing, coaching, following-up on, and evaluating talent management; and
> Critical Success Factors *and* Critical Failure Factors, among others.

Within each case study in this book, you will learn how to:

1. Analyze the need for the specific talent management program;
2. Build a business case for talent management;
3. Identify the audience for the program;
4. Design the program;
5. Implement the design for the program; and
6. Evaluate the effectiveness of the program.

BEST PRACTICES IN TALENT MANAGEMENT

How the World's Leading Corporations Manage, Develop, and Retain Top Talent

MARSHALL GOLDSMITH AND LOUIS CARTER, EDITORS

Pfeiffer
A Wiley Imprint
www.pfeiffer.com

BPI
BEST PRACTICE INSTITUTE

Published by Pfeiffer
An Imprint of Wiley
989 Market Street, San Francisco, CA 94103-1741
www.Pfeiffer.com

Limit of Liability/Disclaimer of Warranty: While the publisher and author have used their best efforts in preparing this book, they make no representations or warranties with respect to the accuracy or completeness of the contents of this book and specifically disclaim any implied warranties of merchantability or fitness for a particular purpose. No warranty may be created or extended by sales representatives or written sales materials. The advice and strategies contained herein may not be suitable for your situation. You should consult with a professional where appropriate. Neither the publisher nor author shall be liable for any loss of profit or any other commercial damages, including but not limited to special, incidental, consequential, or other damages.

Readers should be aware that Internet websites offered as citations and/or sources for further information may have changed or disappeared between the time this was written and when it is read.

For additional copies/bulk purchases of this book in the U.S. please contact 800-274-4434.

Pfeiffer books and products are available through most bookstores. To contact Pfeiffer directly call our Customer Care Department within the U.S. at 800-274-4434, outside the U.S. at 317-572-3985, or fax 317-572-4002, or visit www.pfeiffer.com.

Pfeiffer also publishes its books in a variety of electronic formats. Some content that appears in print may not be available in electronic books.

Library of Congress Cataloging-in-Publication Data
    Best practices in talent management: how the world's leading corporations manage, develop, and retain top talent / Marshall Goldsmith and Louis Carter, editors.
        p.   cm.
    Includes bibliographical references and index.
    ISBN 978-0-470-49961-0 (cloth)
        1.   Executives—Training of.   2. Executive ability.   3. Leadership.   4. Employee retention.   I. Goldsmith, Marshall.   II. Carter, Louis.
    HD30.4.B483 2010
    658.4'07124—dc22
                                                                                2009036634

Acquiring Editor: Matthew Davis   Director of Development: Kathleen Dolan Davies
Production Editor: Dawn Kilgore   Editor: Rebecca Taff
Editorial Assistant: Lindsay Morton   Manufacturing Supervisor: Becky Morgan

Printed in the United States of America   *Printing*   10 9 8 7 6 5 4 3 2

For Crissy

CONTENTS

INTRODUCTION

LOUIS CARTER

The assets of an enterprise can perhaps be divided into two parts: its people, and everything else. While some may measure the value of a company by its real estate, sales, inventories, supply chains, accounts receivable, brand recognition, and the thousands of other pieces that when assembled create an organization's physical and market presence, it may also be said quite simply that a company consists of the human beings who use technology to improve the lives of their fellow citizens.

A dictionary definition of "talent" is people who possess a special aptitude or faculty. There is in this definition the whiff of creativity, of thinking outside the box, of a unique ability to solve a problem. Today's intensely competitive marketplace tolerates no automatons or robotic time-card-punchers who dutifully perform the same task year after year and hope to retire with a gold watch. Companies large and small—both the mom-and-pop corner store and the global Fortune 500 leviathan—must be nimble, creative, and ready to abandon the old reliable methods when challenged by new paradigms. The performance of a task by rote inevitably leads to decline and irrelevance; talent is what infuses the human experience with dynamism and creativity.

In recognition of the importance of human assets to an enterprise, a subject now given stark new importance with the global economic crisis that began in 2008, The Best Practice Institute surveyed a range of enterprises in order to identify leaders in human resource management, and specifically those that had initiated transformative efforts to strengthen organizational leadership. We looked for organizations that had responded to either external or internal challenges—or a combination of both—and successfully created programs that brought out the very best in their existing talent, and helped to recruit and train new talent from outside.

For this book, The Best Practice Institute carefully selected fourteen dynamic enterprises that have succeeded in implementing talent enhancement programs—although to be fair, to call them "programs" is not entirely accurate, as they are in reality vital strategic components integrated into the companies' core operating values. For what we found was that, to be effective, change must happen in the very guts and muscles and bones of a corporate body, and not be a mere cosmetic applied to the visible exterior. The enterprises presented here responded to inevitable evolutionary forces with carefully considered and emphatically administered strategies that not only made a difference to the short-term success of the company but provided a compass setting in the direction of future growth and vigorous health. Indeed, it can be said that a crisis—even such as we are experiencing in the close of the first decade of the 21st century—provides an opportunity for the type of reinvention, renewal, and revolutionary progress that is not likely to be undertaken during more comfortable, less interesting times.

The enterprises we surveyed represent a wide spectrum of industries. They include financial giants in banking and government revenue collection and global leaders in fast food, marketing communications, technology, industrial construction, insurance, and consumer products. Every case was unique, and every solution grew out of each company's strategy for growth. And while it is understood that solutions devised by one company cannot be grafted onto another, it is expected that the diagnostic processes and values embraced by these fourteen success stories may prove to be an inspiration and guide for any enterprise seeking to strengthen its most valuable asset—its talent.

THE ENTERPRISES

In this book we present fourteen organizations that, for a variety of reasons, embarked on a program of self-examination and renewal that focused on enhancing the value of their talent. The companies are varied—indeed, one is a U.S. government agency and one is a not-for-profit health plan—and each was faced with a unique set of circumstances that made change necessary. Each made the evolutionary step and, like the caterpillar that metamorphoses into a butterfly, emerged with the same DNA but somehow permanently altered and more able to thrive in a harsh environment. The fourteen companies are listed in Table I.1.

Avon Products, Inc., is a $10 billion consumer products company that for over one hundred years has promoted the economic empowerment of women around the globe. Bank of America is one of the world's largest financial institutions, serving individual consumers, small and middle market businesses, and large corporations with a full range of banking, investing, asset management, and other financial and risk-management products and services. The company serves more than fifty-nine million consumer and small business relationships in 150 countries.

Drawing on more than 150 years of innovation, Corning is a world leader in specialty glass and ceramics, creating and manufacturing sophisticated components that enable high-technology systems. Ecolab, with more than $6 billion in sales, is a global leader in cleaning, sanitizing, food safety, and infection control products and services. General Electric (GE) is a global infrastructure, finance, and media company producing a wide range of products from everyday light bulbs to fuel cell technology, to cleaner, more efficient jet engines. The subject of our survey is GE Money Americas, the consumer finance brand for GE Consumer Finance worldwide, with more than $163 billion in assets.

TABLE I.1. List of Best Practice Corporations in Talent Management

Company or Division	Industry	Total Employees	Parent Company Revenues ($US)
Avon	Consumer goods	42,000	$10 billion
Bank of America	Banking	243,000	$119 billion*
CES Division	Insurance	38,000	$36 billion
Corning Incorporated	Technology	27,000	$5.95 billion
Ecolab	Industrial products	26,050	$6.14 billion
GE Money Americas	Consumer finance	323,000	$182.52 billion
Internal Revenue Service	U.S. government agency	79,000	$2.7 trillion
Kaiser Permanente Colorado	Health plan	5,400**	$1.9 billion**
McDonald's	Food service	400,000	$23.52 billion
Microsoft SMSG	Software	91,000	$60.42 billion
Murray & Roberts	Construction	33,466	$18.2 billion
Porter Novelli	Marketing communications	70,000	$12.6 billion
Southern Company	Electric utility	26,742	$15.35 billion
Whirlpool	Consumer goods	70,000	$18.91 billion

*2007
**Colorado only

The Internal Revenue Service was established in 1862 by President Abraham Lincoln and helps Americans "understand and meet their tax responsibilities." The IRS has 79,000 full-time employees and in 2007 received $2.7 trillion in tax receipts. Our Fortune 100 insurance company includes our subject, the Customer and Enterprise Services division (CES), which encompasses accounting, call centers, inspections, and even one of the country's largest printing shops.

Founded in 1945, Kaiser Permanente is the nation's largest not-for-profit health plan, serving 8.6 million members, with headquarters in Oakland, California. In this book we focus on Kaiser Permanente Colorado, which has more than 5,400 employees and 2006 revenues of \$1.9 billion. McDonald's operates or franchises more than 30,000 restaurants in 119 countries, and directly employs 47,500 people with a total of 400,000, including franchisees. Microsoft is the worldwide leader in software, services, and solutions that help people and businesses realize their full potential; the Sales Marketing and Services Group (SMSG) employs more than 45,000 people and is responsible for Microsoft sales, marketing, and service initiatives; customer and partner programs; and product support and consulting services worldwide.

South Africa's leading engineering, contracting, and construction services company, Murray & Roberts, has 34,000 employees across five continents. Porter Novelli, a wholly owned subsidiary of Omnicom Group Incorporated, is one of the world's top ten public relations companies with offices in fifty-four countries.

With nearly 4.4 million customers and more than 42,000 megawatts of generating capacity, Atlanta-based Southern Company is the premier energy company serving the Southeast. Whirlpool Corporation is a leader of the \$100 billion global home appliance industry. With a presence in nearly every country around the world, Whirlpool manufactures appliances across all major categories, including fabric care, cooking, refrigeration, dishwashers, countertop appliances, garage organization, and water filtration.

THE BEST PRACTICE INSTITUTE SIX-PHASE SYSTEM TO TALENT MANAGEMENT

As the result of years of research and first-hand involvement with hundreds of top companies, The Best Practice Institute has developed a six-phase system to talent management that brings together lessons and strategies from the most successful case studies:

1. Business diagnosis

2. Assessment

3. Program design

4. Implementation

5. On-the-job support

6. Evaluation

Phase One: Business Diagnosis—The Catalysts for Change

During periods of smooth sailing—growing markets, new products, rising revenues—it is not unusual for companies to take their talent for granted. The human resources office may be unconcerned about turnover and employee satisfaction. The CEO may cast a satisfied eye on his or her realm and pronounce it good. The board may assume that management has everything under control. Golf is played on Mondays.

But sooner or later the system breaks down, is inadequate for growth, or is threatened by an external force. The metrics and practices that were acceptable suddenly look flawed. Profits slump. Employee turnover soars. Markets constrict. Board members start attending meetings.

The fourteen organizations presented here were each faced with a moment of reckoning: at a point in their development when it became clear that painful change was necessary. Each of them turned attention to the question of talent management, and each followed a process of diagnosis, assessment, program design, implementation, on-the-job support, and evaluation. Each was able to transform its talent management and make the company healthier, more competitive, and better able to fulfill its mission. And in every case, the process began with a rigorous, unflinching diagnosis.

Internal Realignment Some of our case studies responded to the perception that the organization itself had become lethargic or was following inappropriate strategies. John Bader, vice president of the Insurance CES division, sensed a qualitative problem with the system's six thousand employees at fourteen locations around the world. Managers were locked into a 19th-century mindset: people were managed like commodities; innovation was nonexistent; growth was stagnant. The customer was someone to be tolerated, not thrilled.

It is a corporate axiom that when hiring executive talent, 60 percent should be promoted from within the organization, and 40 percent on-boarded from outside. This ratio provides a mix of institutional loyalty and experience and new approaches and viewpoints. At Kaiser Permanente, the National Organization realized that 65 percent of its executives were recruited externally, indicating that the organization was not focusing on leadership succession management and that it needed to build an internal pipeline of leaders.

The opposite situation existed at Southern Company. The electric utility, with over 26,000 employees, had traditionally followed a strategy of hiring at the entry level and promoting from within. In 2003, the average age of its executives was fifty-two—and at Southern Company, employees are eligible to retire at age fifty. The company faced a shortage of executives as the retirement wave approached, and embarked on a study to determine how to most effectively produce a sustainable supply of quality leaders.

Capacity Matches Growth At Avon, Inc., CEO Andrea Jung faced a different problem: the company's growth had outpaced organizational capacity. In 2005 the company had achieved a 10 percent annual growth rate and operated in more than forty countries worldwide. But as Avon entered 2006, revenues flattened and operating profits declined. Jung and her team realized that, in order to move forward, the company had to be restructured. After reviewing the company's talent practices, the Talent Management Group identified weaknesses including opacity, excessive complexity, a lack of quantitative measurements, and inconsistency.

Over the past decade, Bank of America has achieved spectacular growth both organically and through acquisitions. As a result, the company must annually recruit and hire and train a significant number of executives. Typically, industry figures suggest that 40 percent of senior managers hired from the outside fail within their first eighteen months on the job (Watkins, 2003). This rate was unacceptable to Bank of America, and the leadership development group needed to quickly and effectively devise strategies to on-board executive leaders from acquired banks.

At Whirlpool, the growth, size, and scale of the company, along with a more demanding consumer marketplace and competition for talent, prompted the company to build a defined set of leadership competencies and put into place an effective talent management system.

In 2001, Ecolab's executive team committed to an aggressive growth goal—they intended to increase revenues at a 15 percent annual growth rate for five years, and by 2007 more than double the company's size. However, they recognized that they did not have the number of qualified leaders required to effectively run an organization twice its current size. The lack of leadership talent and bench strength was identified as a primary constraint to its success.

Building Talent Resources for the Future Corning bases its long-term success on its ability to nurture and grow both talent and technology over the long term—twenty-five and even fifty years. In today's competitive environment, CEO Jamie Houghton realized that the company had to step up the pace of innovation, moving from a target of one to two breakthroughs per decade to two to four breakthroughs.

The Internal Revenue Service has a bigger boss than most other companies: the U.S. Congress. With the passing of the Revenue Reform Act of 1998, the IRS underwent a restructuring and modernization that left it with a shortage of qualified employees. In 2001 Commissioner Charles Rossotti directed a review of IRS leadership competencies, and in 2008 Commissioner Douglas Schulman created the "Workforce of Tomorrow" task force to prepare the IRS for the next fifteen years.

Beginning in 2004, leading global marketing communications company Porter Novelli undertook a fundamental strategic assessment to position itself for growth during the next five years. The senior management group identified the need to restructure human resources management to reflect the company's client-centric focus and encourage employee engagement with the company's vision.

Creating Consistent Internal Systems With more than 45,000 employees, Microsoft's SMSG division had a high-potential development program in each of its thirteen geographical areas. The programs were not aligned to Microsoft's Leadership Career Model and there were no consistent criteria for defining high-potentials, making lateral movement difficult.

Similarly, at Murray & Roberts, with operations spread over Southern Africa, the Middle East, Southeast Asia, Australasia, and North America, talent management processes and practices were not formalized or even were nonexistent. There was no codified succession plan or centralized talent inventory.

At McDonald's, systems existed for evaluating manager performance, but there was no control over validity. Management discovered there was chronic rating inflation for both annual performance (amazingly, 98 percent of managers were rated either "Outstanding" or "Excellent") and potential (78 percent of managers were rated as having the potential to advance in the business at least one level), rendering the system useless and creating a false sense of entitlement.

Toward an Efficient Hiring System Sometimes the process of on-boarding is inefficient and expensive. At GE Money Americas, recruiters realized that the high volume of job applicants was not being managed efficiently: there were too few outlets for applicants to apply, narrow reporting capabilities, unclear processes, the cost per hire was an unacceptable $8,000 each, and the time to fill a position often exceeded three months.

Phase Two: Assessment

The fourteen companies in this book were faced with a wide variety of challenges, both internal and external, and the assessment strategies were unique to each enterprise. Different groups—the CEO, human resources, a task force—took the lead in driving change. In some organizations the focus on change was narrow and involved a select group of potential high-performers; at other organizations the determination was made that the effort had to be company-wide.

It must be pointed out that there is a difference between *evaluating* talent—seeing which employees show up on time and do their jobs and hit their numbers—and *investing* in talent, which requires a much more proactive effort to identify, train, and prepare talent for the future.

Not everyone can be a leader; that's just a fact of life. But surely every person who draws a salary or punches a time card at a company needs to be committed and inspired and empowered to be creative. The kid who gets his first job in the mailroom could work his or her way up the ladder to be CEO—it has happened before and it will happen again. In an ideal world, every employee would receive training appropriate to his or her aspirations and capabilities.

Our fourteen enterprises, having made the decision to evaluate and/or invest in talent, took varied approaches to the scope of the process and the number of participants.

At one end of the spectrum, the Insurance CES's John Bader initially included the division's core leadership team (CLT) in the first "wave" of leadership alignment sessions. The results were so positive that the CLT committed to transforming the entire system—all six thousand employees in fourteen locations around the world. They created a series of waves that included 1,200 employees in groups of three hundred to five hundred, and then a massive one-day event with everyone else.

At the Internal Revenue Service, the Workforce of Tomorrow (WoT) Task Force was charged with restructuring human resource policies and practices that would affect the entire 79,000-member workforce. Murray & Roberts's Leadership Pipeline was created to be accessible to any manager in the company, as were the pipelines at Porter Novelli, Whirlpool, and Southern Company, where succession plans for the top sixty-five positions across the company were formulated.

Ecolab, which also adopted the Leadership Pipeline philosophy, presented an initial launch at an annual meeting where approximately 1,100 key leaders in the company were introduced to the Talent Pipeline in small-group, face-to-face meetings. McDonald's five-part initiative reaches every staff position, with additional investments for executives.

Bank of America's on-boarding program was primarily focused on executives who came to the company from outside, and in the past seven years has tested its approaches on five hundred internal and external hires.

Many companies, however, chose to invest only in identified potential leaders. At Avon, a key plank in the company's approach was to place a few "big bets" on a small number of leaders. With limited funds to spend, Avon followed research that suggested the top 5 to 10 percent of a workforce population was capable of advanced leadership. The company's investment in its highest potential leaders was five to ten times what could be invested in an average performer. The investment included training, coaching, and incentive compensation.

Perhaps because they were seeking program managers with highly specialized technical skills, Corning's two-week Leadership Fundamentals for Program Managers program involved thirty-three incumbent participants. Similarly, Kaiser Permanente, which focused its talent development efforts on building an in internal pipeline to reduce the number of external hires, identified approximately fifty-five incumbents in its first review process. Microsoft's SMSG division targeted less than 4 percent of its population—still, more than 1,600 individuals—for its ExPo Leaders Building Leaders program. At Hewlett-Packard, the executive development process is aimed at understanding the quality, strengths and development needs of the talent at the vice presidential level worldwide.

Phase Three: Program Design

Once the problem was identified and scope of the solution determined, the next step for our fourteen companies was to design the program. In some cases, the solution involved a specific program limited to a set number of individuals; in other cases the transformation was company-wide and affected everyone who drew a salary. In most cases the CEO was personally invested, giving the program the authority of the highest office and energizing the executive layers below. Some efforts were designed and executed wholly in-house, while in other cases outside consultants were brought in to either provide an objective viewpoint or supply specialized expertise. The choice made by our fourteen companies to create a comprehensive plan is in alignment with the results of the Best Practice Institute's recent Talent Management Survey, in which we surveyed forty-five leading companies and found that well over half (60 percent) had a formal talent management plan in place.

Here are a few highlights of the fourteen companies' program designs:

Avon Products

- CEO Andrea Jung and the Talent Management Group (TM) built their talent practices on two guiding principles: execute on the "what" and differentiate on the "how."

- Moved from a regional to a matrix structure; cut management layers; made a significant investment in management talent.

Bank of America

- CEO Ken Lewis personally spearheaded BOA's executive development strategy.

- Created a New Executive Orientation Program with coaching and support.

Corning

- Created a boot camp immersion experience for potential program managers.

- The Corning Management Committee chartered a task team to design a pipeline for program leaders.

Ecolab

- Human Resources formulated key areas and ways through which Ecolab would establish and maintain its competitive advantage—the five key business drivers. These included Talent Development, Leadership, Relationships, Innovation, and Delivering Results.

- HR established the Ecolab Talent Council, composed of the ten most senior Ecolab executives including the CEO, and representing all key business lines, geographies, and critical functions.

GE Money Americas

- With the assistance of a human resources consultant, created a centralized staffing process and a dedicated team.

- Applied the Lean approach to the staffing process to create efficiencies and cut costs.

Insurance CES Division

- Hired consultants to review CES's structure and finances and another set of consultants to perform an assessment survey.

- Got the ball rolling with a no-holds-barred leadership conference.

Internal Revenue Service

- Developed a competency model with twenty-one leadership competencies.

- In collaboration with a consultant, developed the Leadership Succession Review (LSR).

Kaiser Permanente Colorado

- Restructured in collaboration with the Kaiser Permanente National Organization.

- Designed a series of programs including the Peer Network, Leadership Edge, Experience Management, and Executive Coaching.

McDonald's

- Top management asked Human Resources to redesign the performance development system in order to place a stronger focus on accountability for results, increase performance differentiation, and enhance openness to change and innovation.

Microsoft SMSG

- Formed a new program, ExPo Leaders Building Leaders (ExPo stands for Exceptional Potential), drawing on the Corporate Leadership Council's 2005 study "Realizing the Full Potential of Rising Talent."

Murray & Roberts

- A project team was assembled consisting of line managers, HR practitioners, and a consultant. The project team reported to the executive in the Office of the Group CE.

Porter Novelli

- Hired a chief talent officer to work with the executive management group.

- Implemented a Leadership Pipeline program with results-based role definitions.

- In a series of staff interviews, Porter Novelli grappled with the question of defining leadership and management. These concepts were regarded as critically important, but participants stated that neither was well-articulated or easily measured. A client-centered strategy was a key success factor, as was creative thinking.

Southern Company

- The CEO initiated an in-depth review of the company's leadership development and succession processes.

- Chartered a group of executives as the Leadership Action Council, serving as a steering committee for leadership development.

Whirlpool

- Chairman David Whitman and the executive committee spearheaded development of the Whirlpool Leadership Model.

Who says that corporations have no loyalty to their executives? The results of the Best Practice Institute's recent Talent Management Survey found that fully 36.5 percent of corporate respondents were focused on developing talent internally; 59.7 percent were developing both internal and external talent; and only 3.8 percent were focused exclusively on acquiring external talent.

Phase Four: Implementation

The implementations reflect the goals of the respective organizations, the challenges faced, and the scope of the restructuring.

At Bank of America, which has focused on improving the quality of external hires, outside recruiters must understand the bank's culture and leadership requirements, and consequently Human Resources devotes a great deal of attention to its partnerships with executive search firms. Once a candidate is presented to the bank, interviews with the candidate are conducted by one of the bank's Leadership Development Officers (LD Partner) to assess compatibility. Stakeholders, including a leadership development officer (LD), interview candidates; but a complete picture is formed when the LD in turn interviews the interviewers. This 360-degree approach provides a sense of how well the candidate—who may have enjoyed a successful career at another banking institution—will fit into Bank of America's culture and work environment.

GE Money Americas, also concerned with the quality of outside hires, centralized and restructured the application process. The company introduced the Lean Principle, 5S, as the foundation for all improvements focused on Kaizen opportunities.

The Internal Revenue Service created the Leadership Succession Review process, which provides a highly structured and disciplined approach for each IRS Business Unit to prepare qualified leaders. Kaiser Permanente Colorado created the Executive Leadership Program, which provides participants with an opportunity to evaluate and strengthen their leadership approach and skills. Whirlpool initiated the Master Assessor Program, which trains both human resources staff and line managers with frequent hiring needs to identify and evaluate potential leaders.

At Microsoft SMSG, a foundation of the ExPo program is regular interaction between high-potentials and current leaders, in order to build the capability of future leaders and also to give senior leaders greater accountability. Executives demonstrate engagement by conducting ongoing reviews, acting as mentors and coaches, and even accompanying high-potentials on business trips. At Murray & Roberts, managers and subordinates sign a performance contract and development plan that charts a course for success.

At some companies, travel is involved. Insurance CES held a series of leadership retreats, initially with executives but expanded to include all six thousand employees. Corning created "Boot Camp for Program Managers," a two-week program held at the stately old home and newly transformed company conference center of the former CEO Jamie Houghton.

Phase Five: On-the-Job Support

Diagnosing the challenge, assessing the effort, designing the program, and implementing the program are critical steps to organizational transformation. Committed managers know, however, that the lessons learned in program participation must be carried through to the daily grind of business. They must be proven in the field and must translate into measurable results. For this next phase to succeed, companies must support their talent as they put their new confidence and insights into practice.

At Bank of America, new hires are paired with peer coaches (a fellow executive) and a senior advisor at the same level or above. To facilitate a close relationship between the new executive and his or her team, a New Leader-Team Integration session takes place within the first thirty to sixty days of an assignment.

Kaiser Permanente Colorado includes 360-degree feedback, BarOn EQ-i 360-degree feedback, Meyers-Briggs Type Indicator (MBTI), and Insights Assessment. Each potential leader is assigned a case manager who works with him or her on a personal development plan. The Leadership Edge Program has an alumni group that continues to work with the executive team on business solutions.

Follow-up remedial workshops were instituted by Porter Novelli, and in 2007 a performance management workshop focused on skills in creating SMART goals and cascading goals from manager to subordinates in a work team.

At Southern Company, job assignments, developmental moves, and special assignments are the primary methods for developing high-potential individuals. An educational experience for cross-system high-potential managers who are ready to move into officer roles is being created by Human Resources.

Phase Six: Evaluation

Within a company the need for leadership development may exist, but is there an agreed-on standard that will serve as a benchmark or threshold for promotion? Evaluating an existing manager can sometimes be as simple as measuring quarterly revenues. For some companies, a restructured talent development strategy means identifying, hiring, and retaining individuals who have executive qualities that are aligned with existing metrics: work history, project success, skill sets. But in other cases choosing potential leaders for future advancement not unlike consulting the Oracle of Delphi. How do you predict an executive's performance at a new position that is vastly more complex than the previous job? As part of the talent restructuring process, more than a few organizations went back to the drawing board to create a new definition of leadership, one that cut across the existing talent pool and reshaped the company's most fundamental talent characteristics. And, if such a definition could include methods of measurement, so much the better. Today, we can see what the results have been.

The Internal Revenue Service, perhaps not surprisingly, uses a table with numeric scores. On the Leadership Competency Targets by Leadership Level table, candidates are scored 1 through 4 in categories that include Adaptability, Customer Focus, Continual Learning, and Political Savvy. Varying target levels are designated, depending on organizational rank. An executive, for example, should score a "4" in Business Acumen, while a regular employee needs to score only a "1" in the same category. In addition, a matrix is used to rank individuals according to their readiness to assume leadership positions.

Kaiser Permanente uses a Model of Potential, a set of assessments that factors Performance, Abilities, and Predictors of Potential to provide a score of Promotability. At Kaiser, it's important that an executive candidate has the ability to be mobile, and there's a survey tool that gathers information related to a candidate's aspirations, technical skills, and proficiency at VP-level behaviors.

McDonald's initiated five programs, including a set of Talent Reviews, ensuring that the president and lead staff officer of each geographical division are responsible and accountable for addressing the leadership talent needs in their area and are doing so within the framework of the template.

Murray & Roberts adopted the Leadership Pipeline philosophy and moved away from a numeric system to a qualitative approach, which requires managers to apply a thinking model supported by evidence, as opposed to manipulating and arguing about numbers. Performance is defined through a set of symbolic circles that are filled in by lines representing performance dimensions. The more snugly the lines fit into the circle, the higher the probability of success in leadership.

How do we measure overall program success? Is there a bottom-line indicator that tells us that our investment has paid off and our talent is optimized? Many of our companies reported quantitative and qualitative measures of program success:

- At Insurance CES, the wave seminar events produced higher customer satisfaction, increased engagement by customers and employees, and millions of dollars saved over and above the cost of the program.

- Avon reported faster movement of talent into key markets and accelerated development of leaders. There was also a rise in revenue to $11 billion in 2009 from $8 billion in 2005, despite 10 percent fewer Associates.

- Since 2005, Kaiser Permanente Colorado has identified thirteen high-potential leaders, of whom 60 percent have been either promoted or given expanded roles.

- Murray & Roberts reports benefits including job clarity, identification of successors, improved feedback, and cross-company appointments.

- Porter Novelli, after instituting the Leadership Pipeline, experienced a decline in turnover of 24 percent from 2005 to 2006, and in 2006 and 2007 reported zero turnover of identified high-potential managers.

- Whirlpool Corporation's Quality of Hire Metrics indicate that that the Master Assessor Program has had a positive impact on the quality of hires, who perform at high levels and exhibit high levels of job satisfaction.

CONCLUSION

We have seen from our fourteen success stories that when an organization reaches a crossroads in talent management, a consistent and comprehensive approach can provide both a measurable benefit and assurance of long-term growth. Each solution must organically grow from the unique circumstances of a particular moment in time and set of circumstances. While each case is different, valuable lessons can be learned from these examples because together they provide a template showing how to diagnose, assess, and address the challenges that face every organization today. Their commonality lies in the dedication and imagination of the talent that drives every successful enterprise.

As we move into the post-great recession era, challenges will arise that do not have the comfort of familiarity. Solutions must be crafted with integrity, honesty, and an appreciation for the best qualities of the people who every day try to do the very best they can for themselves, their companies, and their communities.

ACKNOWLEDGMENTS

Best Practice Institute Team   *Contributors*

BPI Editorial Team

Louis Carter, CEO

Samantha Francart, Assistant

Dr. William Rothwell

    John Bader, CES Division

    Mike Schechter, CES Division

    Richard O'Leary, Corning

    Heath Topper, Corning

    Bob Barnett, Ecolabs

    Zachary Misko, General Electric

    David Krieg, Internal Revenue Service

    Margaret Turner, Kaiser Permanente

    James Intagliata, McDonald's

    Neal Kulick, McDonald's

    Shannon Wallis, Microsoft

    Brian Underhill, Microsoft

    Zelia Soares, Murray & Roberts

    Greg Waldron, Porter Novelli

    Jim Greene, Southern Company

    Kristen Weirick, Whirlpool

Marc Effron, Avon

Jay Conger, Bank of America

Brian Fishel, Bank of America

Gary Jusela, Corning

HOW TO USE THIS BOOK

PRACTICAL APPLICATION

This book contains step-by-step approaches, tools, instruments, models, and practices for implementing top talent management programs into your organization. The components of this book can be practically leveraged within your work environment to enable a top talent management initiative. The exhibits, forms, and instruments at the back of each chapter may be used within the classroom or by your organization development team and/or learners.

BENCHMARKING, APPLICATION, AND CUSTOMIZATION OF TALENT DEVELOPMENT/MANAGEMENT INTO YOUR ORGANIZATION OR CLIENT ORGANIZATION

The case studies, tools, and research within this book are ideal for managers, executives and consultants who are implementing or managing a talent program, inside of a current talent management program, or are currently seeking a job from one of the organizations in this book. Students of advanced degree courses in management, organization development and behavior, and/or social/organizational psychology should also take notice of this book, as it contains critical information that is useful for your practicum and internship work. This book can be used by any senior vice president, vice president, director, or program manager who is in charge of leadership development and change for his/her organization. Teams of managers—project manager, program managers, HR/OD designers, or other program designers and trainers—should use the case studies in this book as starting points and benchmarks for the success of the organization's initiatives.

This book contains a series of distinct case studies with various corporate needs and objectives. It is your job as the reader to begin the process of diagnosing your company's unique organizational objectives.

When applying and learning from the case studies and research in this book, ask yourself, your team, and each other the following questions:

■ What is our context today?

■ What do we/I want to accomplish? Why?

■ What am I most passionate about leading talent management in? Why?

■ What are the issue(s) and concerns we are challenged with?

- Are we asking the right questions?

- Who are the right stakeholders?

- What approaches have worked in the past before? Why?

- What approaches have failed before? Why?

For more information on Best Practice Institute's benchmark research and executive boards on the most current talent management topics, contact BPI directly on our toll free number at: (800) 718-4274 or via e-mail at: lou@bestpracticesinstitute.org. Please visit us online at https://www.bpiworld.com and https://www.bestpracticeinstitute.org.

If you would like to connect with any expert, practitioner, or author in this book, please e-mail us at lou@bestpracticeinstitute.org. All contributors/authors in this book are listed/known experts within the Best Practice Institute community.

CHAPTER

1

AVON PRODUCTS, INC.

MARC EFFRON

A leadership development and talent turnaround system designed for executives that leverage 360-degree feedback, a leadership skill/competency model, and individual development planning.

- Introduction
- A Success-Driven Challenge
- The Turnaround
- The Talent Challenge
- Execute on the "What," Differentiate with "How"
- From Opaque to Transparent
  - The Avon 360
  - Broad-Based Transparency
- From Complex to Simple
  - Performance Management
  - Engagement Survey

- From Egalitarian to Differentiated
    - Communication to Leadership Teams
    - A Few Big Bets
    - Tools and Processes
- From Episodic to Disciplined
- From Emotional to Factual
- From Meaningless to Consequential
- The Results of a Talent Turnaround
- Measuring the Talent Turnaround's Success

INTRODUCTION

In early 2006, Avon Products, Inc., a global consumer products company focused on the economic empowerment of women around the world, began the most radical restructuring process in its 120-year history. Driving this effort was the belief that Avon could sustain its historically strong financial performance while building the foundation for a larger, more globally integrated organization. The proposed changes would affect every aspect of the organization and would demand an approach to finding, building, and engaging talent that differed from anything tried before.

A SUCCESS-DRIVEN CHALLENGE

Avon Products is a 122-year-old company originally founded by David H. McConnell—a door-to-door book seller who distributed free samples of perfume as an incentive to his customers. He soon discovered that customers were more interested in samples of his rose oil perfumes than in his books and so, in 1886, he founded the California Perfume Company. Renamed Avon Products in 1939, the organization steadily grew to become a leader in the direct selling of cosmetics, fragrances, and skin care products.

By 2005, Avon was an $8 billion company that had achieved a 10 percent cumulative annual growth rate (CAGR) in revenue and a 25 percent CAGR in operating profit from 2000 through 2004. A global company, Avon operated in more than forty countries and received more than 70 percent of its earnings from outside the United States. By all typical financial metrics, Avon was a very successful company.

However, as the company entered 2006 it found itself challenged by flattening revenues and declining operating profits. While the situation had many contributing causes, one underlying issue was that Avon had grown faster than portions of its infrastructure and talent could support. As with many growing organizations, the structures, people, and processes that were right for a $5 billion company weren't necessarily a good fit for a $10 billion company.

THE TURNAROUND

Faced with these challenges, CEO Andrea Jung and her executive team launched a fundamental restructuring of the organization in January 2006. Some of the larger changes announced included:

- **Moving from a Regional to a Matrix Structure:** Geographic regions that had operated with significant latitude were now matrixed with global business functions, including Marketing and Supply Chain.

- **Delayering:** A systematic, six-month process was started to take the organization from fifteen layers of management to eight, including a compensation and benefit reduction of up to 25 percent.

- **Significant Investment in Executive Talent:** Of the CEO's fourteen direct reports, six key roles were replaced externally from 2004 to 2006, including the CFO, head of North America, head of Latin America, and the leaders of Human Resources, Marketing, and Strategy. Five of her other direct reports were in new roles.

- **New Capabilities Were Created:** A major effort to source Brand Management, Marketing Analytics, and Supply Chain capabilities was launched, which brought hundreds of new leaders into Avon.

THE TALENT CHALLENGE

As the turnaround was launched, numerous gaps existed in Avon's existing talent and in its ability to identify and produce talent. While some of those gaps were due to missing or poorly functioning talent processes, an underlying weakness seemed to lie in the overall approach to managing talent and talent practices.

After reviewing Avon's existing talent practices, the talent management group (TM) identified six overriding weaknesses that hurt their effectiveness. They found that existing talent practices were

- **Opaque:** Neither managers nor Associates knew how existing talent practices (that is, performance management, succession planning) worked or what they were intended to do. To the average employee, these processes were a black box.

- **Egalitarian:** While the Avon culture reinforced treating every Associate well, this behavior had morphed into treating every Associate in the same way. High performers weren't enjoying a fundamentally different work experience and low performers weren't being managed effectively.

- **Complex:** The performance management form was ten pages long, and the succession planning process required a full-time employee just to manage the data and assemble thick black binders of information for twice-yearly reviews.

Complexity existed without commensurate value, and the effectiveness rate of the talent practices was low.

■ **Episodic:** Employee surveys, talent reviews, development planning, and succession planning, when done at all, were done at a frequency determined by individual managers around the world.

■ **Emotional:** Decisions on talent movement, promotions, and other key talent activities were often influenced as much by individual knowledge and emotion as by objective facts.

■ **Meaningless:** No talent practice had "teeth." HR couldn't answer the most basic question a manager might ask about talent practices—"What will happen to me if I don't do this?"

EXECUTE ON THE "WHAT," DIFFERENTIATE WITH "HOW"

Our TM group found ourselves in a difficult situation. Fundamental changes were needed in every talent practice, and the practices had to be changed and implemented in time to support the turnaround. This meant that the practices had to be quick to build, easy to use, and, most of all, effective.

Taking our guidance from the *Top Companies for Leaders* study (Effron, Greenslade, & Salob, 2005) and the philosophies of executive coach Marshall Goldsmith (2006), we decided to build our talent practices with two key guiding principles.

1. **Execute on the "what."** The Top Companies for Leaders study found that simple, well-executed talent practices dominated at companies that consistently produced great earnings and great leaders. We similarly believed that fundamental talent practices (that is, performance management or succession planning) would deliver the expected results if they were consistently and flawlessly executed. We decided to build talent practices that were easy to implement and a talent management structure that would ensure they were consistently and flawlessly implemented. More importantly, we decided to . . .

2. **Differentiate on "how."** While disciplined execution could create a strong foundation for success, the six adjectives that described Avon's current processes were largely responsible for their failure. We drew inspiration from Marshall Goldsmith's revolutionary recreation of the executive coaching process. He had taken a staid, academic/therapy model for improving leaders and turned it into a simple but powerful process that was proven effective in changing leaders' behaviors.

With those two guiding principles in place, we began a 180-degree transformation of Avon's talent practices.

FROM OPAQUE TO TRANSPARENT

One of the most simple and powerful changes was to bring as much transparency as possible to every talent practice. TM designed new practices and redesigned existing ones using total transparency as the starting point. Transparency was only removed when confidentiality concerns outweighed the benefits of sharing information. The change in Avon's 360 assessment process was a telling example.

The Avon 360

Avon's 360-degree assessment process was hardly a model of transparency when the turnaround began. When the new TM leader arrived at Avon, he asked for copies of each VP's 360-degree assessment, with the goal of better understanding any common behavioral strengths and weaknesses. He was told by the 360 administrator in his group that he was not allowed to see them. The TM leader explained that his intent wasn't to take any action on an individual VP, simply to learn more about his clients. He was again told "no"—that confidentiality prevented their disclosure.

While the administrator was correct in withholding the information (the participants had been promised 100 percent confidentiality), the fact that the most critical behavioral information about top leaders was not visible to the TM leader (or anyone else) had to change. A new, much simpler 360 was designed and implemented that explicitly stated that proper managerial and leadership behaviors were critical for a leader's success at Avon. Citing that level of importance, the disclosure to all participants and respondents stated that the 360 information could be shown to the participant's manager, HR leader, regional talent leader, and anyone else the Avon's HR team decided was critical to the participant's development. It also stated that the behavioral information could be considered when making decisions about talent moves, including promotions or project assignments.

Helping to make this transition to transparency easier, the new 360 assessment and report differed from typical tools that rate the participant on proficiency in various areas. The Avon 360 borrowed heavily from the "feed-forward" principles of Marshall Goldsmith[1] and showed the participant which behaviors participants wanted to see more of, or less of, going forward. Without the potential stigma of having others seeing you rated as a "bad" manager, openly sharing 360 findings quickly evaporated as an issue.

Broad-Based Transparency

Transparency was woven into every talent process or program in a variety of ways. Examples would include:

- **Career Development Plans:** To provide Associates with more transparency about how to succeed at Avon, the HR team developed "The Deal." The Deal was a simple description of what was required to have a successful career at Avon, and what parts the Associate and Avon needed to play (see Figure 1.1). The Deal made clear

	Potential		
	24+ months 50%	1 level in 2 years 30%	2 levels in 6 years 20%
High 20%	Compensation targets: • Base 50th, Bonus 75th Development investment: • 1.5x average Hi Po Program: No Global Move: No Special Projects: Yes	Compensation targets: • Base 50th, Bonus 75th Development investment: • 2x average Hi Po Program: Consider Global Move: Yes Special Projects: Yes	Compensation targets: • Base 60th, Bonus 90th Development investment: • 5x average Hi Po Program: Yes Global Move: Yes Special Projects: Yes
Mid 60%	Compensation targets: • Base 50th, Bonus 50th Development investment: • .75x average Hi Po Program: No Global Move: No Special Projects: No	Compensation targets: • Base 50th, Bonus 50th Development investment: • Average Hi Po Program: No Global Move: Consider Special Projects: Yes	Compensation targets: • Base 60th, Bonus 60th Development investment: • 2x average Hi Po Program: Consider Global Move: Yes Special Projects: Yes
Low 20%	Compensation targets: • Base 50th, Bonus -- NONE Development investment: • None without TM approval Hi Po Program: No Global Move: No Special Projects: No	Compensation targets: • Base 50th, Bonus 40th Development investment: • Average Hi Po Program: No Global Move: No Special Projects: No	Compensation targets: • Base 50th, Bonus 40th Development investment: • Average Hi Po Program: No Global Move: No Special Projects: Consider

Performance Over Time

FIGURE 1.1. *Talent Investment Matrix*

that every Associate had to deliver results, display proper leadership behaviors, know our unique business, and take advantage of development experiences if they hoped to move forward in the organization.

■ **Development Courses:** Avon acknowledged the unspoken but obvious fact about participating in leadership or functional training courses—of course you're being observed! We believed it was important for participants to understand that we were investing in their future and that monitoring that investment was critical. The larger investment that we made, the more explicitly we made the disclosure. For our Accelerated Development Process (a two-year high-potential development process offered to the top 10 percent of VPs), we let them know that they were now "on Broadway." The lights would be hotter and the critics would be less forgiving. They knew that we would help each of them to be a great actor, but that their successes and failures would be more public and have greater consequences.

■ **Performance Reviews:** Switching from a 3-point scale to a 5-point scale provided additional clarity to participants about their actual progress, as did clarifying the scale definitions. Associates were informed about what performance

Dissertation / Culture Warrior LM —
  Develop a competing model based on CLLM
  theoretical model.?

conversations their managers should be having with them and when. The recommended distribution of ratings across the scale was widely communicated.

FROM COMPLEX TO SIMPLE

One of the most important changes made in Avon's talent practices was the radical simplification of every process. We believed that traditional talent processes would work (that is, grow better talent, faster) if they were effectively executed. However, we understood from our experience and a plethora of research (Hunter, Schmidt, & Judiesch, 1990) that most talent practices were very complex without that complexity adding any significant value. This level of complexity caused managers to avoid using those tools, and so talent wasn't grown at the pace or quality that companies required.

We committed ourselves to radically simplifying every talent process and ensuring that any complexity in those processes was balanced by an equal amount of value (as perceived by managers). Making this work was easier than we had anticipated. As the TM team designed each process, we would start literally with a blank sheet of paper and an open mind. We would set aside our hard-earned knowledge about the "right" way to design these processes and instead ask ourselves these questions:

1. What is the fundamental business benefit that this talent process is trying to achieve?

2. What is the simplest possible way to achieve that benefit?

3. Can we add value to the process that would make it easier for managers to make smarter people decisions?

Using just those three questions, it was amazing how many steps and "bells and whistles" fell away from the existing processes. The two examples below provide helpful illustration.

Performance Management

Aligning Associates with the turnaround goals of the business and ensuring they were fairly evaluated was at the foundation of the business turnaround. As we entered the turnaround, the company had a complex ten-page performance management form with understandably low participation rates. Many Associates had not had a performance review in three, four, or even five years. It would have been impossible to align Associates with the vital few turnaround goals using that tool and process.

■   **The business benefit:** We stated that the fundamental benefit of performance goals and reviews is that they aligned Associates with business goals and caused Associates to work toward those goals with the expectation of fair rewards.

■   **The simplest path:** It seemed obvious that the simplest way of achieving the business goal was simply to have managers tell their Associates what their goals were. It was simple and the value to managers outweighed any complexity. After taking that very small step forward, we literally advanced at the same pace, taking incrementally small steps forward in the design process. At each step, we would ask ourselves, does this step add more value to managers than it does complexity? As long as it did, we added the additional design element. When that complexity/value curve started to level (see Figure 1.2), we very carefully weighed adding any additional elements. And, when we couldn't justify that adding another unit of complexity would add another unit of value, we stopped.

What went away as the design process progressed? Just a few examples would include:

- Goal labels (highly valued, star performer, etc.), which added no value (in fact blurred transparency!) but did add complexity.

- Individual rating of goals, which implied a false precision in the benefit of each goal and encouraged Associates to game the system.

- Behavioral ratings, which were replaced with a focus on behaviors that would help achieve the current goals.

  The output was a one-page form with spaces for listing the goal, the metric, and the outcome. A maximum of four goals was allowed. Two behaviors that supported achievement of the current goal could be listed but were not formally rated. As a result, participation reached nearly 100 percent, and line managers actually thanked the talent team for creating a simple performance management process!

- **Adding Additional Value:** In this process, we didn't find opportunities to add more value than was achieved through simplification alone.

Working Together to Help You Create
a Great Career at Avon

	Grow Avon	Lead Avon	Know Avon	Develop Through Experiences
Your Role	Achieve Results for Our Representatives	Lead Our Associates	Understand Direct Selling	Take on Critical Career Experiences
Avon's Role	Provide Clear Performance Expectations; Let You Know Where You Stand	Provide Feedback on Your Leadership Skills	Provide Training and Exposure	Provide the Right Assignments and Experiences

FIGURE 1.2. *The Avon Deal (Example)*

Engagement Survey

When the turnaround began, no global process for understanding or acting on Associate engagement issues existed. Select regions or departments made efforts of varying effectiveness, but there was no integrated focus on consistent measurement and improvement of engagement. In designing the engagement survey process, we applied the same three questions:

■ **The business benefit:** We accepted the substantial research that showed a correlation (and some that showed causation) between increasing engagement and increasing various business metrics. In addition, we felt that the ability to measure managers' effectiveness through engagement levels and changes would provide an opportunity for driving accountability around this issue. As with performance management, we knew that managers would use this tool if we could make it simple and, ideally, if we could show that it would allow them to more effectively manage their teams.

■ **The simple path:** There were two goals established around simplicity. One goal was to understand as much of what drove engagement as possible, while asking the least number of questions. The second goal was to write the questions as simply as possible, so that if managers needed to improve the score on a question, their options for action would be relatively obvious. The final version of the survey had forty-five questions, which explained 68 percent of the variance in engagement. The questions were quite simple, which had some value in itself, but their true value was multiplied tenfold by the actions described below.

■ **Adding additional value:** We were confident that, if managers took the "right" actions to improve their engagement results, not only would the next year's scores increase, but the business would benefit from the incremental improvement. The challenge was to determine and simply communicate to the manager what the "right" actions were. Working with our external survey provider, we developed a statistical equation model (SEM) that became the "engine" to produce those answers. The SEM allowed us to understand the power of each engagement dimension (for example, Immediate Manager, Empowerment, Senior Management) to increase engagement, and to express that power in an easy-to-understand statement.

For example, we could determine that the relationship between the Immediate Manager dimension and overall engagement was 2:1. This meant that for every two percentage points a manager could increase his or her Immediate Manager dimension score, the overall engagement result would increase by one percentage point. Even better, this model allowed us to tell every manager receiving a report *the specific three or four questions that were the key drivers of engagement for his or her group*.

No longer would managers mistakenly look at the top-ten or bottom-ten questions to guess at which issues needed attention. We could tell them exactly where to focus their efforts. The list of these questions on page five of the survey report essentially reduced a manager's effort to understand his or her survey results to just reading one page.

FROM EGALITARIAN TO DIFFERENTIATED

A critical step in supporting Avon's turnaround was determining the quality of talent we had across the business—an outcome made much easier with transparent processes and conversations. Once we understood our talent inventory, we made a broad and explicit shift to differentiate our investment in talent. While we would still invest in the development of every Associate, we would more effectively match the level of that investment with the expected return. We also differentiated leaders' experiences to ensure that our highest potential leaders were very engaged, very challenged, and very tied to our company.

We made the shift to differentiation in a number of ways, including:

Communication to Leadership Teams

At the start of the turnaround process, presentations were made to each of the regional leadership teams to explain the shift in talent philosophy. The chart below (see Figure 1.3) helped to emphasize that we were serious about differentiation, could be relatively specific about what it meant and how we planned to apply it. Showing the differentiation on our new Performance and Potential matrix also let leaders know that accurately assessing talent on this tool was critical to our making the right talent investments.

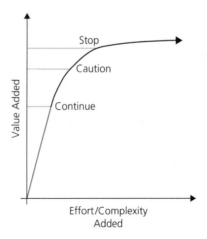

FIGURE 1.3. *The Value/Complexity Curve*

A Few Big Bets

A key plank in our philosophy was that we believed in placing a "few big bets" on a small number of leaders. This approach was informed by the research showing the vastly superior performance of the top 5 to 10 percent of a specific population and by the belief that flawless execution of well-known high-potential development tactics would rapidly accelerate development.[2] With limited funds to spend, we needed to make a decision about what talent bets would truly pay off.

Our monetary investment in our highest-potential leaders was five to ten times what we would invest in an average performer. This investment would include training, coaching, and incentive compensation, but we also invested the highly valuable time of our CEO, executive team, and board members. Our highest-potential leaders would often have an audience with these executives on a regular basis.

Tools and Processes

Our new talent review process and performance review process also emphasized our differentiation philosophy. Our new 5-point performance scale came with a recommended distribution that assumed 15 percent of our leaders would fail to meet some of their goals during the year. We believed that if goals were set at an appropriately challenging level, this was a very reasonable expectation. As a consequence, we saw marginal performers, who typically could have limped along for years with an average rating, receive the appropriate attention to either improve their performance or move out of the business.

Our performance and potential grid (3 by 3) also had recommended distributions, but we found over time that the grid definitions actually better served our differentiation goals. After initially rating leaders as having higher potential (the ability to move a certain number of levels over a certain period of time), over time, managers saw that the movement they predicted didn't occur and those with more potential to move became a smaller, more differentiated group. We also asked managers to "stack rank" Box 6, which contained average performers who were not likely to move a level in the next twenty-four months. This process helped to differentiate "solid average" performers from those who were probably below average and possibly blocking others' career movement.

FROM EPISODIC TO DISCIPLINED

As with many companies, Avon had plenty of well intentioned but very busy managers. Processes like talent reviews, which were administratively complex and difficult to understand, were not going to inspire the typical manager to reorder her priority list. By greatly simplifying these processes, we had removed one barrier to effectiveness, but we hadn't actually moved the process forward. We still needed to build organizational discipline around the execution of these simple new processes. We did that in a number of ways:

- **Consistent global tools and processes:** Many parts of the organization had created their own tools for activities like performance management or individual development. The corporate talent management function was not empowered to push for global consistency, and consequently there was not a common approach to build Avon talent. This changed with a shift to global consistency that was championed by the SVP HR. While all talent practices would now be designed by the corporate TM group, each still had to be vetted with the HR leaders of each geographic region and functional discipline. As a final part of the design process, adjustments were made to tools and processes to ensure they met needs around the world.

- **Adding talent management structure globally:** We created the role of "regional talent management leader," a manager- or director-level role responsible for the local implementation of the global processes. Five of these positions were created—one in each key geographic region—and the improved process discipline can be credited to them and their HR leaders. Regular meetings and calls between regional leaders and the corporate TM group helped ensure great dialogue and consistent improvements in the processes.

- **A committed CEO:** Our CEO, Andrea Jung, showed herself to be a tremendous supporter of effective talent processes. Both through her role modeling (conducting performance reviews and setting clear goals for her team) and instilling process discipline (she held formal talent review meetings with each direct report and an executive committee talent calibration meeting twice each year), she signaled that these processes had value.

This new level of discipline was an incredibly strong lever in our ability to assess and develop our talent. By holding talent processes every six months, we were able to drive transparency around talent issues on a regular basis and instill accountability to take action on issues before the next cycle.

FROM EMOTIONAL TO FACTUAL

Avon was a company with genuine, heart-felt concern for its Associates and an organization in which strong relationships were built over a lifetime of employment. As the organization grew, a leader's personal knowledge of other Associates' performance or development needs often served as a key factor in determining talent movement. While in many cases a leader's individual knowledge was relatively accurate, it's likely that a more calibrated point of view or additional quantitative facts may have allowed a richer discussion or more confidence in decision making.

The TM team worked to inject more fact-based decision making into talent discussions. Some of those facts were qualitative and others quantitative, but as a whole, they allowed a more complete discussion of an individual's performance and potential.

- **Qualitative facts added:** Additional qualitative facts were found everywhere from talent reviews to leadership and functional courses. In talent reviews, calibration discussions were added at each level so that individual managers could justify individual potential ratings to their peers. Those ratings might also be reviewed an additional time at the next level. Regional talent management leaders would facilitate many of those meetings to help leaders have complete and honest discussions, helping to ensure that the qualitative data was accurate. Additional qualitative data was also added from a leader's participation in leadership or functional development programs. Senior line managers would sponsor those programs, frequently attending the entire one-, two-, or three-week process. Those managers would then bring rich observations to the talent discussions about an individual's performance in those classes.

- **Quantitative facts added:** Two of the new tools discussed above, the 360 and the engagement survey, provided quantitative facts that helped Avon assess talent. Progress against engagement goals or individual behavior improvement (or lack of it) was often a key indicator of readiness for additional development.

FROM MEANINGLESS TO CONSEQUENTIAL

Injecting managerial accountability for talent practices was a key factor in their effectiveness. Prior to the turnaround, accountability for those practices did not exist, with some managers taking personal responsibility to implement them and others doing very little. In creating the new talent practices, we tried to inject accountability into each one, answering that critical question, "Why should I do this"?

- **Monetary accountability:** Varying a leader's pay for successfully or unsuccessfully managing talent is a dream of many HR and compensation leaders. We chose to use that lever in a very targeted way when we applied it to engagement survey improvement. The executive team believed that the survey provided a strong enough measure of a manager's focus on people issues that they could be held accountable for its improvement. The executive committee established year-over-year improvement in engagement scores as a goal in every VP's performance plan.

- **Associate-led accountability:** To encourage the timely completion of the performance management process steps, we empowered Associates to hold their managers accountable. A memo was sent to every Associate at the beginning of each year informing them of the specific action steps and corresponding dates their managers should be taking to set goals. A similar note was sent for mid-year and end-of-year reviews. The notes asked the Associates to let their local HR leaders know if those steps weren't occurring.

■ **CEO-led accountability:** Every six months each executive team member would meet to present his or her talent review to the CEO. Actions promised at the last meeting were reviewed and progress noted. Leaders knew that promises were being tracked and reviewed, and that progress would need to be shown at the next meeting.

While accountability was applied in many different ways, the common outcome was that leaders understood that focusing on talent during the turnaround (and after) mattered, and that they were responsible for getting it done.

The progress made on talent issues was helped by the various factors discussed above, from a committed CEO and SVP HR to the urgency of a turnaround to the dramatic change in talent practices. But it would not have been possible without the desire of every manager at Avon to do the right thing. We started with a culture that valued every Associate, and we channeled that positive spirit using sound processes and unflinching discipline. We didn't delude ourselves into thinking that those talent changes would have been possible without the Avon culture.

THE RESULTS OF A TALENT TURNAROUND

We described the six weaknesses in Avon's talent practices at the beginning of this chapter. Over the initial turnaround period (twelve to eighteen months), we moved those talent processes:

■ **From opaque to transparent:** Leaders now know what's required to be successful, how we'll measure that, how we'll help them, and the consequences of higher and lower performance. They know their performance ratings, their potential ratings, and how they can change each of those.

■ **From egalitarian to differentiated:** We actively differentiated levels of Avon talent and provided each level with the appropriate experience. Our highest-potential leaders understand how we feel about them, and they see a commensurate investment. Our lower-performing leaders get the attention they need.

■ **From complex to simple:** Managers now do the right thing for their Associates both because we've lowered the barriers we previously built and because we've helped them with value-added tools and information.

■ **From episodic to disciplined:** Processes now happen on schedule and consistently around the world.

- **From emotional to factual:** Talent decisions are made with an additional layer of qualitative and quantitative information drawn from across many different leader experiences.

- **From meaningless to consequential:** Leaders know that they must build talent the Avon way for both their short- and long-term success.

MEASURING THE TALENT TURNAROUND'S SUCCESS

The specific talent practices we targeted have seen significant improvements in effectiveness. Ratings of Immediate Manager (including items such as clear goal setting, frequent feedback, and development planning) have increased up to 17 percent, with directors and vice presidents giving their immediate managers nearly a 90 percent approval rating. The ratings of "people effectiveness" (which captures many HR and talent practices) increased up to 16 percent, including strong gains on questions related to dealing appropriately with low performers and holding leaders accountable for their results.

More transparency has allowed faster movement of talent into key markets. Simpler processes have allowed us to accelerate the development of leaders. Holding leaders accountable for their behaviors has improved the work experience for Associates around the world.

While these changes were hard-fought and we believe created much more effective processes, a more important set of metrics exists. Avon has achieved all of its expense savings goals since the start of the turnaround and has recently reinforced its commitments to even greater expense reductions. Even with this lower cost base and 10 percent fewer Associates, Avon has grown from revenues of $8B in 2005 to nearly $11B in projected 2009 revenues while delivering strong single-digit earnings growth.

We can't say with certainty that our new talent practices contributed to either those cost savings or our revenue increases. We are confident, however, that the talent practices now in place will deliver better leaders, faster, to help Avon meet its business goals.

REFERENCES

Effron, M., Greenslade, S., & Salob, M. (2005, September). Growing great leaders: Does it really matter? *Human Resource Planning Journal, 28*(3), 18–23.

Goldsmith, M. (2006). Try feed *forward* instead of feedback. In M. Goldsmith & L. Lyons, *Coaching for Leadership* (pp. 45–49). San Francisco: Pfeiffer.

Hunter, J.E., Schmidt, F.L., & Judiesch, M.K. (1990). Individual differences in output variability as a function of job complexity. *Journal of Applied Psychology, 75*(1), 28–42.

Jones, C. (1986). *Programming productivity*. New York: McGraw-Hill.

Marc Effron helps companies build better talent, faster. As a talent management leader, Effron has worked for, and consulted to, some of the world's largest and most successful companies, including Bank of America, Citigroup, Philips Electronics, Reliance Industries (India), and Alcoa. He applies a simplicity-based approach to building leaders, which emphasizes transparency and managerial accountability. Effron's recent experience includes serving as vice president, Global Talent Management, for Avon Products and as the global practice leader for Leadership Consulting at Hewitt Associates. At Hewitt, Effron created the *Top Companies for Leaders* study, which is now an annual cover story in Fortune magazine. He was also senior vice president, leadership development, at Bank of America and held other corporate and consulting positions. Effron's latest book is *One Page Talent Management: How to Build Better Leaders, Faster* (Harvard Business Press, 2010) with co-author Miriam Ort. He has co-authored two books on leadership, written chapters in eight edited books, and is a frequent speaker at industry events. He is the founder of the New Talent Management Network, the world's largest organization for talent management professionals.

CHAPTER

2

BANK OF AMERICA

BRIAN FISHEL AND JAY CONGER

A comprehensive, multi-phased executive on-boarding program that leverages multiple sources of feedback, coaching, and leadership and cultural competencies.

INTRODUCTION

The Bank of America is the first true national retail banking brand in the United States. Over the last two decades, the bank has grown dramatically, primarily through acquisitions. It began as the small regional North Carolina National Bank and has become one of the largest companies in the world. As a financial institution, it serves individual consumers, small- and middle-market businesses, and large corporations with a full range of banking, investing, asset management, and other financial and risk-management products and services. Following the acquisition of Merrill Lynch on January 1, 2009, Bank of America is among the world's leading wealth management companies and is a global leader in corporate and investment banking and trading across a broad range of asset classes serving corporations, governments, institutions, and individuals around the world. The company serves clients in more than 150 countries.

In this chapter, we will describe the Bank of America's executive on-boarding programs. Through a multi-phased approach supported by comprehensive feedback and coaching mechanisms, the bank's programs have proven highly effective at both pre-empting leadership failures and for accelerating the knowledge and relationships necessary to step into an executive role. Our insights are drawn from an in-depth case analysis of these on-boarding programs at the Bank of America.

Company Background

The Bank of America example is one of the most comprehensive approaches to executive on-boarding in the field today. It also has a proven track record of seven years with successful results. For example, the Bank of America hired 196 externally hired executives between 2001 and May 2008 and had experienced twenty-four terminations—a new hire turnover rate of approximately 12 percent. This compares to estimates as high as 40 percent turnover in large corporations (Watkins, 2003). The Bank of America has tested its approaches out on a very large sample of on-boarded executives—over five hundred internal and external over the last seven years. Over the last decade, the Bank of America has been actively involved in acquisitions as well as organic growth. As a result, the organization must annually on-board a significant number of executives—both externally and internally sourced. This demand has created many opportunities to learn about the efficacy of various executive on-boarding interventions.

In addition, the Bank of America's on-boarding program is expressly designed to help new executives learn to be facile at navigating the bank's large matrixed organization as well as building and leveraging networks of relationships for career success and for implementing company initiatives. These same demands are common in most large corporations today. We feel that this particular case holds lessons that readers in a wide range of organizations will therefore find useful.

The Leadership Dilemma

The first-time executive leader faces three dilemmas as he or she steps into a new role. In a brief period of time, the leader must gain mastery over a complex and demanding role.

The learning demands are often the most pronounced in a manager's career. Second, expectations are high. It is assumed that the incoming executive already has the seasoning to lead in the new situation. After all, most executives have already spent years in managerial roles beforehand. As a result, there is little developmental feedback for those at the top of organizations. These two challenges produce the third dilemma. The probability of the incoming executive's derailment is high. Complex new role demands combined with a lack of developmental support can produce a "perfect storm" in terms of failure on the job.

As can easily be imagined, the price of leadership failures in the executive ranks is very costly for any organization. Beyond the direct costs of on-the-job development, severance, and recruitment, there are more significant costs to the organization, such as stalled organizational initiatives, loss of business knowledge, damage to customer and staff relationships, dampened employee morale, and lost opportunities. In addition, there are the costs of recruiting a replacement as well as the replacement's time in gaining mastery of the job and setting his or her own agenda. Given these high costs, there is a tremendous need for developmental interventions that place an emphasis on pre-empting failures in senior leadership roles.

While some organizations have developed formal on-boarding interventions, the typical approach tends to be quite limited in scope and does little to effectively on-board an executive leader. Most are simple orientation programs offering an opportunity to network with the CEO and the executive team. They may also provide some form of overview of the corporation, its financials, and its activities. A handful of organizations such as General Electric and Toyota do have more sophisticated on-boarding programs at the executive and general manager level (Fulmer & Conger, 2003), but such programs are very rare in the corporate world. Instead interventions to pre-empt leadership derailments tend to be dependent on performance appraisals and talent management practices. The underlying premise is that failures at the executive level can best be avoided through continuous formal performance feedback to a manager and through the careful selection of jobs and bosses over the *life span* of a manager's career (McCall, 1988). While we share this view, we also believe that developmental interventions focused solely on the transition to the executive role are a necessity. Companies such as General Electric and PepsiCo have long designed their leadership education programs around career transitions, especially at executive levels (Conger & Benjamin, 1999). In other words, a comprehensive on-boarding program at the executive level has an essential place in any organization's portfolio of leadership development initiatives.

The Need for On-Boarding Interventions at the Executive Leadership Level

The transition from line management to an executive role is a significant jump in terms of scale and complexity of the job. Executives operate at the boundary between their organization and the external environment, whereas most managers are more organizationally and functionally oriented. Executives must also formulate company-wide strategies and play a critical role in their implementation—roles which they played to a far lesser degree prior to their executive appointments. Their decisions around staffing, rewards, measurement systems, and culture create a context that shapes the strategic choices made by managers and specialists throughout the organization.

The executive role comes with enormous visibility and accountability. It is extremely demanding with little time for learning on the job. At the same time, developmental feedback and coaching for executives tend to be minimal. There are the occasional opportunities for formal coaching and executive education programs. But beyond these interventions, there is usually little else. In conclusion, for many managers, the promotion to an executive leadership role will be the steepest jump in their career history, and paradoxically the one with the least amount of transition support.

The limited developmental support is a result of several factors. First it is assumed by most organizations that their senior-most talent is well seasoned, given the many years of managerial experiences required for entry into the executive suite. Yet positions in functional line management roles are rarely broad enough to provide sufficient preparatory experience.

Second, the promotion itself and the many years of prior management experience can produce an often misplaced self-confidence in new executives that they are up to the task. This sense of self-assurance may discourage new executives from seeking out developmental feedback and from being more proactive in self-reflection and learning. There is a natural desire to appear in charge—in other words, to be seen as an effective leader immediately. Seeking coaching and feedback would dispel this impression, and therefore executives may be hesitant to seek either.

Third, in the executive suite, the environment is also more politicized. Peers at the executive level are often competitors jousting for the top roles. As a result, developmental support and feedback from colleagues tend to be far more difficult to obtain. In addition, many CEOs do not see coaching their executives as an essential part of their role. So the new executive's superior may provide limited or no developmental guidance.

All of these forces coalesce to increase the probability of leadership derailments at the senior-most levels of organizations. The problem is even more extreme for organizations when outsiders are hired into executive jobs. As noted earlier, one estimate is that 40 percent of senior managers hired from the outside fail within their first eighteen months in the role (Watkins, 2003). Given the above discussion, it is easy to see why a developmentally oriented program to help transition managers into executive leadership roles might not only be helpful but essential. But what exactly should be the aim of such interventions and how best to design them?

Ideally, a well-designed on-boarding intervention can and should achieve three outcomes. The first is to *minimize the possibility of derailment* on the job. By accelerating the new executive's understanding of the role demands and by providing support through constructive feedback, coaching, and follow-up, a well-designed program can and should preempt failures. The second outcome is to *accelerate the performance results* of the new leader. For example, research suggests that a senior-level manager requires an average of 6.2 months to reach a break-even point—the moment at which the new leader's contribution to the organization exceeds the costs of bringing him or her on board and he or she has acquired a critical base of insight into the job (Watkins, 2003). Effective on-boarding interventions should shorten this cycle of learning by accelerating the development of a network of critical relationships, clarifying leadership and performance expectations, and facilitating the formulation of more realistic short- and medium-term performance objectives.

A third outcome for on-boarding interventions concerns organizations that are aggressively pursuing acquisitions or experiencing high growth rates. In both cases, they must grapple with socializing an influx of outside senior managers. An effective on-boarding intervention *should facilitate a far smoother integration and socialization experience* for these incoming executives. It accomplishes this by helping them to rapidly acquire an understanding of the business environment, socializing them into the organization's culture and politics, building a network of critical relationships, and familiarizing them with the operating dynamics of the executive team. In the sections to follow, readers will see how the Bank of America on-boarding programs successfully achieves these outcomes.

LEADERSHIP DEVELOPMENT ACTIVITIES FOR EXECUTIVE LEADERS

The impetus for the Bank of America's interest in executive on-boarding is a product of its own corporate history. Over the last two decades, the bank has experienced dramatic growth through acquisitions. It began as a small regional North Carolina bank (North Carolina National Bank) and has grown into one of the largest companies in the world. As a result of this history of aggressive acquisitions, it discovered a need to more effectively on-board executive leaders from acquired companies and to quickly assimilate them into the Bank of America's standards and expectations for performance. The organization's leadership development group was very familiar with the research on executive derailment, which showed high failure rates for executives who were on-boarded into acquiring companies. In response, the bank developed on-boarding interventions. Over time, these programs have been expanded to the organization's internal executive promotions to ensure that these individuals will succeed as well as feel that they were receiving attention equal to the outsiders.

It is important to note, however, that executive on-boarding is only one of several processes that the Bank of America deploys for the leadership development of its senior talent. While we explore this one activity in depth in this chapter, the bank's success with leadership talent is a product of its multi-faceted approach to development at the executive level, along with Mr. Lewis' and his executive leadership team's unwavering support for leadership development. The latter is a critical driver of the bank's success in this area. As illustrated in Figure 2.1, the range of the bank's executive leadership development activities is extensive and includes selection, on-boarding, performance management, processes to upgrade executive talent, developmental experiences, and compensation.

A critical factor is that the executive development strategy is championed by the bank's CEO Ken Lewis. In overview fashion, Figure 2.1 highlights the core dimensions of executive development at the bank. In addition, Lewis meets every summer with his top executives to review the organizational health and development strategies of each business. In two- to three-hour sessions with each executive, Lewis probes the people, financial, and operational issues that will drive growth over the next twenty-four months, with the majority of time spent discussing the key leaders, critical leadership roles necessary to achieving the company's growth targets, and organizational structure. These meetings are personal in nature, with no presentation decks or thick books outlining HR procedures. But they are rigorous. Business leaders come to the sessions with a concise document (the goal being three pages or fewer to ensure simplicity) that describes strengths and weaknesses in their units' leadership talent pipelines, given business challenges and goals. During these conversations, executives make specific commitments regarding current or potential leaders—identifying the next assignment, special projects, promotions, and the like. Lewis follows up with his executives in his quarterly business reviews to ensure that they have fulfilled their commitments. With this active commitment at the very top of the organization, leaders throughout the Bank of America sense that leadership development is a critical activity for the company. As a result, it is a widely held belief that leadership talent directly

FIGURE 2.1. *Executive Development at Bank of America*

affects the performance of the bank. This belief sets up a mandate for the organization—to hire and keep great leadership talent.

Finally, the organizational culture promoted by Lewis is one that encourages candor, trust, teamwork, and accountability at all levels in the organization, especially at the executive level. The company has a deep comfort with differentiating individual performance (based on what is achieved as well as on how these achievements are attained). There is also a belief that today's top performers are not necessarily tomorrow's—that even the best leaders can fall behind or derail. As a result, the corporate culture is one in which the truth is more highly valued than politeness or tolerance for average or poor performance. These beliefs drive what and how the Bank of America builds and measures leadership success, whether it is in programs, performance management, or selection. This overarching environment is critical to the success of the bank's executive on-boarding program. One cannot understand the on-boarding process without first appreciating the bank's commitment to leadership and high performance.

The Design Assumptions Underlying the Bank of America's Executive On-Boarding Process

Underpinning the Bank of America's on-boarding interventions is a set of fundamental assumptions that have shaped its design features. These assumptions are the product of "lessons learned" from earlier experiences with on-boarding interventions and experiments. The baseline assumption is that successful on-boarding occurs *over time*—specifically during the executive's first twelve to eighteen months on the job. Thus, any on-boarding process must be supported by *multiple interventions* instead of a single event, say at entry into the executive role. Interventions must occur at *intervals* over the executive's first year to eighteen months, rather than solely within the first few months into the job. To be effective, on-boarding must also be supported by *multiple resources*, especially in terms of *stakeholder* resources. To engage solely the new executive's superior (the hiring executive) is not sufficient to ensure a successful on-boarding experience. Instead the fullest possible spectrum of stakeholders must be involved in the new executive's selection, entry, and on-boarding. Finally, interventions are completely dependent on the quality of the *interaction* between the executive and his or her stakeholders. A purely paperwork-driven or bureaucratic process will not produce optimum results. The approach must therefore focus on the quality of *dialogue* and interaction, rather than on documentation and formal processes.

These assumptions have directly shaped the on-boarding interventions that the Bank of America deploys. For example, the bank's program is designed around multiple phases. Different kinds of interventions occur in each phase. It engages the new executive's many stakeholders in a simple, transparent process, with the aim of achieving a broad range of outcomes. Dialogue and feedback are at the core of all of the various interventions. In the discussion that follows, we will examine how these design assumptions play out in each of the major phases of the on-boarding process.

The Bank of America's Executive On-Boarding Program: Phases and Interventions

The on-boarding experience spans four core phases—selection of the new executive, initial entry into the executive role, a mid-point phase of 100 to 130 days on the job, and a final review phase at the end of the first year. We will examine each of these phases, its central activities, and its goals.

Selection Phase The first element of a successful on-boarding process is the selection process itself. While expertise and experience are the overriding criterion, there are additional dimensions when it comes to selection at the Bank of America: leadership ability and cultural fit. If the new executive is lacking leadership and interpersonal skills and cultural sensitivity, he or she will have a much higher probability of derailing. To ensure this does not happen, the human resources function at the Bank of America devotes a great deal of attention to its partnerships with executive search firms. Recruiters must understand the bank's culture and leadership requirements when hired to conduct an executive-level search. In addition, a leadership development officer from HR ("LD partner" in the bank's terminology) will often interview the candidate to assess cultural fit with bank, value to the team, and leadership approach. This information is meant to complement data from other potential stakeholders who are interviewing the candidate about his or her expertise and experience. The LD partner will solicit responses to the following types of questions from all the interviewers:

1. "Would you personally trust your career to this person [the candidate]?"

2. "Do you see yourself learning from him or her?"

3. "Is this person capable of putting enterprise objectives ahead of his or her own goals and working well across lines of business and constituents?"

4. "Would this person complement the direct team that he or she would be a part of?"

5. "Would this person be able to accept, process, and apply candid coaching and feedback in order to continuously improve?"

6. "Does he or she have the drive and passion to be part of a winning team?"

7. "Can you see this person leading from and living the company's core values? Would he or she fit our culture?"

8. "Does this person have the potential to assume more responsibility in the future?"

Answers to these questions provide insights into the candidate's potential for a fit or misfit with the bank's culture and for his or her credibility as a leader. If the candidate is hired, the answers to these and other interview questions are then provided to the individual upon his or her arrival into the job. The sources of feedback, however, remain anonymous.

Job design is another essential part of the selection process. A clear and calibrated job specification is spelled out and supported by stakeholders before a search begins. Critical stakeholders will be interviewed by the LD and/or HR partners about what is required in the job, as well as other dimensions that are not critical but helpful for the candidate to possess. This selection process is designed so that the hiring executive does not make a blind selection—say hiring someone with a similar style to his or her own. The multi-stakeholder involvement also ensures that the hiring executive has a clear sense of the demands of the job from the perspectives of the widest range of stakeholders.

Critical to this phase is the role of the LD partner. This individual acts as a "chief talent officer" during the hiring process and on-boarding process of each new executive. Usually with ten to fifteen years of experience, they normally possess a leadership development and/or organization development background. Most have deep experience in hiring and developing executives. As a result, these LD partners have a strong degree of credibility in the eyes of the new executive and his or her stakeholders. The LD partners' responsibilities are broad. They essentially "own" the executives' on-boarding process from beginning to end.

Entry Phase Following hiring, the new executive's initial few weeks on the job are critical ones. During this time, he or she must accomplish four outcomes: (1) develop business acumen specific to the new role, (2) learn the organizational culture, (3) master the role's leadership demands, and (4) build critical organizational relationships.

From the standpoint of business acumen, the new executive must be able to efficiently and quickly learn customer and financial information specific to the new role. In turn, he or she must set realistic goals and objectives based on this information. On the cultural dimension, he or she must acquire an understanding of the written and unwritten norms of behavior within the organization. From the standpoint of leadership demands, new executives must be able to rapidly determine the organization's expectations of them as well as establish leadership expectations within their teams. Finally, it is imperative that the new executive be able to identify and build relationships with key organizational stakeholders.

To meet these demands, three major categories of interventions are used: (1) tools and processes, (2) orientation forums, and (3) coaching and support. Tools and processes include an on-boarding plan and new leader/team and new leader/peer integration processes. Orientation forums include a general new employee orientation and a new executive orientation program. For coaching and support, there are three primary providers: the hiring executive, an HR generalist, and the LD partner. Each of these interventions is described below.

During the first week on the job, the LD partner prepares the on-boarding plan for the executive. This early engagement with the LD partner ensures that from the very start the LD partner will be viewed as a critical resource for the newly appointed executive. The integration plan itself has two primary outcomes. One is to provide the new leaders with basic yet critical information about the business they will soon be leading. They are given an overview of their units' financials, the units' business plans, key initiatives, assessments of their teams' leadership talent, and other important background information such as biographies of key managers, customer surveys, and recent presentations on key issues in the units. The second outcome is to have the executives define successes for their first ninety days on the job. They must identify these along three dimensions: financial, leadership, and organizational. The plan also explores early obstacles the executives are likely to face in terms of people, processes, and technology. The new executives must look at their own developmental issues and how they can best address these. At this time, the executives are given the names of their peer coaches (fellow executives) and senior advisors (typically at the same level or above). The peer coaches are resources for "insider" information. They will have benefited from having their own peer coaches in the past, and therefore see the importance of their role. To accelerate the relationship between executives and peer coaches, the LD partners will often try to find some common ground in backgrounds, such as attending the same college or experience in similar industries or companies. Consideration is also given to those who are known internally to be good coaches and who will be candid with the new executives. The senior advisors provide the new executives with mentoring around their careers. In contrast to the peer coaches, the advisors have a broader view of the organization, given their seniority. Often these are people with whom the new executives may need to undertake extensive near-term projects. They often are chosen from outside the lines of business as the newly hired individuals, as projects at the executive level often require cross-company partnerships.

In the first one to three weeks, further planning is used to identify emerging challenges in the new role, people-related issues, key relationships that must be built, and ongoing management processes that need to be established. This planning is captured in the New Leader-Team Integration Session—a critical experience in the entry phase. The objective of this process is to facilitate an effective working relationship between the new leader and his or her team. The process creates an opportunity for both the leader and the team to establish open channels of communication, exchange views, and become more acquainted with their respective operating styles and expectations. When this planning process is done well, it can dramatically shorten the time required for the new executive to become effective on the job.

The New Leader-Team Integration Session ideally occurs within the first thirty to sixty days of the new assignment. The process involves three steps, all of which are facilitated by the LD partner (sometimes and often in partnership with an HR partner). In the first step, the LD partner meets with the new executive leader prior to the integration session. The LD partner provides the new executive with an overview of the integration session's objectives and mechanics, identifies the executive's own objectives for the session, and selects the questions that will be used to create a mutually beneficial dialogue between the executive and his or her new team. In addition, the LD partner gauges the new leader's interests and concerns. Questions to solicit this information for the new executive include:

1. "What do you need to know about your team?"

2. "What don't you know about your team?"

3. "What are your concerns?"

4. "What things are most important to you as a leader?"

5. "What does the team need to know about your expectations and operating style?"

6. "How can the team best support you in your transition into the new role?"

7. "What key messages would you like to send to the team?"

Following this meeting with the executive, the LD partner meets with the new leader's team—either individually or preferably and more often as a group—without the new leader. The purpose of this second step is to develop a preliminary understanding of the group's issues and concerns. Typically, the LD partner will solicit this information using questions such as the following:

1. "What do you already know about the new executive?"

2. "What don't you know, but would like to know?"

3. "What advice do you have for the new executive that will help him or her be even more effective?"

4. "What questions do you have for the new executive?"

5. "What are your concerns about him or her becoming the leader of the team?"

6. "What major obstacles are you encountering as a team? What opportunities exist?"

7. "What is going well that you would like to keep? What is not going well that you would like to change?"

8. "What do you need from the new executive to allow us to be even more effective?"

Following these two preliminary meetings for data-gathering, the New Leader-Team Integration Session is conducted over a half-day period. After describing the meeting objectives and ground rules, the team goes off without the executive to gather responses to their new superior's "questions to the team." In the meantime, the new leader is debriefed on the group's interview responses, and he or she prepares responses to these for the team. The team and the leader then meet together for two hours of dialogue. The environment is a non-threatening one. The LD partner begins by reviewing the group's overall messages to the leader. For example, an insight might emerge that direct reports are interpreting certain of their superior's behavior in a negative light. The leader comments on the team's responses as well as communicates his or her key messages to the team and how he or she plans to address the feedback. Facilitated by the LD partner, both the leader and the team establish formal commitments to one another and identify future issues to be addressed. For example, the new executive may commit to a new behavior or set of actions or a clearer vision. The leader might shift his or her management practices so that more time is spent on addressing future issues.

In addition to the New Leader-Team Integration Session, there is also a New Peer Integration Session, which is also held within the first thirty to sixty days of the new executive's arrival. This session creates an opportunity for the executive to network with new peers, to seek advice and guidance on on-boarding, to learn about norms, and to obtain general support. It also allows the individual's peers to learn about their new colleague's background, operating style, and priorities and to build an initial working relationship. Similar in design to the New Leader-Team Integration Session, it involves three stages. First, the LD partner meets with the new executive to describe the process, select discussion questions, and explore special issues and concerns. Typical interview questions for the preparation phase include:

1. "What would you like your new peers to know about you?"

2. "What would you like to know about your new peers?"

3. "Provide a summary of your personal and work history that others might not know."

4. "What are you interested in outside of work?"

5. "How can your new peers support you as you transition into the executive team?"

The LD partner then meets with the executive's new peers and solicits responses to the following questions:

1. "What advice do you have for your new peer?"

2. "How would you describe the team's written and unwritten rules?"

3. "What would you like your new peer to know about the team?"

4. "The things that make a person successful on this team include. . . ."

5. "The things that can derail a person on this team include. . . ."

6. "The things that help a person integrate well into this company include. . . ."

7. "What can you tell your new peer about each team member's operating style?"

In addition to responses to these questions, the LD partner also gathers from members of the peer team information on their areas of competence for which they might serve as a resource to the new executive, their interests outside of work, and the names of their spouses and children. This data is recorded on index cards for the new executive.

The integration session is broken into three parts. There is a short overview, a setting of objectives, and an introduction of the team and the new peer. This is followed by the peer team and the new peer gathering responses to each other's questions in separate rooms. Each side's responses are recorded on flip charts. The team and their new peer then gather together in a conference room. Facilitated by the LD partner, there is sharing of the responses and dialogue. Basically, the session enables transparency and partnering—both cornerstones of success in the Bank of America's culture. It drives joint ownership for success as well, and, like the New Team Integration Session, it facilitates the acceleration of relationships with peers—individually and collectively.

Earlier, we had mentioned that orientation programs were a component of the entry phase. Within the first week on the job, the new leader attends a welcome orientation (providing an overview of the Bank's business, history, culture, values), which is run on every Monday for all new employees. Leaders then meet with their LD partners to discuss the on-boarding plan. Within the leaders' first few months, they are automatically registered to attend the New Executive Orientation Program. This program is sponsored directly by the CEO. Its purpose is for the executive to network with other new executives as well as the CEO and with his executive team as well as other executives previously hired into the bank from the outside. The program itself is one-and-a-half days long. On the first day of the program, there is an informal panel with executives who have been hired into the bank within the last two years. The panel of executives shares their own on-boarding experiences. They explain their experiences, what the new executives can expect, their personal "lessons learned." This is followed by presentations by the CEO and top executives, who cover topics such as the corporate values and culture, leadership philosophies and expectations, company strategy and finances, as well as other key business units' growth strategies and key enterprise initiatives. A social networking event then follows hosted by Ken Lewis and his direct reports. This orientation provides the new executives with insights into the business, the bank's culture, Ken's expectations for leaders, and how executives can derail. Beyond the information provided in the orientation, a parallel goal is to create a cohort identity for the new executives. This is important, as they will likely need to work with one another on key projects or business initiatives in the future. The cohort also provides the new executives with a safe haven or resource group to ask questions and to help navigate the complexities of the bank.

Mid-Point Phase (100 to 130 days): Three to four months into their new assignments, the executives take part in the Key Stakeholder Check-In Session. This intervention involves receiving written and verbal feedback from a select list of their key stakeholders. The experience is designed to accelerate the development of effective working relationships between the new leaders and the stakeholders, who now share responsibility for the new leaders' success. It also aids in helping the newly hired executives understand the feedback and coaching culture that is unique to Bank of America's rich feedback environment. It is essentially a process for the new leaders to seek and receive early feedback regarding how their stakeholders view the leaders' on-boarding process, operating style, leadership approach, and cultural fit. It can uncover whether there are potential disconnects between others' perceptions and the leaders' actual intentions. It can also further clarify the expectations of key stakeholders. Most importantly, it can be used to allow the executives to make early adjustments in their approaches and in turn avoid their own potential derailment. Like the earlier integration sessions, it also gives voice to the stakeholders. They can take advantage of a process that permits them to surface potentially sensitive issues or concerns in an anonymous manner. They can share organizational insights that are not readily apparent to the new leaders. They can also communicate special needs to their new leaders.

In terms of its timing, the bank discovered (using a six sigma process and tools) that stakeholder reviews held close to a new leader's entry were not effective. The executive did not always have sufficient self-confidence to respond positively to the feedback received from stakeholders. Similarly, staff did not possess well-formed opinions of their superiors or peers before the three-month timeframe. They may not have seen enough of a particular behavior to determine whether it was a pattern or not. On the other hand, within three to four months, patterns in the executive's behavior become quite clear. With a timeframe within 130 days, it was harder for new executives to discount feedback that was more critical of their approach. They could not claim that their behavior was simply due to a one-time event. That said, delaying feedback to the executive until the six-month mark or later created a serious dilemma. By that point, the executive's behavior may become typecast. After six months in the job, it was very difficult for the executive to escape the label. For this reason, the feedback occurs ideally by the 130-day milestone.

The process behind the Key Stakeholder Check-In involves an initial planning session with the new leader and the LD partner in which they review and revise the questions that will be used to solicit insights. For example, the LD partner will identify specific areas in which the leader would like to receive feedback and from whom. The LD partner then contacts the leader's key stakeholders to conduct an anonymous fifteen-to thirty-minute interview with each stakeholder. Beyond the questions identified by the new leader, there are additional questions to stakeholders. These often include:

1. "What are your initial impressions of your new leader's strengths?"

2. "What are the potential landmines/obstacles that he or she may come up against?"

3. "What advice would you give to the new leader to be even more effective and to accelerate performance in the role?"

4. "What one to three things do you specifically need from this individual?"

5. "To increase effectiveness, what does this individual need to (1) continue doing, (2) stop doing, and (3) start doing?"

The LD partner then organizes the interview responses, identifies themes, and records specific verbatim comments from specific stakeholders. They then meet with the new leader and share the interview results. In the review session, the executive constructs an action plan to address specific feedback items and prepares for a discussion with their boss. With their superior, they review the action plan and the overall on-boarding experience overall. The LD partner and the leader hold follow-up meetings to evaluate progress on the action plan and for further coaching. Sometimes these discussions will uncover a problem that even the individual's boss was unaware of. It is worth noting that the boss is not one of the people the LD partner interviews for this very reason. *in this phase.*

This comprehensive check-in process brings great clarity to identifying the new leader's strengths but also highlights development needs and problem areas. For example, new executives might learn that they possess strong interpersonal skills and are perceived as highly competent and action-oriented. On the other hand, the same executives might learn that they still need to build stronger connections with key leaders and learn various business strategies and initiatives at a more granular level. They also may receive feedback that they must spend more time on developing a clearer business vision and communicating to their team. Staff might wish more one-on-one time with the executive. Out of the action planning process, concrete steps will be identified that this executive must undertake over the coming months to build on the identified strengths and address the problem areas.

The Final Phase (one to one and a half years) Typically twelve to eighteen months after their stakeholder reviews, the new executives will receive a 360-degree feedback assessment, which provides the leaders with feedback on their leadership competencies (see Figure 2.2 for the Bank of America's leadership competencies). The timing is designed so that the executives have had an opportunity to make significant progress on the development areas identified in their stakeholder reviews. They now also have had complete performance cycles under their belts. If executives are successful, their improvements will show up in the 360 feedback data. The tool itself is designed around the bank's leadership model as well as common derailing behaviors. When leaders receive their 360 feedback, they will again sit down with their LD partners to review it, compare it to stakeholder feedback, and use the outputs to further shape their development plans and actions. This process also triggers another more formal development discussion between the individual executive and his or her boss. The 360 feedback is used along with other data and feedback mechanisms as input into the individual's performance ratings and reviews.

TO GET RESULTS, LEADERS SIMULTANEOUSLY...			
I. Grow the Business	II. Lead People to Perform	III. Drive Execution	IV. Sustain Intensity and Optimism
A. Demonstrate deep and broad business acumen B. Create competitive and innovative business plans C. Build customer/ client-driven environment D. Institutionalize error free quality processes E. Excel at risk/ reward trade-off	A. Align enterprise capabilities B. Recruit and grow great talent C. Inspire commitment and followership D. Communicate crisply and candidly	A. Instill management focus and discipline B. Build partnerships to achieve swift adoption C. Demonstrate sound judgement and act with speed	A. Constantly raise the bar B. Display personal courage C. Continuously learn and adapt
LIVE OUR VALUES...			
Winning – Leadership – Inclusive Meritocracy – Doing the Right Thing – Trusting and Teamwork			

WHILE NOT EXHIBITING DERAILING BEHAVIORS...	
• Failing to deliver results • Betraying trust • Resisting change	• Being exclusive vs. inclusive • Failing to take a stand • Over leading and under managing

FIGURE 2.2. *Bank of America's Senior Leadership Model*

LESSONS FOR DESIGNING ON-BOARDING FOR EXECUTIVE LEADERS

Sooner or later in their first year in the executive role, most leaders will face some type of major stumbling block. An executive on-boarding process can and should provide the support and feedback that will assist executives in successfully addressing hurdles. The most effective programs also act as early warning systems that allow the executive and the organization to preempt the possibility of derailment. As we have noted, the process must be supported by multiple interventions that occur at intervals over the executive's first year rather than solely at the moment of entry into the job. It must also proactively engage the new executive's multiple stakeholders from the moment of selection to the end of the on-boarding cycle. Effective engagement is completely dependent on the quality of interaction between the new executives and their full range of stakeholders. In addition, stakeholders must feel a high degree of ownership in the process itself, which increases their ownership in the executives' success.

In assessing how well your own organization on-boards its senior most talent, there are several critical questions to ask. Does your organization treat on-boarding

Application

as a one-time orientation event or as a longitudinal process? What is the breadth of interventions it employs from integration tools to coaches to formal feedback? Does it proactively engage all the new executive's stakeholders in a candid process that generates constructive feedback and clarifies expectations? Does the process deploy interventions at regular intervals throughout the first year for the new executive? Are these "toll gates" built around critical learning and feedback windows or are they more arbitrary or shaped by the corporate calendar? Are the interventions in time to gather critical and valid feedback for the new executive so that he or she can constructively respond and maintain credibility?

While such programs have traditionally been geared to external executive hires, internally promoted executives can benefit as greatly from formal on-boarding. While the internal hire may understand the corporate culture well, the role demands of executive leadership are as great for the internal hire as the external one. So it is useful to ask whether your organization treats its insider promotions differently. Does the organization assume they do not need on-boarding support? What are patterns in how insider promotions fail? What might be done to assist insiders in a more proactive and constructive manner in their own on-boarding experiences?

In the case of the Bank of America, their use of LD partners and the various dialogue and feedback-based integration experiences allow the new executives to obtain rich, candid, and ongoing information on their progress over the first year. What vehicles if any does your organization provide to new executives to rapidly gain constructive feedback on their leadership approaches and performance? What support does your organization provide in helping the executives to act on that information?

For on-boarding to be effective, a number of individuals need to "own" the new leader's success. In this regard, one of the more important lessons from the Bank of America example is the pivotal role of the LD and HR partner. This individual in essence owns the executive's success from the moment of selection to the end of his or her first year on the job. Their job is to make certain the executives successfully on-board. In addition, they engage the new executives' superior, several peers, and the subordinates in the ownership process. Therefore some questions to ask about your own organization's process include: Does your organization have individuals who are dedicated to ensuring the success of new executives? Are they influential at all stages of the executives' on-boarding experience? Ideally, there are multiple owners such as peers and senior advisors. What ways, if any, does your organization engage the peers and superiors of the new executives in supporting their successful on-boarding?

As we noted at the beginning of this chapter, an effective on-boarding process does not exist in a vacuum. It is highly dependent on a supportive culture. As we close this chapter, it is important to assess more broadly your organization's commitment to talent management. Questions to ask would include: How deeply committed are your CEO and senior team to leadership development? Does the firm have a clear talent strategy? Does the culture encourage individuals to learn and adapt? Is it a culture in which candid constructive feedback is available and rewarded? What are the breadth and depth of your organization's talent management and development interventions? Are they supported by well-aligned rewards, performance feedback processes, useful metrics, and the culture?

REFERENCES

Conger, J., & Benjamin, B. (1999). *Building leaders: How successful companies develop the next generation.* San Francisco: Jossey-Bass.

Conger, J., & Fulmer, B. (2004). *Growing your company's leaders: How great organizations use succession management to sustain competitive advantage.* New York: AMACOM.

McCall, M. (1988). *High flyers: Developing the next generation of leaders.* Boston: Harvard Business School Press.

Watkins, M. (2003). *The first 90 days: Critical success strategies for new leaders at all levels.* Boston: Harvard Business School Press.

Brian Fishel has over twenty years of broad human resources experience across various industries. He has specific expertise in global talent management, executive development, executive assessment and coaching, learning, staffing, and employee relations. He currently heads Bank of America's Enterprise Learning and Talent Management group, as well as leadership development efforts for the Consumer and Retail Bank and Risk Management Divisions. He has been with Bank of America since 1999 and has held various senior-level leadership and organization development and learning roles at the enterprise level as well as faced off directly with most of the company's major lines of business and functional disciplines. Prior to Bank of America, Mr. Fishel held various senior-level organization development and human resource generalist roles focused on The Coca-Cola Company's international operations and previous to that Pizza Hut, at the time a subsidiary of PepsiCo. He is a frequent national speaker on the topics of talent management and leadership and executive development. He is a member of the Conference Board's Learning and Organizational Performance committee and a founding board member of The Best Practices Institute. He holds bachelor's and master's degrees in education, both from Miami University of Ohio.

Jay Conger is the Henry Kravis Chaired Professor of Leadership at Claremont McKenna College in California and a visiting professor at the London Business School. He is one of the world's experts on leadership. In recognition of his extensive work with companies, *BusinessWeek* named him the best business school professor to teach leadership and one of the top five management education teachers worldwide. Author of over one hundred articles and book chapters and fourteen books, he researches leadership, organizational change, boards of directors, and the training and development of leaders and managers. He is one of a handful of authors who have published multiple articles in the *Harvard Business Review*. His most recent books include *Boardroom*

Realities (2009), *The Practice of Leadership* (2007), *Growing Your Company's Leaders* (2003), *Shared Leadership* (2002), *Corporate Boards: New Strategies for Adding Value at the Top* (2001), *The Leader's Change Handbook* (1999), *Building Leaders* (1999), and *Winning 'Em Over: A New Model for Management in the Age of Persuasion* (1998). As an executive educator and management consultant, he has worked with over three hundred companies during his career.

CHAPTER

3

CORNING INCORPORATED

CREATING THE NEXT GENERATION OF INNOVATION LEADERS

RICHARD A. O'LEARY, GARY JUSELA, AND HEATH N. TOPPER

- Week One—Running a Program
- Interim Period—Leadership Connections
- Week Two—Launching a Business
- Outcomes and Next Steps for Growing the Talent Pipeline of Program Leaders
- Next Steps

INTRODUCTION

Corning has established a leadership position in glass and ceramics based on a commitment and ability to out-innovate the competition. The company has had a devotion to R&D investment and the delivery of value through applied science since its very origins 157 years ago. In the past decade the company has come to appear as something of an anomaly within Corporate America, given the continued devotion to investing at least 10 percent of annual revenue into fundamental research and development. Many comparison companies have pursued a game of financial engineering. Most competitor companies have off-shored critical competencies in both product development and manufacturing, which has created short-term wins and prosperity for senior leadership at the sacrifice of long-term viability in sustaining a product pipeline and wealth creation for a broad domestic workforce. These companies have diverted available capital into stock repurchase programs as well as internal remuneration schemes rather than investment in organic growth.

Corning leadership has built a strategy for the future founded on distinctive value creation through internally owned innovation. While the practice of applied science is not new to the company, the senior leadership has become more sophisticated in the practice of innovation and they have accelerated their objectives for new product development. The new mantra is to expand from a target of one to two breakthroughs per decade to a much more aggressive two to four. Companion with this objective is the company's acknowledgement that this goal can only be achieved through a dedicated investment in new leadership development, both through attracting talent with new domain expertise from outside and systematically broadening the capabilities of high-potential internal talent. Our objective in this chapter is to identify both the fundamental assumptions underlying innovation at Corning and the internal process for grooming the requisite talent to enable achievement of the top-level strategy.

Navigating the Storms

Corning, comparable to other companies with a long history of endurance, has experienced waves of success punctuated by market turns and the demand for learning, adaptation, and strategic agility. As the company laid claim to the new path of talent management of innovation leaders, Corning had recently found a new stride, having emerged from a market meltdown in telecommunications. In the early to middle part of the past decade, Corning saw a decline in telecommunications revenue of nearly 67 percent and a decline of shareholder value of close to 99 percent. Jamie Houghton was re-recruited to take the helm as CEO, and his task became that of radically restructuring the enterprise through a reduction in force, spinning off of non-essential businesses to generate needed cash, and reinvesting in and repositioning product development across sectors whose potential had been far from realized and mostly sharply underestimated. In his own humble way, Houghton characterized his role as merely that of "cheerleading" the rest of the team, although in reality his impact was both profoundly strategic and inspiring of the values that have given the company enduring sustainability.

In their story about the innovation history of Corning, Bowen and Purrington (2008) identified the company's essential turbulence navigation skills. The foundation begins with a combination of both financial strength (assuring that the company always has more cash than debt) and patiently nurturing the investment of capital in the future of product development. The creation of successful keystone components often requires an investment in internal learning that may run to decades before yielding meaningful rates of return and profitability.

A key lesson out of the telecommunications market meltdown was the importance of diversification of technology development. The company resisted strong external guidance to shut down all development outside of telecom support. While the diversification had not been sufficient to stave off a near disastrous disintegration of the company, there was marginally sufficient diversity to give the company the necessary toehold to recreate itself. Within five years, Display Technology established itself as the new growth engine for the company, supplanting the role formerly held by the fiber business and optical networking. This lesson has once again come to the fore within the context of the 2009 economic crisis, as further diversification is required to create balance against assaults on the automotive and consumer electronics markets and the consequent reduction in demand for Corning's keystone components in these sectors.

Deeply understanding the needs and business models of customers is a fourth dimension of economic navigation. With respect to the telecom sector, Corning did not recognize the magnitude of the overbuilding in which the collection of customers engaged and the extent to which this put the viability of many of these companies fatally at risk. The ability to navigate successfully in multiple technologies required identifying a finite set of acutely wise customers who were technology leaders within their respective domains. Customers are not created equally in their ability to accurately characterize their needs and the real opportunities inherent within their markets. The telecom meltdown was an archetypal example of excessive exuberance precipitating a catastrophic market collapse. Engaging customers and reading the markets effectively are critical skills not only to navigating broad turbulence but also to shepherding new programs from the laboratory to scalable production and commercial success.

Finally, Corning has demonstrated a core set of values that distinguish the company primarily through a deep and long-term commitment to employees, especially the internal talent pool of scientists, technologists, market specialists, and developers of manufacturing processes. Where many companies have come to treat the workforce as expendable, Corning premises its long-term success on the ability to nurture and grow both people and technology over periods of twenty-five to forty years. Embedded within the company is a deep DNA of beliefs in the criticality of integrity, performance, innovation, and the sanctity of the individual. It is the development and consistent practice of these navigational skills that provide both the durability of the company over its extended history and the ability to guide discrete technologies through the five stages of innovation to a successful launch.

The Art and Science of Innovation

Innovation is the lifeblood for the enterprise to secure a sustainable future. The continuous funding of R&D is a cornerstone for innovation success. Yet Corning's ability to win in the game of innovation is premised not simply on a financial commitment, but on the creation of the requisite internal culture and the reservoir of multidisciplinary talent to foster new product development. Innovation is not simply a task of research but is a function of creative problem solving and "imagineering" rooted in a deep capacity for extracting wisdom and learning from relevant audiences. Wendell Weeks, the current Corning CEO, has characterized program management as a "truth discovery" process. This implies that the innovation leaders must set the charge to ensure that they and their teams conduct an inquiry into the nature of reality and question every assumption underlying the program.

Five-Stage Model of Innovation Process

Corning has been devoted to both total quality management and high performance over the last three decades. Under the leadership of Tom MacAvoy, former president and vice chairman of the company, innovation was brought under the spotlight of quality improvement and was refined and systematized as a set of custom disciplines. But unlike companies that tend to over-define the steps of new product development in minute detail, Corning was committed to creating a flexible framework. The intent of the new innovation process was to provide an ordered structure to invention that could be applied using common sense and thoughtful judgment based on a cultivated understanding of the technical, market, and manufacturing nuances of a given product. The model was formalized as a set of reliable tools that could be accessed both through the Internet and through a classroom curriculum and ancillary physical materials. While the five-stage model as depicted in Figure 3.1 has an appearance of linearity, it is in fact intended as a guide to be used in an iterative fashion based on the fluid process of learning across an array of dynamic social and technical networks and through a parallel process of integrating the commercial, technical, and manufacturing functions. Programs will frequently function simultaneously in more than one stage and just as frequently reverse course along the way to retreat to an earlier stage to refine or rework prior understandings before forging ahead to scale program development. See Figure 3.1.

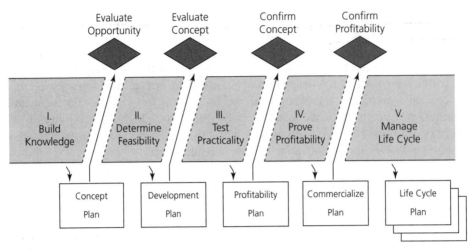

FIGURE 3.1. *Five-Stage Innovation Model*
© Corning Incorporated

A Mandate for Cultivating Effective Program Leadership

While the five-stage model provided the quality and process framework for successful innovation and new value creation, the model and tools did not provide sufficient support to cultivate the needed program leadership. The Corning Management Committee chartered the task team to pursue their draft plan for building the pipeline of program leaders both through effective career and performance management and through the design and deployment of a new program for high potential program and functional leaders that was initially conceived to be a "Boot Camp for Program Managers."

Corning's ongoing recipe for innovation could only be realized through the initiative of effective, committed, and inspiring leaders. The company management was clear that no given product line or business division could singularly guarantee the sustained profitability of the company. Program managers would continue to have the primary role within the company for assuring the effective adaptation to market opportunities and the creation of new value streams.

THE BUSINESS CASE FOR THE ACCELERATED DEVELOPMENT OF CORNING PROGRAM MANAGERS

In early 2007, Joe Miller, the chief technology officer, detailed a proposal for doubling the rate of productive innovation. The pipeline was and is full of a number of promising technologies that require wise stewardship to enhance successful implementation. Mark Newhouse, senior vice president, had just completed a review of innovation successes and failures across the past thirty years within Corning. Some common themes emerged and were addressed in the formation of a "Strategic Growth Organization" designed to shepherd new opportunities that did not fit within an existing business. In addition, a corporate technology council and a strategy and growth council were formed to provide broad oversight and guidance to new innovative ideas moving through the pipeline. The pace of learning was addressed by an initiative driven by Charlie Craig and Bruce Kirk, science and technology executives, to revitalize the innovation model. This effort resulted in the development and deployment of innovation black belts to support the increased tempo of R&D.

These foundational steps led directly to the focus on leadership. The research done by Mark Newhouse, Deb Mills, David Charlton, and others within Science and Technology suggested that a new type of leader would be needed who might be different from those found within existing business leadership.

After a long and difficult journey of dialogue and discovery, the role of an innovation program manager was formed with the support of a detailed voice of the customer and validation of the role with senior management. Given the ideal, Corning tested the model of program manager competencies against existing project managers, managers of large initiatives within Corning, and general managers of company business divisions.

The two champions of this work, Peter Volanakis, president and COO of Corning, and Joe Miller, chief technology officer, charged Rick O'Leary, then director of human resources for the Technology Community, to work with human resource leadership, Charlie Craig, and a small team of internal and external resources to test whether there could be a way to design a set of experiences to develop a program to address the needs of emerging program managers. Corning reached out to Gary Jusela, who had led a similar intervention with The Boeing Company and was a deep expert in learning design, to partner in the creation of a boot-camp type of immersion experience for those who had the potential to become program managers.

Engaging Internal Experts to Shape the Design for the Innovation Leadership Program

The effort to groom the future cadre of program leaders began as a collaboration among Rick O'Leary, Charlie Craig, and Gary Jusela. The initial work scoped out the definition of the role of program managers within the company and addressed both the current state of the art for grooming the required talent and the important areas of opportunity for strengthening this critical resource pool. This analysis identified career rotation, talent and performance management processes, and the design and creation of the needed communities of practice to shepherd development of both functional and program management practitioners. A tailored curriculum was viewed as an important component of program talent development but would only account for, at most, 10 percent of the career growth process.

Existing leadership curricula within the company primarily addressed project management rather than full program leadership. As part of the early planning, the task team created a differentiation of the project versus program roles as described in Figure 3.2.

Critical Activities	Project Management	Program Management
Stage gate management	◕	●
Quality, cost, schedule management	●	●
People performance management	●	●
Develop understanding of market and customers, create demand	○	●
Broad-scale stakeholder engagement and resource management	○	●
Boundary-spanning among technology, commercial, and manufacturing organizations	○	●
Supplier/partner management/engagement	◐	●
Deep knowledge of complete business model and leveraging resources across company	○	●
Effectively managing manufacturing launch	○	●
Broad awareness of global reach of business	○	●
Continuous improvement mindset	◐	●

FIGURE 3.2.   *Critical Activities Attributes: Project/Program Manager*
© Corning Incorporated

Based on a review with the Management Committee of the current state, vision, and next steps in talent development of program leaders, the task team was given the go-ahead to gain insight, ownership, and guidance from a diverse focal group of internal leaders serving as the voice of the customer. This panel then provided a foundation for initiating the detailed design process to create a robust learning intervention.

Voice of the Customer—Key Themes

The interviews with the host of influential community members provided a good foundation of understanding as preparation for the work with the multi-functional design team. The major themes included the following:

How Do You See the Role of Program Managers Within the Company?

- Program managers need to know when to firm up the program and structure and when to keep things loose—boundary management is a critical skill set; you need to know when to keep on pushing for innovation and when to lock down on a path to develop a product.

- Program managers are innovation managers; their role is beyond technology; it encompasses technology, marketing, and manufacturing.

- Program management is really the advanced course in leadership; it is a great training ground for general management.

- You have to be able to deal with messiness and ambiguity and make many decisions with insufficient information.

- You have to start the conversation on the manufacturing process already in Stages I and II, because 80 to 85 percent of the manufacturing cost is locked in by early Stage III.

What Are the Key Program Management Success Factors?

- You need to understand both the market and the technical domain as well as the internal Corning culture with respect to integrity and how we make decisions.

- You need to be able to set up a well-composed steering committee with key leaders who can help you access the needed resources.

- You must be effective in engaging with customers; you have to be able to win them over even when many things are up in the air, such as during Stage II; you have to be confident even in the face of doubts, and you need to sort out who the customer decision-makers are and connect with them.

- You need to understand where value comes from when you do something new, and then you must capture a meaningful amount of that; this requires that you know how the industry works and also that you be prepared to walk away from a deal if necessary.

- Understand the innovation process—you have to be smart to use it well, with consistency yet flexibility; it forces you to include the voice of technology, commercial, and manufacturing at every stage.

- Internally within the company you have to be ruthlessly honest about what you are doing and where you have made mistakes.

What Are the Most Common Ways That Program Managers Get into Trouble?

- Inability to articulate the business proposition.

- Inability to scale from a small project to the bigger picture; you need to have a grasp of scaling, pacing, and letting go if you are to follow the growth curve.

- Failing to manage the inevitable conflicts among the technical, commercial, and manufacturing communities, especially balancing between the technical community that wants clarity to come late and the manufacturing community that wants clarity to come as early as possible.

What Will Be Especially Important to Address in the New Development Program for Program Managers?

- Understanding the emergent nature of new-new programs (that is, new technology addressing a new market), you have to create your tool set as you go; there is a lot of uncertainty and ambiguity; you need an extra measure of creativity and entrepreneurship.

■ Learn how to sniff out the truth about the program as you proceed.

■ Address the criticality of appropriate domain expertise; you can't groom people for that; you have to hire the right external players.

■ You have to learn how to work outside of your comfort zone and have a broad feedback clock cycle dealing with both near-term and longer-term issues; help people develop good judgment quickly.

■ Focus on having tough conversations; learn how to address what went wrong openly.

These themes were reviewed in the gathering of the design team as a way to begin to build a broad shared database of critical information for setting the direction for the new curriculum.

Convening Wisdom—Foundational Design Team to Set Direction, Purpose, and Core Content

In order to build a framework for learning that would have the right aim and deep internal ownership, the core designers met with the program sponsors, Peter Volanakis and Joe Miller, as well as with the head of human resources, Christy Pambianchi, to identify a balanced set of participants to serve as a seasoned design group. Our objective was to gather a team who collectively had experience across all of the stages of the innovation process and who among them could speak to the technical, commercial, and engineering/manufacturing dimensions of new product development. The assembled group met all of these criteria, as well as covering a broad set of international experience and product programs addressing either new technology and new markets or a variation of new technology in existing markets or existing technology in new markets.

The process for creating the plan began with the initial formation of the design circle through in-depth personal introductions that brought both the spirit and the experience base of each participant into the context of the team. Following the building of the team, the conveners shared the model of **D**ata—**P**urpose—**P**lan—**E**valuate (**DPPE**) as a reliable method for building the learning structure. Within the group, we built the database through the sharing of all members' personal stories, reviewing the themes that emerged from the Voice of the Customer interviews, and engaging in collective inquiry and dialogue about the nature of innovation and new product development as practiced within Corning.

Purpose: The team was able to coalesce around four high-level themes that would need to be addressed in the learning event. These included:

1. Managing the transitions in moving through the innovation Stages I to III.

2. Building the value proposition/business case for the program.

3. Navigating corporate politics/understanding governance.

4. Providing effective leadership and managing the multiple challenges within the context of good moments and bad.

These topics were examined further and gave us a sense of the richness that could be explored in preparing the participants for effective leadership of new product development. Part of the learning would need to address the internal model of innovation, and another part would be heavily dependent on effective engagement and negotiation with customers with respect to value creation and the sharing of the benefits of new technology between Corning and these lead customers. The design team also discussed in considerable depth the role of internal governance structures, including the Program Steering Committee, the Corporate Technology Council, and the Growth and Strategy Council. And finally full consideration was given to the leadership requirements to be successful as a program manager, including realistic optimism, how to deal with the "dark nights of the soul" that occur, how to manage risk, and how to select, build, and engage a multifunctional team.

This discussion of what had to be covered in the curriculum was ultimately distilled into a focused and lean statement of purpose. One of the design members declared that what we were creating was a learning vehicle that recognized that new product programs were effectively the engines for growth for Corning. The course title was settled on as "Leadership Fundamentals for Program Managers," and the purpose statement was agreed as follows:

Leadership Fundamentals for Program Managers

Purpose: Prepare program managers (and supporting staff) who can move programs efficiently through the development phases as indicated by:

■ More efficient use of critical resources

■ Higher hit rate

■ Pacing to meet market needs

■ Killing things that need to be killed earlier

■ Capturing our fair share of the value

This statement came to serve as the North Star for the further refinement of the program and the build-out of the learning architecture. Before this initial design meeting was concluded, we succeeded in identifying an abundance of content detail from which to construct a series of modules and an overall system for individual and collective engagement.

Plan—Executive Development as Catalyst for Change: The design deliberations enabled the team to achieve an understanding of the difference we would need to make to not only create a cadre of future leaders for new product development, but to strengthen the innovation process and the inner workings of the company. The team clarified that innovation inevitably required a smart balance of structure and fluidity, that there was no simple cookbook or recipe to follow mechanistically toward a product or program goal. If the learning process was to be as powerful as possible, the design would have to engage the participants in a thoughtful interrogation of reality as well as in a deep exploration of what the company did particularly well and what aspects of internal practice had to be improved to better harness technology in the service of both the market and business needs.

The conversations started in the design meeting and then continued in the following months with different members of this group and an expanding circle of subject-matter experts and executive presenters. Along the way the process yielded several important components that would have to come to life within the design. Jim Nagel, the business development director and vice president of Corning Environmental Technologies, brought our attention to the Schrello questions associated with building a business case and evaluating a program's viability. He also pointed us to the concept of "judgment calls" as elaborated by Noel Tichy and Warren Bennis in an article within the *Harvard Business Review.*

The Schrello questions—Is it real? Can we win? Is it worth it?—provide the basis for determining and defending whether a program can justify its existence. Mark Beck, vice president and general manager of Corning Life Sciences, used the slide shown in Figure 3.3 to illustrate the process of internal interrogation and scrutiny that a program is repeatedly subjected to as it evolves through the stage gate model. Answering the questions posed requires incisive analysis along the lines of technology, commercial/market reception, and the manufacturing process. Yet there is rarely available an analysis so definitive as to yield perfectly defined outcomes delivered on an exact timetable. Program management is a process requiring finesse, judgment, and approximations of target timing. Hitting the window of opportunity on time is continuously an aspiration, but rarely a precise achievement.

Capturing both strategic control within a product domain and sustainable competitive advantage requires a blend of cognition with respect to the playing field and action in the midst of uncertainty based on the exercise of educated yet imperfect judgment. Our task as learning designers was to make these dilemmas real in a powerful true-to-life format and engage the participants in an inquiry without simple or obvious answers. A significant objective in our work was to help the students cultivate a thoughtful point of view about the reality within which they would be working in leading new product programs. See Figure 3.3.

Questions must be addressed not only to establish a clear business case and value proposition but also to assess progress through the innovation process. The expectation was articulated that the participants in the new program should have completed prerequisite training in Project Management and the Basics of Corning Innovation. Moreover, there was the hope that members of the class should have had significant assignments in two of the three major program disciplines, that is, technology, commercial development, and engineering/manufacturing. At a foundational level, Corning team members learn the vocabulary of innovation through their career experiences, combined with specific classroom training. In the advanced course, the objective would be to strengthen the players' judgment about how to use the innovation process.

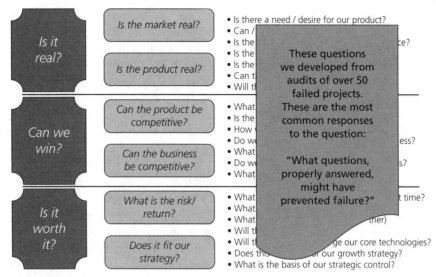

FIGURE 3.3. *Building a Business Case*
© Corning Incorporated

Effective innovation requires discernment with regard to which questions to attend to and which to ignore, depending on the technology, market, or manufacturing process at a given point, and how to engage deeply in truth discovery to differentiate solid ground from false assumptions. The executive faculty would organize their material to share both the wisdom of experience and unanswered questions in search of new knowledge. Perhaps what was most captivating about the role of program management was the simple fact that the role and task were (and are) simultaneously enormously creative and bursting with opportunities for learning, experimentation, and risk taking. Corning is not only committed to the strategic imperative of bringing new products to market but equally to continuously improving every aspect of the innovation process, starting from the first germ of a technical idea all the way to the full-scale build-up of supply chains, manufacturing partnerships, product sales, and distribution and customer service. The Leadership Fundamentals for Program Managers would serve as a platform to address both building the pipeline of innovation talent and strengthening the organization's understanding and capability of delivering new product value.

Senior leadership engagement and sponsorship. A key aspect of this approach is the understanding and commitment that the course would be taught primarily by internal senior leaders, including management committee members when appropriate; these included the CEO, the president and COO, and the chief technology officer. Two examples of leveraging the talent and wisdom of leadership are the following:

Peter Volanakis wanted to ensure that potential program managers knew what success would look like, in addition to the competencies and fundamental knowledge required. He chose to give a fireside chat as his contribution to the program. Things he would like in a program manager, in addition to being "really smart," included "telling the truth, getting out there, listening, rolling up sleeves and getting involved, staying the course, reducing complexity, resolving ambiguity where possible, and demonstrating courage and emotional resilience." This led to a sharing session of his own journey as a program manager and ended with friendly advice to a prospective program leader, "Be a chief detective, balance data with judgment, level with stakeholders, build a tight team, be there for your team, get to the customer, focus on the relationship and value proposition, identify the competition, and, above all, demand personal leadership of yourself and others."

Wendell Weeks signed up to lead the discussion on "game changers" that helped shape specific programs within Corning, and he identified some core principles contributing to competitive success. He spoke to the truth-discovery process within innovation and noted that the program manager is the creative director shaping the convergence of technology, manufacturing, and commercialization. He also encouraged leaders to embrace the tensions of the program manager role. In Wendell's view, winning program leaders make leadership personal and themselves accountable, find experts who can help, listen to customers, confront reality, stay open to new possibilities, and, above all, lead others into new program territory with confidence and yet full awareness that not all programs will succeed.

The design was sculpted through a series of conversations with senior leaders and experts and integrating the important learning objectives into leaders' presentations, case study documents, and learning team assignments. At each stage of program development, the key leaders were briefed, asked for their perspectives and commitment, and leveraged for their ideas and contributions to message development and delivery. The result was a course that had a committed leadership cadre, available and willing to serve this important initiative critical to Corning's success.

THE DESIGN FLOW: TWO WEEKS OF EXPERIENTIAL LEARNING WITH AN INTERIM PERIOD OF COACHING AND MENTORING

Out of the treasure chest of the purpose statement and the plethora of potential design elements, the structure of Leadership Fundamentals for Program Managers emerged. A smaller group of designers, both internal and external to the company, settled on a framework that would encapsulate the inquiry and content to address the North Star purpose statement and provide a living experience—a learning laboratory—to explore both the possibilities of individual development and the opportunities for improving innovation within Corning. The design would be composed of two discrete weeks, each with a focus on a segment of the Stage Gate Model. Week One would take on the origins of a program and explore the intentional evolution and development focusing primarily on ideas moving from mid-Stage II up through the end of Stage III. This would cover the heart of program development with all of the richness and intensity of the interplay among the commercial, technical, and manufacturing aspects of product development. This is a period of high uncertainty and risk in which there is a maximum of alternative paths. While Week One would have the character of "Running a Program," Week Two would have the overarching theme of managing the transition from running a program to "Launching a Business." This second week would address the large-scale ramp-up of the new product organization, addressing capital investment in manufacturing, globalization, market development, and managing the knife-edge tension between converging on a given product definition and market plan, versus diverging and staying open to new learning and insight with respect to technical, commercial, and manufacturing options.

Week One—Running a Program

Each day was given a theme, and the days together flowed through a simulation of real program development built around two case studies. The community came together on a Sunday at the stately old home and newly transformed company conference center of the former CEO Jamie Houghton. From the beginning, the design connected the participants to each other through the power of their personal histories and the choices they had faced in their careers and their lives. They came together from around the world, representing some ten different countries and even more different businesses from across the company. Each had seen new product development from the ground up, although some had been through the process many more times and in greater depth than others. All came from the cadre of managers who were viewed as promising prospects for providing bold program leadership for the future. The learning design would seek to create the opportunity for the participants to learn from each other as much as they would gain insight from topic experts brought in to share their perspectives with the group. The framework for this first week is captured in the schematic in Figure 3.4.

In order to bring the concept of program management to life, participants were assigned to one of two case studies, and in each instance the one with which they had a minimum of prior exposure or experience. The first case came out of the Environmental Technologies Division. This case was that of the Light Duty Diesel Filter, a product designed initially for a passenger car product with the launch customer being Volkswagen and the vehicle engineering center partner being based in Germany. This was a product that fell within an existing line of business, but one that required significant new technical development and the solidification of a completely new manufacturing process. The new material to be used in this filter had to be selected from among multiple options with divergent preferences expressed between the Corning team and the lead customer. This material and the fully formed filter would have to be produced at scale for a product line that was rapidly closing in on its production launch with projected volumes of millions of vehicles.

The second case study came out of the Life Sciences Division within Corning, the Epic System. This product would address a new market and would require entirely

	Sunday, April 6 **Day 1** Forming the Team	Monday, April 7 **Day 2** Beginnings Determine Endings	Tuesday, April 8 **Day 3** Engaging the Customer/Creating Value	Wednesday, April 9 **Day 4** Managing Competitive Dynamics	Thursday, April 10 **Day 5** Managing Complexity in a Growing Program Ecosystem	Friday, April 11 **Day 6** Delivering Value/ Assuming a New Identity
Morning		• Beginnings—Stage 1 (Case Teams) • "Thinking About Programs—Defining the Territory" M. Newhouse and J. Steiner • Taking Charge in Stage 2 (Case Teams)	• "Building the Technology Organization Within the Program" JP Mazeau • Engaging the Customer at Stage 2 to define and create Value Panel with Program Business Leaders • Stage 2 Customer Engagement (Case Teams)	• Prelimary Value Proposition Presentation (Case Teams) Business Leader Panel • Personal/Team Resilience—The Corporate Athlete	• Stage 3 Customer Panel • "Manufacturing Transition: Moving from Making Some to Making Many" M. Giroux • Managing Stage 3 Production and Customer and Team Dynamics (Case Teams)	• Value Proposition Working Session (Case Teams) • Value Proposition Team Presentation to Corning Executive Panel (M. Beck, T. Hinman, JP Mazeau, L. McRae, S. Miller, M. McClusky)
Afternoon	• Program Intro—R. O'Leary/C. Pambianchi • Program purpose and agenda—G. Jusela • Team formation • "Picking Programs and Making Them Work"—D. Morse • Social time	• "Building the Value Proposition/Business Case" M. Beck/ T. Hinman • Diagnosing Stage 2 Realities—Commercial/ Technical/Adv. Engineering • Preliminary Value Proposition (Case Teams)	• "Building the Value Proposition—Managing for Strategic Control" D. Charlton • "Early Stage Manufacturing" Process Leaders • Late Stage 2 Considerations (Case Teams) • Physical Activity	• Personal/Team Resilience—The Corporate Athlete • "Game Changers and Competitive Resilience...Stage 3" W. Weeks • Managing Through Game Changers (Case Teams)	• "Program Governance—Managing Promises, Expectations, and Stakeholder Relationships" P. Schneider • Value Proposition Working Session (Case Teams)	• Leadership Learnings: On Becoming a Program Manager • Discovering Our Strengths • Closing Round: Personal and Group Reflections on the Week • Adjourn for the Interim Period
Evening	• Dinner and Conversation with J. Miller and D. Morse: "The Program as an Engine of Growth"	• Dinner and Panel Discussion with M. Lauroesch, R. Snyder, L. Beall: "Managing Technology and Risk: IP Protection"	• Dinner and Conversation with Business Leader: "Engaging the Customer and Negotiating Value" • Late Night with Case Teams—Preparation of Preliminary Value Proposition Presentation	• Dinner and Fireside Conversation with P. Volanakis: "Personal Resilience in a Program Environment—Surviving Success or Failure"	• Dinner and Conversation with D. Morse and R. Henderson (MIT): "Innovation: A Process of Creative Tension"	

FIGURE 3.4. *Program Snapshot—Week One*
© Corning Incorporated

new technology to be developed within the company and also in conjunction with external design partners. The product was intended to make a significant contribution to shortening the cycle and improving the accuracy of new drug discovery and development within the pharmaceutical industry. This new market domain would require the importation of new players and new knowledge to the company and the pursuit of rapidly evolving technologies and customer interests. The case study, as well as the real-life program, were rife with complexity and challenged everyone involved with a highly difficult sense-making innovation task. There was nothing simple about any aspect of the technology, the market, or the building of the prototype products.

Both the core design team and an external design partner, Newry Corporation, working in conjunction with the Corning leaders responsible for these respective programs, shaped the case materials. By design, the learning teams received the relevant information piecemeal to have them engage with the content associated with these development efforts at a pace and sequence consistent with reality. Concrete learning objectives were developed for each day of the overall program design and each element of the case-study simulations. The design was built in a way that posed decision dilemmas and critical choice points facing the program team, without spelling out the actual path selected by the real teams. In both real-life programs, choices were made that led down blind alleys in some instances and opened up positive possibilities in others. The learning intent was not to display the one right path through the technical, commercial, and manufacturing minefields, but rather to educate the participants in how to marshal evidence and create the needed database to make educated decisions and defend and make a value proposition to customers and a defensible business case to Corning management.

With the thread of the two case studies running through the program, content pieces were introduced to create both the needed knowledge base from which to explore new product creation and to pose the dilemmas that would need to be addressed in these simulations and in future new business undertakings. Senior executive presenters were invited to share with the group important principles for managing their legs of the knowledge base and to open up territory within their respective domains that were fair game for new insights and continuous improvement. By design, the presenters were invited to set the stage for high-level inquiry into the innovation process and the discovery of new truths and value-adding insights.

In order to create an appropriate level of performance anxiety and tension, the participants were also asked to develop and make real presentations connected to the transition of their respect programs from Stage II to Stage III and from Stage III to Stage IV. The recipients of these respective presentations to be made on Day 4 and Day 6 in Week One were high-level executives within the company who themselves served on real governing bodies at either the division or the corporate level. These panels were directed to make the theater of these presentations as realistic as possible while supporting the primary objectives of creating a great learning experience with regard to developing and defending a well-composed value proposition and business case for a new product.

Parallel to the journey through the first three phases of a program's life, this first week provided a vehicle for exploring the personal leadership required in the navigation of new product development and the practices that would support personal resilience in the face of seemingly insurmountable obstacles, challenges, and ambiguities. Specific presented content as well as introspection and personal planning addressed the self-management disciplines that would enable the participants to maintain their sense of well-being in the face of all forms of adversity. Before concluding the week, each person was asked to reflect on his or her understanding of the program leadership role and to identify his or her own primary targets for learning and development in the interim period in advance of Week Two.

Interim Period—Leadership Connections

During the interim period between Week One and Week Two, the participants were each connected with a Corning executive as a mentor through the process called "Leadership Connections." This component engaged participants in a 360-degree assessment and provided them with three one-on-one coaching sessions with a member of Corning's senior management. The purpose of this component was to enhance each participant's classroom learning experience by providing specific feedback that focused on key individual development needs related to program management core competencies. In addition, the coaching sessions provided participants with an additional opportunity to have access to senior-level management to grow their networks throughout the organization.

Assessment Process: Prior to Week One, participants completed a 360-degree assessment that measured their capability against sixteen core leadership competencies specific to program management at Corning (see Program Manager Competency Model, Figure 3.5). Each participant selected up to seven feedback providers, including their managers, peers, direct reports, and themselves. The assessment was web-based and administered by a third-party company.

Once collected, the feedback was aggregated into a personal competency profile. Each profile contained an overview of the competency model, along with competency definitions; a guide to help the participants interpret the feedback; and their actual results. Also, the profile highlighted where the participant had hidden strengths or blind spots, along with written comments offered by the feedback providers.

The competency profiles were treated as confidential and were only viewed by one member of the facilitation team and the participant. Once the profiles were completed, a facilitation team member met with each participant to review his or her respective profile. This session typically took about an hour, and the purpose was to assist them in identifying areas of development that they were interested in working on with the coach to whom they would be assigned.

Coaching Framework: The facilitation team administered a process to pair participants with coaches based on the development areas that they selected and their functional growth opportunities within the business. The coaches were generally members of Corning's Management Group (CMG), which consists of the two hundred most-senior managers within the organization. The goal was to pair participants with coaches who were known to be subject-matter experts with depth in the area that the

Leadership Competencies			
Create Vision and Strategy	**Execute Strategy**	**Mobilize and Develop People**	**Manage Self**
• Managing Vision and Purpose • Strategic Agility • Creativity • Managerial Courage	• Organizational Agility • Priority Setting	• Motivating Others • Compassion • Building Effective Teams • Sizing Up People • Directing Others • Developing Others	• Dealing with Ambiguity • Presentation Skills • Resilience • Perseverance

Technical Competencies
Manufacturing
Commercial / Business
Technical / Innovation

FIGURE 3.5. *Program Manager Competency Model*
© Corning Incorporated

participant was interested in developing and who came from a different part of the business from where the participant was based. The intent was to broaden each person's network across the organization.

Once the pairings were completed, the coaches were notified and provided with a biography of the participants they would be coaching. In addition, each coach received a two-hour orientation summarizing the program manager competency model, as well as a model for how to structure the coaching sessions.

The participants were notified of who their coaches would be during the last day of Week One. They were provided with their coaches' biographies, along with an overview of what was expected during the coaching process. The participants were responsible for scheduling and completing three coaching sessions during the twelve-week period between Week One and Week Two of the classroom learning.

The coaching sessions were intended to provide participants with an internal support system that would help them to make real and lasting improvement. The first session was meant solely to build rapport between the participant and the coach and allow them to get to know one another's backgrounds. During session two, the coach and participant discussed the development area on which the participant would like to focus. During session three, the coach assisted the participant in creating an individual development plan. Then during Week Two of the classroom learning, each participant reviewed his or her development plan with a facilitation team member. Additional coaching sessions following Week Two were scheduled on a mutually agreed-on basis.

Summary: The Leadership Connections component of the program complemented the classroom learning activity by providing the participants with individual feedback specific to program management leadership competencies. This feedback was instrumental in helping the participants understand what area(s) they needed to further develop in order to become exceptional program managers at Corning. In addition, the Leadership Connections process provided tailored development and strengthened each individual's linkages to members of the Corning management group.

Week Two—Launching a Business

Stage IV and Stage V provide the focus for Week Two, with all of the attendant choice points regarding locking down on a technical configuration, ramping up production to support large-scale delivery, zeroing in on a target market, and managing profitability. The risks associated with program decisions at this stage become larger by several orders of magnitude, which brings even greater attention to sorting out options as early in the innovation process as possible. Mistakes made in the manufacturing design at Stage IV in the innovation sequence become truly painfully substantial, so the consequences of choices at this point bring an increasing level of management scrutiny. The beginning of this week brings attention to critical scaling issues associated with the production process and tracking cash utilization relative to market returns. Good growth, by definition, must generate a return on investment that exceeds the rate of cash burn to create a net positive business return and management willingness to press ahead with the program. Kate Asbeck, corporate senior vice president of finance, made a strong case for what would be required of a program to generate good growth, supported by the objectives shown in Figure 3.6.

A continuing narrative with regard to the Light Duty Diesel and the Epic System case studies again anchors the design for Week Two. The participants are asked to marshal arguments to justify their recommended decisions on the program direction in the transition from Stage IV to Stage V in the innovation model, and they are required to make their respective cases to a senior management panel consisting of senior leaders from the Life Sciences and Environmental Technologies businesses.

The design has the layout shown in Figure 3.7, which balances the evolving case study with content related to later stage technical development, refinement of the market strategy, and scalable manufacturing, as well as special attention devoted to program staffing, people development, leadership challenges and the requirements for effective program termination.

A fundamental question behind every program at these later stages in development is "Are we having fun?" Essential to a positive answer to this question is whether or not the program can be justified financially as a major source of profitability. The program must not only be technically and commercially viable with a robust manufacturing process, but it must also generate returns to exceed the weighted average cost of capital. In this second week, the participants engage in data gathering from actual program customers as well as from the plant teams responsible for late stage production. They are also asked to contemplate some of the ways programs may run off track at these stages and to bring to the table specific leadership dilemmas they are facing on programs and projects they are connected with in their back-home assignments. The learning teams within the class provide a forum to generate options for addressing

---

Corning's Metrics and Goals

✓ Growth
  – Sales: Aspire to 10% CAGR over 5 years (minimum 7.5%)
  – EPS: Aspire to 10% CAGR "over a cycle" ... trough to trough or peak to peak. Better during surges and expect retreats.

✓ Return on invested capital (ROIC)
  – ROIC > WACC (Weighted average cost of capital)

✓ Cash flow
  – Aspire to be positive cash flow every year
  – Goal 5% of sales 5 year average

✓ Shareholder value
  – Track and report TSR versus markets and competitive comparators
  – Track and report metrics that drive TSR in theory
  – Do not adopt formal TSR goal

FIGURE 3.6. *Corning's Metrics and Goals*
© Corning Incorporated

	Monday, June 22	Tuesday, June 23	Wednesday, June 24	Thursday, June 25	Friday, June 26
	Day 7 Mid-life crises and organization renewal	**Day 8** Investment choice points	**Day 9** Being a business	**Day 10** Innovation leadership in Stage IV and V	**Day 11** Holding on and letting go
Morning	• Reconnecting from the interim • "Thriving in Stage 4—Critical Competencies for Going Commercial" D. McCabe • Personal/Team Resilience—The corporate athlete	• Choice Points in Building a Manufacturing Organization—Plant Tour • Case study teams: -Plant tour debrief -Preparation for customers	• "Scaling Up and Growing a Global Business" — L. Ferrero • "Asian markets—The view for the future"—Eric Musser • Preparation for Memo to Corning Senior Leadership on the State of Program Management Within the Company • "Killing Programs Not People" —C. Craig	• Stage IV to V Stage Gate Review with Division Leadership—T. Hinman, J. Nagel, M. Beck, R. Verkleeren, Case Study Teams • "Managing Our Most Important Assets—People" C. Pambianchi	• "Securing the Value Proposition/Transitioning to the Business" Panel: Business Leaders • "Completing the Past, Embracing the Future, and Being True to Oneself": R. O'Leary, G. Jusela, Teams
Afternoon	• Personal/Team Resilience—The corporate athlete "What Is "Good" Growth?" (Finance 303)—K. Asbeck • "Case Study—Stage IV Divergence/Convergence	• Engaging with Customers (Case Study) • Preparation for Stage IV to V Stage Gate Review • Preparation for Memo to Corning Senior Leadership on the Stage of Program Management Within the Company	• "Is This Show Ready for Broadway?—Late Stage Failures and Recoveries" M. Curran • Preparation for Memo to Corning Senior Leadership on the Stage of Program Management Within the Company • Preparation for Stage IV to V Stage Gate Review	• Leadership Challenges—Learning Teams • "Innovation Revisited" B. Kirk • Final Draft of Memo to Senior Leadership	• Reflections on Program Management Within Corning—Round Table with W. Weeks, P. Volanakis and J. Miller • "Innovation Leadership—Our Heritage/Our Future" J. Houghton • Closing Round • Adjourn
Evening	• Dinner and Conversation with L. McRae and M. Newhouse: "Beyond Convention—Strategic Alternatives in Business Architecture and Domain Expertise"	• An Evening of Self-Expression - Theater of Innovation "Face the Music" —Blues Improvisation 171 Cedar Street Performing Arts Center	• Social Hour/Dinner—LC/HQ? • Case Teams—Preparation for Stage V Stage Gate Review	• Evening of Celebration at CMoG	

FIGURE 3.7. *Program Snapshot—Week Two*
© Corning Incorporated

55

personal leadership dilemmas and to expand the circle of relevant resources to be tapped outside of the class.

The final piece of the design explores the strengths and weaknesses of the innovation process within the company. Bruce Kirk, the process owner for the innovation model and the supporting online and classroom-based tools, engages the class in an examination of systemic opportunities for building on the company history in innovation. The participants take the opportunity to capture their collected insights in the form of formal feedback to the senior most executives about what can and must be done at both the program level and the management committee level to continue to improve the yield from the company's investment in innovation. Punctuating this dialogue with the senior leaders is a reflection on the Corning legacy and future of innovation by Jamie Houghton and a shared round of closing contemplation among all present for what is possible and what represents each person's highest hopes as a program leader.

OUTCOMES AND NEXT STEPS FOR GROWING THE TALENT PIPELINE OF PROGRAM LEADERS

So what happened? Thirty-three bright and motivated participants showed up, we received overwhelming positive feedback from the attendees as well as from management committee members and key leaders, and all were highly engaged. Participants came away with a deeper understanding and appreciation of Corning's commitment to innovation leadership as a strategy and the program manager's vital role in sustaining the growth engine of Corning.

Key Observations

- Participants enjoyed learning from executives and from each other.

- Diverse global representation of businesses, functions, and backgrounds adds to the program effectiveness.

- Leaders as teachers brought real-world experience and credibility to the content.

- Using case studies of real and current Corning programs was a useful device for learning.

- Strategic control/intellectual property were important topics.

- Supporting personal resilience was valued.

- Extensive focus on the value proposition/business case and presenting to the mock strategy and growth council were traumatic and quite helpful.

- Strong messaging about the need for early and balanced involvement of the commercial, technical, and manufacturing functions was important.

- Keeping the customer point of view embedded in the learning was effective.

Opportunities for Strengthening the Design

- Deepen the exploration of leadership behaviors and people skills required for success, especially in the later stages of program scale-up.

- Provide more specific tools on how to kill a program effectively when appropriate.

- Enrich the process and value of the interim coaching.

- Refine the engagement of key customers in the delivery of the program and further explore the nuances of effective customer interaction.

- Expand the case study materials and activities addressing Stages IV and V.

- Leverage the alumni of the first class in teaching and mentoring the second class.

NEXT STEPS

Program management is a highly valued function within the company and a key role to the ongoing deployment of Corning's innovation strategy. Inherent in the function is a serious risk of failure in any given program, yet that goes with the territory of new product creation. The participants wanted assurances that they could survive individual moments of reversal in the fortunes of any specific program, and they were seeking to understand plausible future trajectories for program leaders. There was a keen interest in understanding preferred developmental paths and a community of practice to share learning, insight, and peer-to-peer consultative guidance. Peter Volanakis was explicit in his perspective that program management is a vital and valuable proving ground on the path toward general management. Program managers have many options in front of them as they continue to progress with the company. Besides the GM roles, there are comparably important functions as country managers and senior functional positions within the technical, commercial, and manufacturing communities.

There could be few opportunities richer than what is afforded by program management for cultivating a diverse set of perspectives on Corning's business and testing and growing the mettle, resilience, and judgment of the highest-potential leaders within the company. There is more to be done to put in place a fully robust talent management process to support the growth of this cadre. The Leadership Fundamentals for Program Managers is an essential building block to strengthen both the innovation leaders and the innovation processes. (See Figure 3.8.) Systematic career movement, talent reviews, performance management, coaching, and practice exchange forums will better equip leaders for strategic innovation responsibilities. It is these leaders who will in turn assure the flow of new products through the innovation pipeline that is so critical to Corning's future.

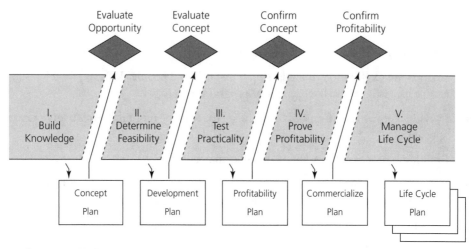

FIGURE 3.8. *Five-Stage Innovation Model*
© Corning Incorporated

REFERENCES

Bowen, H.K., & Purrington, C. (2008, March). *Corning: 156 years of innovation*. Harvard Business School Case Study N9–608–108.

Day, G.S. (2007, December). Is it real? Can we win? Is it worth doing? Managing risk and reward in an innovation portfolio. *Harvard Business Review*.

Tichy, N.M., & Bennis, W.G. (2007, October). Making judgment calls. *Harvard Business Review*.

Dr. Richard A. O'Leary joined Corning in April 2001 as director of human resources and diversity for Science and Technology. In 2003, he assumed additional responsibilities for the Corporate Legal and Patent group, and in 2005 assumed responsibility for the global Manufacturing, Technology, and Engineering organization. Effective January 1, 2009, he was appointed global director, human resources, International Regions. Prior to joining Corning, O'Leary was vice president, human resources, at Cytometrics, Inc., a biomedical high-technology start-up in Philadelphia. He has also held director-level human resource positions at the Public Service Electric & Gas Corporation and at Owens-Corning Corporation. O'Leary is nationally recognized for his expertise in organization development and human resources practices. O'Leary is an adjunct faculty member of the University of New Jersey, School of Medicine, and is a Lt. Col. in the Air National Guard, with twenty-one years of service. He serves on the boards of Watson Homestead, the Best Practice Institute, and The Alternative School for Math and Science. O'Leary holds a bachelor's degree in sociology and a master's degree in counseling from the University of Delaware, and a doctorate in counseling psychology from Western Michigan University. He was awarded Corning's President's Excellence Award in 2001, the Distinguished Alumni Award from Western Michigan in 2002, the Paul Harris Fellow Award from Rotary International in June 2004, the Awareness Quality Improvement Team Tower Award in 2005, and the Awareness Quality Improvement Team Outstanding Contributor Award in 2006, and was awarded two Meritorious Service Medals from the Air Force in 2005 and 2007.

Gary E. Jusela, Ph.D., consults globally with leading companies on customized learning design, innovation management, leadership development, and organization change. He has previously held the role of vice president of learning and/or organization development at Boeing, Cisco Systems, Lucent Technologies, and The Home Depot. He has served on the board of directors of ASTD, The Principals' Leadership Institute of the Seattle Public Schools, and the Church Council of Greater Seattle, as well as on the Service Quality Committee of Group Health Cooperative. He presently serves on the board of advisors for the Center for Leadership, Innovation, and Change at the Indian School of Business in Hyderabad, India, and on the Board Quality Committee of Swedish Medical Center in Seattle. He holds a bachelor of science degree in psychology from the University of Michigan, and an M.A., M.Phil., and Ph.D. in organizational behavior from Yale University.

Heath N. Topper joined Corning in August 2007 as organizational effectiveness director, strategic growth, within Science and Technology. Prior to joining Corning, Topper held the position of vice president, human resources, at Covalence Specialty Materials Corporation, a custom flexible packaging manufacturer in Minneapolis, Minnesota. He has also held director-level human resource positions at Tyco International and AutoNation, along with generalist positions at the Pepsi Bottling Group and Siemens. He was a leader for HR processes, including employee relations, people planning, staffing, and organizational development, for these corporations. Topper holds a bachelor's degree in business administration from the York College of Pennsylvania.

CHAPTER

4

CUSTOMER AND ENTERPRISE SERVICES (CES) DIVISION OF A FORTUNE 100 ORGANIZATION

MICHAEL SCHECTER, JOHN PARKER, AND JUDY ZAUCHA

How transforming the talent management systems and culture of a Fortune 100 insurance company's operations division created new profits, decreased costs, and improved productivity.

- Business Background and Challenges
- The Roots of the CES Transformation: Leadership and Process
  - The Personal Transformation of John Parker
  - Assessment Drives the Need for a Whole System Transformation
  - The Process to Transform CES's Whole Body

- Diagnosing and Designing the Whole System Transformation: The Leadership Alignment Event
    - Aligning Behind the Common Vision: Thrill Our Customer
    - Aligning Behind Common Values: Wholehearted and Inclusive Behavior
    - Designing the Whole System Transformation
    - Evaluation of the Leadership Alignment Event
- Implementing the Whole System Transformation: The Waves
- Supporting and Reinforcing the Whole System Transformation
    - The Hybrid Waves
    - Sustaining the Change
- Evaluation of the CES Whole System Transformation

The Customer and Enterprise Services Division ("CES") of a Fortune 100 company transformed the experiences of its clients, the internal satisfaction of its talent, and its fortunes by transforming all of its systems, including its talent management systems: It assessed each system that comprises its business, changed how those systems worked, and aligned each system with an over-arching and empowering vision. CES accomplished this change through an organization development process that emphasizes vision and values and strong leadership that created the transformation. Today, the talent in CES is more engaged, efficient, and happy; and CES is more productive and profitable.

BUSINESS BACKGROUND AND CHALLENGES

CES division is the back office to one of the largest and best-known insurance companies in the United States. It encompasses all call centers, accounting, inspections, and one of the largest printing shops in the country. It handles nearly twenty-two million phone calls, sells over 250,000 new financial products, and produces about three hundred million mailings. Historically, CES had been divided into two separate and distinct divisions. It duplicated accounting, customer service, and other services, plus related files and procedures. Because of this division, external clients experienced different responses from different people, missed follow-through due to miscommunications, and re-told their stories because the databases weren't necessarily shared.

Many managers in CES had inherited and maintained nineteenth century, industrialist leadership principles. It managed its people like commodities: The people executed tasks for forty hours a week without a need or desire for their personality or creativity. The managers measured and held their talent accountable to internal benchmarks of time and units produced, with little regard to external factors such as customer or employee satisfaction. This management attitude was passed through generations of CES leaders, creating an impermeable and static culture.

Managers marshaled no significant gain nor saw a significant decline in any major category such as production or efficiencies. Nothing changed.

Beneath this crust, employees toiled silently with disappointment and hopelessness. The manager's perception of clock-punchers was correct. Employees parked their personalities and lives at the door, did their duties mechanically, were careful to not question or create in any way that might suggest difference, boss-watched fearfully, and waited for the evening or weekend. It was a monochrome existence.

In short, CES division was inefficient, stunted, and frustrating to employees and clients alike. The client dissatisfaction was becoming more pronounced, staging the need for immediate change.

THE ROOTS OF THE CES TRANSFORMATION: LEADERSHIP AND PROCESS

In writing this chapter, a debate materialized whether CES transformed its talent management process because of its vice president's leadership or the whole system transformation process used. The CES team, with the exception of Parker himself, swears it was John Parker. The external consultants, who perhaps benefit from seeing this transformation regularly, emphasize the process, which changes the whole body, including the leader. The debate is reminiscent of Yeats' famous line, "O body swayed to music, O brightening glance, How can we know the dancer from the dance?"

Roland Sullivan, one of the external consultants, echoes this indistinction in two emails sent on the same day:

> *"It was the [process that moved] countless number of individuals and teams [to] surface the fantastic ideas to move CES forward. . . . The design team must get strong credit. [Nicole Lorenzetti's] role was key. . . . Then the most important people were the 1,000 or so people who attended the waves. All other people and teams only help set the stage for the phenomenal success."*

> *"The . . . theory says that the most critical person to model new behavior and attitudes is the top person of the organization. . . . I have had a number of cases where the top person could not change and the effort results were pale in terms of the [CES] case."*

Similarly, CES's transformation harmonized the dancer and the dance. Its leader, John Parker, embraced change before the external consultants arrived, welcomed the formal process and consultants, courageously committed to change, modeled and (when necessary) enforced change, and inspired employees to believe again in CES. The transformation process created safety to engage, enabled people with critical knowledge to contribute in inclusive ways, provided exercises and forums to showcase CES leadership's humanity, and built and sustained the momentum through phased interventions. In sum, the story of CES's transformation shows the individual qualities and successes of John Parker, choreographed with the whole system transformation process.

The Personal Transformation of John Parker

Today, John Parker walks through the office halls in a pressed white dress shirt, open collar, dress slacks, no coat, and an easy smile. Eyes follow him, half as star-gazers and half hoping he will stop and talk. His presence infects the staff. You might mistake him for a celebrity and not the vice president of the CES division. You might never guess that a few years ago he held a Darth Vader reputation for managing projects versus people. Before CES even recognized its need to change, its pump was primed with the personal transformation of John Parker. Parker rediscovered the value of relational leadership skills and embraced new language of wholehearted and inclusive behaviors. He then brought these values and language to CES and, in so doing, changed and affected the change of CES.

Parker began his career in a team-centric environment. They trusted each other, supported one another, created together. It was fun and engaging. Successes earned him the promotion to lead one of the technology divisions, where there were more employees to manage and they were not structured to work in teams. He got new mentors who taught him task-master leadership techniques, where a leader made sure that employees met or exceeded internally set measurables. Parker realized that the technology division could exceed its numbers and still fail because the numbers had little real meaning. But he did not challenge the system. It was not the CES way. He knuckled down and enforced. When asked, he acknowledges that he was not liked; he was feared, and he deserved it.

Then a friend, one of his mentors, died from a heart attack. He was fifty-four years old.

Parker had a personal crisis. His friend spent most of his life with the company and with its people. He treated the people transactionally and was remembered by some in CES transactionally. His legacy reflected his management style. The scene to Parker was like a visit from the ghost of Christmas future: Parker realized that he was like Scrooge following in Marley's footsteps and felt the rush of urgency to change. "Mankind was his business," and his management needed to reflect this humanity.

In OD nomenclature, he had a personal appreciative inquiry moment. He remembered the meaning and values of his past, discarded the bad parts, kept valuable skills, and drew a line to design a new future. Without any OD training, he decided that he had three stages to his career. Stage two was over. He now set the vision for stage three.

Stage three, he chose, will be to lead through relationships and create a people-centric environment. He began by re-learning talent management skills to communicate, give and receive feedback, and make people feel more included and safe in conversations. He found a common language on inclusion (from the Kaleel-Jamison Consulting Group) to train the department that would instill and sustain these behaviors. He moved his being from uber-executive to human.

Parker's personal change was highlighted first by his decision to be wholehearted, which means bringing your whole self to work. The alternative, parking your personality with your car, made the workplace transactional and unsatisfying. Without the opportunities to create, express, inquire, or otherwise be oneself, people will disengage, stop innovating, and show low energy. In short, they'll hate being at work.

Co-workers similarly can tell when they are being treated as a transaction. By becoming wholehearted, Parker discovered new creativities, ideas, and, consequently, opportunities. He began to challenge co-workers to bring more of themselves to work—to think for themselves, question when processes made no sense, feel empowered to try new ways of doing things, and be rewarded for their passion in addition to their results.

In short, rather than tell, Parker began to ask.

Parker's second significant realization was the hierarchy of being: Think, Do, Be. At the first, thinking level, a person learns what is or should be done. It is best characterized by the six-year-old who, morning after morning, is ready to leave for school but forgot his socks. He is reminded and, the next morning, again comes to breakfast sockless. He knows about the socks. He just hasn't reached the Do stage yet.

The Do stage is when the boy remembers. Think now of the goals we set for ourselves, like eating healthier. Doing becomes a challenge for most to do consistently. Ironically, many corporate training programs are geared to Do. We create exercises and training how to be accountable, for instance, and the Doing lasts as long as a carrot is offered or the stick is threatened.

CES was stuck in the Do stage. It wanted its employees to perform per unit, show up to work a number of hours per day and days per year, and sustain per volume. It was a definition of Do disconnected from less quantifiable and more human characteristics. It was action measurable and thereby could be made accountable, and so CES trained its employees informally to Do and not complain.

Being is the third, desired stage, when the doing becomes engrained into our definition of ourselves. We hold the door for the elderly not because we remember or are practicing, but because that simply is who we are. Being connects what we do with our desire of who we want to Be as a person. Questioning and choosing who we Be defines our humanity and empowers us to do difficult, scary, inspiring, or exotic things.

In his sunset months with the technology division, Parker discovered and re-defined his sense of being and living wholeheartedly. He became more humble, more inviting of feedback, more relatable and encouraging. His change became the prelude to CES's transformation.

Assessment Drives the Need for a Whole System Transformation

At the same time as Parker's new-look technology division began to take hold, opportunity struck when several executives left. The sudden vacuum in leadership raised business questions: Did it make sense to have a divided organization? Were there redundancies? Why was CES never improving? Why were CES employees asking to transfer to other departments? Why were CES internal clients asking to have work fulfilled by external vendors?

One of the senior vice presidents asked Parker to look into these questions. She gave Parker no directive or clear mandate, meaning that Parker did not have her blessing or her limitation. Parker hired outside consultants to review CES's structure and finances, as expected, and another set of consultants to review CES's culture by interviewing and surveying CES employees and clients. It is difficult to emphasize how novel or brave this act was. Within CES, culture was an irrelevant criteria. By showing an openness to deviate from the engrained culture and ask questions of change, Parker entered new (meaning risky) terrain without clear support.

The consultants performed the assessment survey, discovering and documenting the culture within CES. The results showed deeper problems than mere system redundancies, prompting the consultants to suggest addressing all of the systems. These results and recommendations had meaning because Parker was receptive to them. He then acted on the results by reaching out to Kris Kammerer.

Kammerer has sandy blonde hair, a smile warmed by the rose in her cheeks, and a sureness in her voice when she talks about organization development theory or training practices. Unlike Parker, who is with the corporate offices in Chicago, Kammerer is based in Texas as an internal education and training specialist. She was planning a leadership retreat for CES's vice presidents and division heads when she received from Parker, to her surprise, the analysis of CES's internal culture.

Her theme for the leadership retreat changed. She purchased and distributed one of John Kotter's books, made copies of the assessment data, and created ways to share the data with the leaders—a full, transparent discussion. She intended to create the burning platform, but without creating fear: To unfold the data carefully so it would be accepted more than challenged, reveal missed possibilities, and suggest that CES could choose to be different. She did so by weaving employee stories and experiences with the numbers and committing to inclusive conversation practices.

Opportunity then again graced CES. On the eve of the leadership event, Parker was named the new vice president in charge of the merged CES. The announcement surprised everyone, including Parker and Kammerer. Its timing, however, gave Kammerer the political backing and confidence to engage in the leadership conference fully.

If this were a military campaign, we might talk about the leadership conference as the turning point in the war. Leaders going into the meeting had the deluded sense that the CES culture was nice, fulfilling the needs of its clients and company according to its own internal measurements, and although not growing in revenue or efficiency, was fulfilling its mission. The conference would be like any other: Talk with those you normally don't see, pretend to learn something, and eat well. It would be something between a vacation and a waste of time.

Parker and Kammerer, with advice and help of an outside consultant, unfolded the cultural data carefully, created the case for urgent change, and then called them to arms. As leaders of one of the world's most famous institutions, the call to arms was greeted with an immediate and obvious response: The report was wrong, the assessment was biased or improperly performed, and the data was irrelevant. This quick response came from one table in particular: the table where Kammerer had seated the more entrenched and likely resisters. And they did not disappoint. Their table's energy quickly united and their response was thick. Kammerer and Parker let them protest, patiently, and exhausted their list of protests.

Other tables had nodded to parts of the report and had experienced some of its conclusions. The more the "resisters table" talked, the more it became alienated. And then someone else spoke up—the resisters table did not speak for him. Then another spoke up and, soon, the resisters table was in the minority. A more open dialogue ensued, permitting more people to share critical information. Parker encouraged this conversation and insisted on the safety necessary for them to risk contributing their opinions.

In this moment, CES cracked the 19th century concrete in its culture and considered a new perspective of itself. Its leaders saw through their management practices, glimpsed the truth of its culture, and found an opportunity to do things differently. Nicole Lorenzetti, a director in CES, describes:

> "[The] leadership meeting was to gather together all of our CES leaders with our new leader, John, and discuss expectations for the new organization. The theme was the 'iceberg is melting' . . . and the discussion focused on how we must change our approach to our work in order to be successful: Specifically, our internal clients saw us as expensive and slow, while we saw ourselves as doing a great job. I did see the call of action and the need to change based on interviews shared with us of our internal business partners, and always felt it was safe to change."

The key to the success, safety, was created by sharing the data and personal experiences openly, permitting open dialogue, emphasizing inclusive behaviors, and having Parker and Kammerer model these behaviors.

The Process to Transform CES's Whole Body

Parker and Kammerer had identified the need and created leadership support for the case for change. They had never transformed a whole system, however, and did not know the next steps. In his next courageous act, Parker committed dollars to a team of outside change agents, Gina Lavery, Jen Todd, and Roland Sullivan, and their whole system change methodology. Parker recalls:

> "I think [I committed to the process because of the] many conversations with our OD consultants asking me to trust the process. . . . What I didn't understand until afterwards was really the entire process has to do with transformation of many people in many different ways, including myself, and trusting the process is sometimes part of that type of learning. I was given a number of books to read and peruse that did talk about the process and talk about the theory. We spent some time on theory and it made sense to me, but ultimately working with trusted partners really helped, and I was allowed to learn, thank goodness, through the process as to how to transform myself not only as me personally but as a leader within the organization."

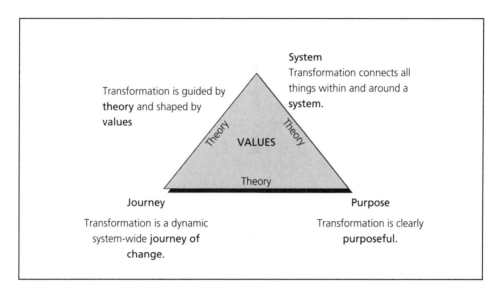

FIGURE 4.1. *The Five Truths of Whole System Transformation*
Source: W.J. Rothwell and R.L. Sullivan. (2005). *Practicing Organization Development*. San Francisco: Pfeiffer.

This courage resulted in part from his earlier personal transformation and commitments, and from the safety provided by the outside consultants. They offered confidence in their experience, theory that supported their beliefs, and a process that promised success.

The whole system transformation process addresses human fears and hopes. It balances the needs for courage and safety, and permits all elements in the system to voice thoughts and be heard by all the other systems. It is based on sociological theory, truth perspectives shared through facilitated dialogue, and the import of a communicated vision. One of the external consultants, Sullivan, illustrates these factors in Figure 4.1.

The process is (1) gather data on the system's culture and functionality of its processes; (2) share the data with the leader and, upon approval, the core leadership group; (3) create and align the core leadership group behind a vision; (4) empower the systems to change; (5) involve and engage the vision and value to a max mix gathering[1] of the system for the purpose of furthering the vision and identifying action items to make the vision alive; and (6) consistently solicit feedback from the system and adjust per the feedback.

This process works because the vision and actions reinforce the message of value—that the company and leadership value the employee as a person. The process:

■ Asks for information, rather than telling;

■ Involves all systems, giving a feeling of ownership and value to all employees;

- Trusts information to be shared with the systems, and people are hungry to share and receive information;

- Emphasizes ideas and growth—personality characteristics that connect people to each other; and

- Empowers people at all levels in the hierarchy to be experts on the tasks they do and to use and share their expertise.

In short, this process first suggests a new vision for organization and then values the human experience within the systems. The employees can relate to the vision and find a sense of identity from it, and feel valued by participating in designing the change.

The success of the process is something between magic and science. Magic because the results, the personal and systematic excitement, look miraculous. Science because the process can be duplicated with new organizations and the ability transferred to new people. For CES, this was a perfect match. Sullivan was very experienced with organization development theories and methodologies, could use Lavery and Todd as local extensions, and could train CES's internal trainers, Kammerer, Ginger Whitson, and Ginny Chiappetta, to make CES self-sufficient. If CES was going to sustain a change initiative among six thousand employees around the world and manage the initiative long term, it was going to have to develop internal competency. The outside consultants unselfishly promoted this transference.

DIAGNOSING AND DESIGNING THE WHOLE SYSTEM TRANSFORMATION: THE LEADERSHIP ALIGNMENT EVENT

The first step in the process was a leadership retreat with Parker's core leaders. The iceberg leadership retreat established the case for change among a broader group. Now, CES needed to identify and assemble its core leadership group to find a common vision.

The leadership alignment event followed the appreciative inquiry format. The external and internal change agents used the assessment data to help confront the past and redefine who they would choose to "be in the future." The data compelled the recognition that CES must change or die. The CES core team first looked at their accountability in the culture, what difference they could make, and what actions could make a difference. They then let go of the past and committed to action steps to involve and transform the whole system. They finally aligned with three important decisions: (1) a common vision, (2) core values, and (3) a journey to involve and change the whole system.

Aligning Behind the Common Vision: Thrill Our Customer

The vision identifies the common purpose that unites a team. The common purpose provides direction, promotes safety and trust, spurs momentum, creates value, and helps people become more human than transactional. For instance, many people decide to go to work to earn money. They punch the clock, do their time, and cash their checks. Although a vision or a purpose, it has nothing in common with those of others and lacks the fairy dust feeling of value.

A common purpose depends on relationships. Identifying a vision that shows how we decide to relate to others becomes more powerful naturally and harder to dismiss. Rather than sound transactional, it invokes feeling and thereby engenders wholeheartedness and inclusive behaviors. Starting from the heart and valuing a relational vision are fundamental to dialogue, dispute resolution, feedback, feedforward, and transformation practices. It is a different way to manage talent.

For CES, the leadership team identified the vision at the leadership alignment retreat, but the language changed later when a front-line employee expressed it perfectly: "Thrill Our Customer." The team also established the number one duty of each employee:

"Major Responsibility #1" (MR1) has become prevalent, from a main theme in every training to the first criteria used in each employee's annual review. It is CES's "prime directive." Although MR1 may seem similar to other platitudes from other companies, what makes MR1 special is that—stated so and used so—it is each employee's first major responsibility, from the front line to the vice president. Leaders hold employees accountable first to being inclusive, open, and relational, and then to numbers.

This vision invokes change. Their job had been to satisfy units and the customer, but their vision now is to "thrill" the customer. Create an experience. Be memorable. Don't count papers; deliver smiles.

With this realization, the core leadership team found the next piece of its change language: Get Different. In the past, CES had preached to work smarter, better, more efficiently. Although these sound bites have been pop in management circles, they also have become caricatures of disconnected leaders. Rather than motivate employees, the terms are heard as criticisms for being dumb, inferior, or unfocused. Jen Todd reflected that this new language, "get different," recognized that CES could not "get different results without getting different ourselves. It is about a deep paradigm shift. It is about a breakthrough." At a more basic level, getting different simply asked employees to try something new. Not "better," just different. This simple permission created great freedom and provided the space for innovation and empowerment, failure and success.

Major Responsibility #1—Our employees be accountable and highly engaged to deliver unbeatable service by:

1. Modeling and supporting an inclusive environment

2. Referrals when needed, coaching, and helping to retain talent

3. Removing barriers

Aligning Behind Common Values: Wholehearted and Inclusive Behavior

The next key ingredient is to show and teach how to value one another. Any relational environment depends on respectful treatment. Fears, politics, money, and other business factors can undermine this feeling of respect. More commonly, the transactional side of business predominates the discussion and so, while a conversation may not be disrespectful, it can undermine respect by feeling like a command (devaluing the other's input, feedback, or circumstances).

Best decisions are made when all the information enters the dialogue. This means creating an environment of safety. Parker had discovered the language of wholeheartedness and inclusive behaviors and brought these lessons to the CES core leadership team. These lessons included language to lean into uncomfortable conversations, how to give and receive feedback, and how to make others feel included in the vision and direction of the group. The core team further committed to involve all systems in the change effort and to value all voices in the system. This commitment meant trusting and empowering all systems to participate in the change.

Designing the Whole System Transformation

The core team finally committed to a journey map that would lead CES to change all its systems. Following the Kathy Dannemiller "Whole-Scale Change" methodology, it designed four large group transformation events, called waves. The waves would be built along the max mix model at all levels. To achieve the max mix representation of location, hierarchy, and all other attributes, attendees would need to fly in for the wave. This included flying non-exempt employees who never had flown for the company before (some never had been on an airplane before!), hosting them in at a nice hotel, and providing meals. The core team treated each person as an executive.

Again, all these decisions were made without a budget or clear mandate from above!

One key factor in the success was the leadership team's commitment to the change exemplified in one simple yet dramatic act. The leadership team made its schedule subject to the change initiative. That meant that the team designing the wave could book and plan the event, and the leader would adjust his or her schedule accordingly. Meetings, travel, deadlines, and vacations took a back seat. The leaders became subject to the same planning as all employees, except that the leaders needed to attend all wave events.

Evaluation of the Leadership Alignment Event

Everyone in CES considers this leadership alignment event as the critical victory in its transformation. It took three days to align the leadership group to the new vision and to commit to the waves. Since that time, each leader has been "on message" and has helped to create a roadmap to complete the transformation. Parker recalls:

> "[The] top team alignment was totally different than other sessions that I had been through. It was focused on really speaking as one voice, taking our core leadership team of seven folks and making sure that as we went into our transformation of the organization that we were speaking of one voice so that people could trust us and trust what we were all about. What shifted for the team in the session really was all of the background of the two organizations and the leaders at the top going through the process and actually changing."

Equally as important, the leaders got human with each other, meaning they identified with each other as a person rather than a position, shared their hearts, and, in the process, built trust in one another and greater commitment toward and accountability for their relationships. Parker again recalls:

"[The leaders] were all competitive with one another, they didn't trust one another, they had spent years with their leaders working on that lack of trust and that competitiveness and, as a result, were not optimizing and supporting one another in what we needed to do, even though that would be a desired effect. We had to leave our baggage behind and we had to get to know one another and then agree that we were going to leave it behind and come out speaking as one voice and take the organization in a different direction. That happened in the session.

"What also happened in the session was the CLT, the core leadership team, understanding and ownership of what it is we were going to do in the organization . . . to change the way we were going to conduct business: Moving from a shared service organization totally focused on process, efficiency, and effectiveness, [and] being internally measured; to a valued service provider . . . providing and proving the value that we provide to the corporation. . . . [The CLT] took total ownership of that strategy in that session as well as getting to know one another. And as a result, we came out with a purpose, with guiding principles, with operating norms as a team, and truly started to operate as a team of one. Even though there were seven of us, our voices were the same. . . . It was unbelievable."

CLT never wavered and still has not wavered, from the vision and value principle determined at this event.

IMPLEMENTING THE WHOLE SYSTEM TRANSFORMATION: THE WAVES

The leadership team committed during its alignment event to transform the whole system, or roughly six thousand employees in fourteen locations around the world. Rather than engage the whole system at one time, the leaders decided to engage the 20 percent tipping point amount in four waves, with roughly 300 to 550 people in each wave. The wave events were planned for two and a half days and were rooted in the Dannemiller-Tyson formula for change:

$$\text{Dissatisfaction} * \text{Vision} * \text{First Steps} = \text{Transformation}[2]$$

Accordingly, each wave included all of these elements with an emphasis, or "thrust", on one element. This emphasis evolved from wave to wave, building momentum. The process is shown in Figure 4.2.

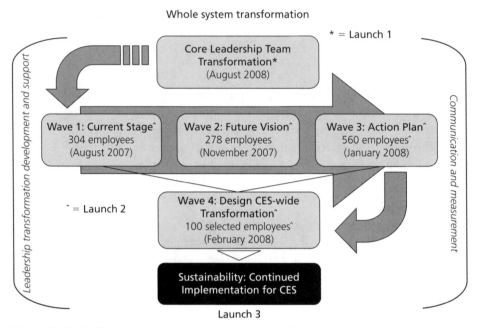

FIGURE 4.2. *Whole System Transformation Process*

As seen in Figure 4.2, the first wave's thrust was on the dissatisfaction, the past, and how things have been. It created thoughts and conclusions that were presented to the second wave, which focused on what was working at CES and the vision of what CES could be. The third wave picked up the vision and focused further on what CES could and should become. The fourth wave brought together all the thoughts and recommendations and mapped the journey to sustained change.

For CES, the dissatisfaction lay with its business and premium-paying customers. They struggled dealing with CES. This customer dissatisfaction created business problems that were addressable by cultural changes that the core team had considered in the vision. CES was going to be about thrilling the customer, getting different, and fulfilling the MR1. How this vision became action depended on the input and recommendations of the wave.

The waves therefore focused on the entire system, following the Dannemiller star model (depicted by the figure of a star in which the top, true north, is strategic direction, and each following point is processes and systems, form, resources, and shared information). For instance, in reviewing where CES had been and where it could go, each wave considered each point of the star and what resources it might need or processes to adjust. Action items were created at local and system levels.

The process also designed ways to grow and sustain the change. The following graph in Figure 4.3 depicts the attention CES gave to the post-wave experience, adopting a QUEST formula to continue to involve and emphasize the work done in the waves.

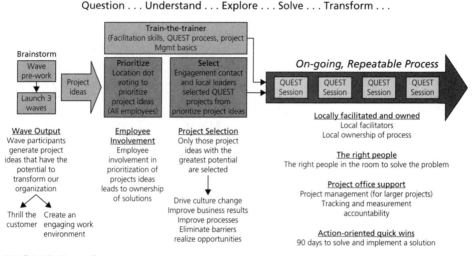

FIGURE 4.3. *QUEST Sustainability Process*

As Figure 4.3 shows, the transformation began with leadership, expanded to large groups through the waves, and then began focusing more on the local and personal responsibilities. Individuals were required to question processes on an ongoing basis and create new solutions that would improve how CES thrilled its customers. This focus on empowerment, questioning, and improvement became the momentum of constant transformation.

Each wave was co-planned by members of the core leadership team, managers, and front-line employees, including employees in the location of the event. Each event followed the max mix belief in each stage (from planning to table groups), in organization chart rank, and in attitude (from cheerleaders to sourpusses). PowerPoint was banned. A "no stripes" policy was enforced. Leaders were seated at tables anonymously without titles. Parker explained:

> *"It was a very inclusive process, all parties represented, all levels, all parts of the organization regardless of geography, and it was designed that way. It really was designed to bring everybody together for the first time and break down the walls of the kingdoms and queendoms that existed, and the result was incredible. People found out for the first time who they were talking to on the other side of the phone when they were working through their horizontal business processes and began to talk about how almost immediately how to make them better. That was what we were after and that's what we got."*

Each wave began with a keynote from "Saint" Judy Zaucha, John Parker's executive assistant, and discovered inspirational speaker. Each wave then included room greeting activity, a presentation of "what is CES," a candid interview with John Parker (literally, someone interviewed him on-stage, live, with unapproved questions), craft activities, and an "elephant box" where any question could be posed to expose the elephant in the room. Each step was calculated to value the opinion and presence of each attendee, knock down barriers, become human or inclusive with one another, and show commitment to the vision.

Parker, especially, got personal and unprotected. He answered tough questions. He talked regretfully and emotionally about the manager he was. He confessed to getting drunk in college, getting hit by a bus, and breaking a lot of bones. And learning. He also did shots with his son when his son graduated college. Employees were shocked to hear their boss having life experiences, even stupid ones, like everyone else. Parker became a person, not just a suit. He showed himself to be vulnerable and wholehearted.

To change the culture, CES needed to become more inclusive, transparent, appreciating and empowering. In short, they needed to Thrill Our Customer and fulfill MR1. The waves explored how each person could do this. For instance, the "Stop/Start/Continue" exercise in Wave 1 asked participants to create flip charts answering this question:

In order to thrill our customers, we must:

- Start doing?

- Stop doing?

- Continue doing?

The groups then discussed what "Thrill Our Customer" meant in the context of their work and to create solutions within their departments that would further this goal.

The waves also had fun activities that reinforced the themes. For instance, in Wave 2, CES did a "fearless" activity in which the group divided into twos and shared with their partners a moment when they were fearless or witnessed fearlessness. They used these stories to prompt a discussion of what it takes to act and be fearless. The discussion then became concrete—the participants created guidelines on being fearless and thriving in the transformed organization. Finally, each person was asked to advertise their fearless guidelines in an arts and crafts project. They made capes, decorated them with their guidelines, and showed them to others. The discussion created new creative energy about being unafraid to show initiative. A similar exercise in Wave 3 created superhero shields that would allow employees "to step out of our comfort zones and feel empowered to achieve MR1."

The waves also looked at external experiences. For instance, an activity divided the teams into two groups. Group 1 put itself in the shoes of an external, premium-paying customer, and Group 2 was an internal customer. The two groups created lists of needs and wants and then shared the lists. Finally, the wave as a whole discussed how CES could support both sets of needs.

Some changes were almost instantaneous. For instance, some people had worked on opposite ends of an issue, and even had spoken on the phone, but never met. They began to get a fuller view of the processes, realized barriers in how they did things, and made connections for how to improve them. People also made personal connections to the change, talked about it and how it affected others. Many had to leave the room at times to gather themselves or reflect on what was happening.

Everyone remembers "Johny." She is a front-line, non-exempt, shy, plain-shirted employee who had been with the company for thirty-four years. She had seen it all, didn't want any part of it, and didn't want to contribute or even attend the wave. They flew her out anyway. Then she heard from Zaucha and Parker and participated in the conversations. She found new hope. And courage. She went on stage and publicly addressed the six hundred wave attendees: "This is the first time anyone at [the company] asked me about my job and how to do better." She confessed that she had been cynical and wanted to be happy and involved. She challenged her role in the company and her role in her personal life, and saw how choosing a new attitude and new perspective could create new possibilities within CES and her personal life. She cried and made others cry with her. "I can't wait to go back to my desk and begin making it better," she concluded.

The success with Wave 1 helped grow future successes. Another employee wrote, "For Wave 2 one person from my department volunteered due to the information and excitement I came back with. . . . I learned so much. The hotel [CES] put us up in was just beautiful and the food was great. I will ask for my name to be submitted to attend Wave 4."

Following the wave, a department leader immediately identified the need to be in closer relationships with her co-workers and develop relational leadership skills.

> *"Personally, it was a wake-up call for me. I have found myself being more focused on the personal relationships of the folks I work with. I can honestly say I am listening more earnestly, driving folks to become engaged at all levels and looking at my co-workers with more respect, acknowledging that everyone has value and can add value."*

She sustained this effort, became a more effective manager whose results soon became apparent in her team, and was promoted to director. This promotion reinforced the new values CES encouraged.

Another employee declared an end to triangle conversations. Her manager, who had not yet attended a wave but was impressed with the impact, reported: "She would not entertain any more 'negative' comments. If someone had something to complain about, then [he should] come up with a solution to the issue."

The waves' impacts also were transformational in the magic way. One woman wrote the design committee:

> *"Thanks again for everything you and everyone else did that made last week such a huge success. I try explaining to people that it was not only business related, that it*

touched a spiritual level as well. Through what I learned last week, not only can I become a better employee, but a better spouse and a better mom. It was truly amazing. As a matter of fact, I bought a black long-sleeve shirt and got "GET DIFFERENT" in big white letters. I am wearing it proudly today."

Ginny Chiappetta says that, after the wave events, her family said she couldn't stop smiling. She even used the OD process with her sixteen-year-old daughter, helping to transform that relationship.

Parker became a rock star or touchstone to many employees—the leader who understood his employees and worked toward real solutions. Today he gets emails from dozens of employees at all stations asking his advice, sharing stories, and giving feedback. He tries to respond to all of them. One employee commented after Wave 1: "The buzz is still humming here about Wave 1. And I think I'm going to start a John Parker fan club. A photo he took with one of our attendees is now her screensaver. No joke."

The waves were transformational, meaning that attendees moved from disengaged and disenchanted to energized by a shared vision, a feeling of empowerment to achieve it, and a sense of value that being wholehearted at work is desired. Transformation speaks to the "be" state and includes both business and personal relations. Following Wave 2 in Ohio, one transformed participant, Tony, wrote to his table:

"The experience that I had in Ohio was a humbling experience. It made me see that no matter where you come from most people are all the same. Except for Table 24. An extraordinary group of people I have had the great pleasure of meeting and being in the company of. The compassion that each of you show for each other was overwhelming. And it made me rethink the type of person that I am. I have always tried to better myself each and every day. When I wake up in the morning and look in the mirror, the first thing I say is 'okay what can I do to make Tony a better person today?' I won't have to look any further. Because the little notes that you all wrote about me say it all. They are posted on my mirror so in the morning I just look at one and read it. It has inspired me to become even more of a better person. Not just about a person inside. But also a better human being. . . . What I mean by that is to think more logically . . . all of you guys at Table 24 have made the difference in my life. And I am pretty sure a lot of your good qualities have rubbed off on me. . . . So can one person make a difference. If that is true that I'm a very lucky person because I have had seven people make a difference in my life. P.S. if any of you guys ever happen to be in Chicago give me a call. I extend my hospitality out to you with open arms. Also you can drop me a personal e-mail at. . . . Your friend Tony."

Table participants responded hours later, including the following:

"I did get this email from Tony, and honestly I've been touched ever since. . . . What he comments is very true, all expectations on my side were blown away for the best and

you are all greatly responsible for it . . . so I thank you that. I believe it is important that we not only keep alive Wave 2 but also the friendship that was born in Table 24!!! I know I will see again Jen and Kris because I do go to Virginia at least ten times a year (family and Tech games), and I also go to TX to visit my old peers and friends. . . . did promise Tony that I would visit Chicago, during 2008 so that only leaves me with the promise of making an effort to go around Ohio to see everybody else!!! Please stay in touch!!! Your friend, Edgar"

Another incredible, albeit sadder story, occurred when CES closed one of its offices. The employees cheered. They were crushed for losing their jobs but thankful for the way in which Allstate held the conversations. Rather than humiliated and lost, they felt appreciated and supported. CES included them in the transformation process and considered them part of CES, even after the decision was made to close the office. Further, the decision was communicated early and respectfully, and support offered. Again, the story of how CES valued these employees spread, proving that management could be trusted to fulfill the intention of the waves.

SUPPORTING AND REINFORCING THE WHOLE SYSTEM TRANSFORMATION

The Hybrid Waves

The success of the four waves bred new energies. First, the leadership team believed that the 20 percent tipping point had been achieved, but the division was not tipping fast enough. Employees who did not attend the events had not learned the language of feedback or communication, and either felt left out or were being left behind. Second, they wanted to support and reinforce the learning in the waves with the other employees. And not unimportantly, the leadership team was so moved by the personal transformations of those who attended the waves that they felt all should attend a wave—all six thousand employees.

The transformational energy tugged at their emotions. For instance, one wave attendee wrote to the core team:

"I was also blessed to be at the first wave in Dallas, and am still calling to mind the experience I had there on a regular basis. I'm so grateful to be a part of the CES & the . . . corporation. I pray the rest of the CES team that hasn't gone to a wave will feel the same excitement that is brought back from each of the waves and start to transform their thinking."

Other success stories, like the employee who used to make others miserable who returned from a wave ready to be a good teammate, highlighted the urgency in achieving the possible quickly. Or, as Harry said to Sally, "When you realize you want to spend the rest of your life with somebody, you want the rest of your life to begin as soon as possible." [*When Harry Met Sally.* Castle Rock Entertainment.]

For the first time, though, budget became a concern. CES already had spent dollars on the alignment and four waves, reaching the 20 percent tipping point. Although it would be repaid multifold in savings, reaching the remaining 80 percent was budgetarily daunting.

In another defining moment, CES did not relent to failure. True to its vision to "Get Different," CES decided to do a one-day hybrid wave.

The consultants said no. Although it was a good idea, you simply cannot get transformation in a one-day event. It was better to trust the process, trust the tipping point, and plan more waves over a longer period of time. This process could be designed efficiently, respecting budget concerns and to guard against burnout.

CES stuck to its opinion. It really wanted more employees to have a wave experience, did not want to wait, and felt capable of designing and handling a hybrid one-day event. Today, they credit the outside consultants for building this internal competence through education and coaching. They then exercised this confidence and overrode the consultants' decision, created the new hybrid wave, and took full ownership of their transformative journey.

To make up for the shortened time of the event, the hybrid wave provided pre-event training explaining transformation, what the prior waves had done and accomplished, and CES's language for feedback and inclusion. Another day of training was added after the event to follow up on the one-day event. These pre- and post-events were local, saving cost and time.

The one-day events followed the roadmap of the larger events, just shortened. They shared the work of the prior waves, explained the new language being developed to create and sustain the change, and invited the employees to join in the change effort. Specifically, each person was given the chance to own his or her position and performance and suggest different ways of accomplishing the task. For instance, one exercise asked participants to read the CES mission statement out loud and then discuss what part their team played in accomplishing that mission. They further created flip charts showing how they could initiate acts that would move their teams toward success and in the direction of the vision.

The one-day mini waves were extraordinarily successful, due in part to the hybrid planning and the fact that a critical mass had experienced the prior waves and paved the road for the hybrid waves. The hybrid waves let participants learn first-hand the new language of change, question and experience the sincerity in MR1, and feel personally included. Not coincidentally, the numbers improved immediately. Parker saw higher customer satisfaction and unforeseen money savings:

"Following the transformation we saw things start to happen in our measurements immediately. Our post-call survey results, a survey that our customers opt to take when they make a phone call to our call centers, started to immediately jump. Years had gone by and there had been no movement. We saw seven months in a row of improvement. . . . We saw our ability to execute and manage our expenses change this year. Without asking, without driving, we're going to come in millions of dollars

under plan and have been able to use that money in really buying more advertising for our direct sales teams and providing resources back to the organization."

In addition to saving money and performing at higher levels, employees were happier and more engaged. More employees began attending and leading work activities from department meetings to corrective action teams.

Sustaining the Change

CES values the change it made and wants it sustained. As discussed above, it designed in its wave process the post-wave QUEST process, empowering employees to continue to question procedures, engage and solve problems, and transform the processes in the system. It also provided concrete guidance to drive this questioning and confront problems early.

Figure 4.4 shows first that CES is looking at its whole system and how those systems are supported and related. Within the systems, CES emphasizes maintaining the language of change, engaging actively in feedback, creating a rewards and recognition program, now learning about feed-forward, continuing personal and business growth, and keeping the MR1 in focus. In short, sustainability is a sustained campaign that is behavior and attitude focused and feedback and accountability driven.

In living this model, CES approved a new position requested by a wave. The engagement catalyst's job duty is to make sure that CES is continually changing on the personal, skill development, and professional levels. Parker explains, "We have to constantly be changing. We have to constantly adapt to the changes that are put in

FIGURE 4.4. *Output for the Waves*

front of us, and we have to [be] open and willing to do that." The engagement catalysts provide consistent training and reinforcement of the transformation.

CES also monitors its progress and regressions with internal focused pulse surveys. Numbers that historically had been in the two or three out of five range consistently have climbed and maintained a 3 to 4.5 rating. Figure 4.5 shows improved satisfaction in every system.

When a survey identifies setbacks in an area or location, an engagement catalyst jumps in or a focus group is created. In a focus group, a facilitator gathers a max mix sample in one or several locations and dives deeper into the issues, like a wave event. A year ago, these groups might not have worked because they were foreign and there was lack of trust about how the results would be used. Today, there is a common language and trust that these events are co-designed by employees to improve the system and will have a good impact.

CES also pays attention to how it performs in comparison with other industries. For instance, it has conducted surveys with Chris Worley measuring CES's performance in key categories, shown in Table 4.1.

As the pulse survey shows, CES scores higher consistently than similar departments in other industries. Another survey (seen in Table 4.2) shows that, because of the successes in CES, leadership is able to spend more time building future business.

These surveys further show no glaring problematic culture. Worley's initial conclusions suggest that CES's culture is progressive, innovative, and agile.

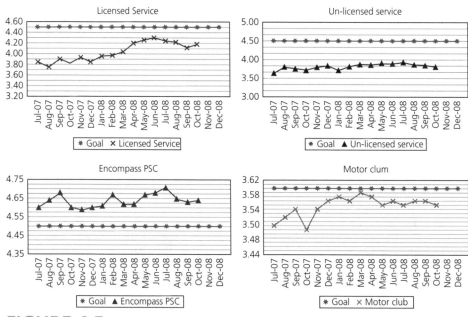

FIGURE 4.5. *CES Business Results*

TABLE 4.1. Pulse Survey Results, CES

Descriptive Statistics	OVERALL CES		Insurance		Financial Services		Health Care Services	
	Mean	S.D.	Mean	S.D.	Mean	S.D.	Mean	S.D.
Sense of Shared Purpose	4.12	0.87						
Develops Robust Strategies	3.99	0.91	3.18	0.66	3.82	0.63	4.30	0.46
Encourages Innovation	4.02	0.92						
Change-Friendly Identity	3.90	0.91	3.05	0.58	3.56	0.74	4.23	0.48
Strong Future Focus	3.94	0.98	3.33	0.67	3.87	0.60	4.34	0.46
Flexible Structure (Surface Area)	3.78	0.84	3.12	0.52	3.71	0.60	3.97	0.55
Information Transparency	3.88	0.95	3.07	0.83	4.00	0.57	3.98	0.47
Shares Power	3.74	1.09						
Flexible Resources	3.68	0.96	2.75	0.82	3.05	0.89	3.58	0.90
Development Orientation	3.98	1.02	3.39	0.48	3.74	0.54	4.19	0.44
Flexible Reward System	3.50	0.86	3.07	0.65	3.85	0.59	3.97	0.64
Shared Leadership	3.84	1.03	3.00	0.55	3.64	0.74	4.28	0.46
Change Capability	3.92	0.92	2.59	0.66	3.49	0.69	4.08	0.47
Learning Capability	3.81	0.97						

CES Response scale: (1) = Not at all; (2) = A little; (3) = To some extent; (4) = To a moderate extent; (5) = To a large extent.
Pilot Survey Response scale: (1) = Strongly Disagree; (2) Disagree; (3) Neither; (4) Agree; (5) Strongly Agree.

TABLE 4.2. Pulse Survey Results, Management Attention

Management Attention (Percentage)	OVERALL CES		Support		Service		Bus / Admin		Facilities		Cust / OpEx		Educ / Comm	
	Mean	S.D.	Mean	S.D.	Mean	S.D.	Mean	S.D.	Mean	S.D.	Mean	S.D.	Mean	S.D.
Time spent fixing the business	28.39	17.74	28.74	17.42	28.74	18.24	28.09	17.89	29.53	16.10	25.48	23.36	27.13	17.14
Time spent running the business	41.69	20.96	38.56	19.33	45.11	21.99	42.15	21.43	37.11	18.82	53.81	24.96	43.52	21.69
Time spent building the future business	29.92	18.48	32.70	18.40	26.15	16.94	29.76	18.36	33.36	20.84	20.71	14.03	29.35	24.98

Of Parker, his team is grateful that they have "seen very little of the old John" and appreciative that he "lets us lead." In a recent survey, almost all leaders expressed gratitude that Parker supported creativity, was patient, and stepped out of day-to-day issues. In short, he let leaders lead and got out of their way to empower them to do so. Parker also has kept the pressure on change by making it an expectation. He holds periodic knee-to-knee chats with managers and directors, providing encouragement and accountability. And he warns about the un-popped kernels.

Parker understands that you need to take the bag out of the microwave at some point. He accepts giving the kernels a little extra time to pop. However, he won't let the rest of the popcorn burn. As with popcorn, he is being patient in giving time to slower managers to embrace the new vision and way of being. As they show genuine progress, there is hope. However, at some point, Parker will make the difficult decision that time is up and, if not transformed, the managers could be removed to non-managerial duties or let go.

On the one hand, this tactic runs counter to the theory that change can only happen by invitation and not by force. On the other hand, businesses can reach a point of expectation that its workforce be a certain way and how a manager leads will reinforce this culture. The un-popped kernel metaphor tries to strike the balance between patience for the individual and impatience for the team, and make all accountable for the feedback and culture they helped to create. They reinforce the new criteria CES uses to evaluate and promote its talent.

EVALUATION OF THE CES WHOLE SYSTEM TRANSFORMATION

CES's greatest difficulties today are in the pockets of managers who haven't yet "got it." These pockets may seem alarming to those in the trenches, but Parker is both confident and happy. CES never before has been so productive or engaged, and it is attracting good talent rather than losing desired talent. The flock has turned and is progressing. The stragglers are the exception and, over time, hopefully they will join the fold.

Parker believes the greatest lesson learned from this process is commitment. "If you're thinking about doing a whole system transformation, you have to be signed up for the whole thing." Although in hindsight Parker can show that he recovered millions of dollars more in savings than the money spent on the change and that the change improved system functions and satisfactions across the board, he did not have hindsight when he made his commitment. To the OD practitioner or the executive considering a whole system change, Parker's words ring a promise and a warning. Whole system change offers much. It also takes much courage and faith to take the leap.

The story and lessons of Parker and the success of CES are helpful to anyone contemplating a whole system change. Success depends on finding a mixture of courage, trusting the process, diligently enforcing the vision and value, and committing to the whole thing. When one embraces these practices, he or she becomes the kind of leader who can transform an organization and create a community.

NOTES

1. The max mix gathering is a microcosm of the company or a minimum number of representatives at the maximum levels within the company. The microcosm reflects the locations, cultures, diversities, and systems of the company, and can answer all questions that would be presented to the system as a whole. For transformations, the microcosm should be at least 20 percent of the whole organization to generate a tipping point when re-integrated into the whole system.

2. CES and the external consultants also co-created a new formula for change, based in part on the Richard Beckhard DVF formula on creating a collective paradigm shift.

$$(D * A * F * B) = T > CR$$

"D" means allowing participants to voice dissatisfactions with the current state. "A" stands for their aspirations, which describes their yearning for a new future state. Aspiration better fit CES's internal desire because it felt empowering to them. Aspiration was more than the absence of pain in the current situation—it was a desire to become the beautiful butterfly. The "F" stands for first steps. CES was all about getting committed to the right action that would make the difference. The "B" standing for belief was added. CES felt that if critical mass really believed they could change, anything was possible. There is incredible human talent within the organization. The talent just needed to be set free. "T" stood for the transformative leap to being dramatically different. The "CR" stands for the total of D * A * F * B becoming greater than any "change resistance." The formula suggests that it is impossible for an organization to return to its old ways of being once it has achieved the breakthrough and the paradigm shifts.

Michael Schechter is a mediator and the general counsel and senior managing director of ChartHouse International Learning Corporation, the creator of FISH! organization development and training programs. He graduated from New York University School of Law, was awarded the Minnesota State Bar Association's President's award, and has helped clients from healthcare to construction.

John Parker is the vice president of CES division. He has been with the company for thirty-two years and enjoys each and every day.

Judy Zaucha is the executive administrative assistant to John Parker. She has been with the company for twenty-eight years and feels extremely privileged to have been a part of such a dynamic team in working through the CES transformation.

CHAPTER

5

ECOLAB, INC.

**ROBERT C. BARNETT, MICHAEL L. MEYER,
SARAH J. MURPHY, AND SUSAN M. METCALF**

A long-term effort to build a full pipeline of capable leaders at all levels in the organization to help the company achieve aggressive growth goals.

INTRODUCTION

This chapter describes the talent management framework, models, and approach implemented by Ecolab, Inc., for building their leadership bench strength to support growth in their business. Ecolab's approach is based on implementing leadership development systems that promote individual action planning and career mobility. Their efforts have preserved the best elements of Ecolab's results-focused culture and added a well-defined roadmap for individual and leadership development.

COMPANY BACKGROUND

Ecolab is the global leader in cleaning, sanitizing, food safety, and infection control products and services. Founded in 1923 and headquartered in St. Paul, Minnesota, Ecolab serves customers in more than 160 countries across North America, Europe, Asia Pacific, Latin America, the Middle East, and Africa. Ecolab delivers programs and services to the food service, food and beverage processing, hospitality, healthcare, government and education, retail, textile care, commercial facilities, and vehicle wash industries. Ecolab is committed to assisting customers worldwide with their unique needs by providing them with comprehensive, value-added solutions and professional, personal service.

Over half of Ecolab's 26,000 associates are employed in sales, service, and related positions. With more than 14,000 sales and service experts, Ecolab employs the industry's largest and best-trained direct sales and service force. Ecolab sales and service associates are on the ground where their customers are located to provide advice and assistance regarding a full range of cleaning, sanitation, and service needs.

Although the company provides superior products, it is the quality of the relationships it has with customers, its ability to solve problems and satisfy needs, and its intention to deliver nothing less than the best possible service that differentiates Ecolab from its competitors. Ecolab has been recognized for sales and service excellence. For example, Ecolab was ranked in the top ten of *Selling Power* magazine's "Best Manufacturing Companies to Sell For" list in 2007, and again in 2008. Rankings are determined through a detailed rating system that analyses compensation; sales skill and product training; and career management, retention, and promotion data.

Ecolab genuinely depends on the quality of its people. They recognize that in an organization whose success depends on providing superior sales and service, they need leaders who can attract, motivate, and develop the highest performing associates. Sound talent management strategies are central to Ecolab's success.

ECOLAB'S 2002–2007 STRATEGIC PLAN

In 2001, Ecolab reported net sales of approximately $2.3 billion. As the company considered its future, the executive team (the CEO and his direct reports—the ten executives responsible for major business lines and functions) committed to an aggressive growth goal—they intended to increase revenues at a 15 percent annual growth rate for five years, which would more than double the company's size by 2007. Ecolab's growth strategy was multi-faceted:

- Capitalize on success to capture greater share in markets in which they were established leaders.

- Find and enter a new segment that represented a considerable growth opportunity.

- Develop a broader range of cleaning and sanitizing products and services they could offer customers.

- Significantly expand efforts and operations globally.

Ecolab had achieved market leadership in several segments (food service, hospitality, food and beverage processing), but saw that significantly greater penetration was possible in these markets. In addition, they targeted the healthcare market as a major new opportunity. However, the Ecolab executives immediately recognized that they did not have the number of qualified leaders required to effectively run an organization that would grow to twice its current size. The need for additional leadership talent and bench strength was identified as a critical success factor.

As Ecolab's leaders considered their strategic objectives, they began to educate themselves about a variety of possible approaches they might take to develop their bench strength of leadership talent. Among the ideas they reviewed was the framework described in *The Leadership Pipeline* (Charan, Drotter, & Noel, 2001). Ecolab's leaders quickly resonated with this approach. They found that it captured and explained a sound way to build a supply of talent for the organization in a pragmatic yet powerful manner. The pipeline framework is based on the natural hierarchy of work that exists in most organizations. Each leadership level in an organization calls for new skills and a different focus to effectively execute new and more complex responsibilities. Movement up the hierarchy requires transition through a series of critical leadership passages made possible by the development of the skills required at the next level. The pipeline framework is shown graphically in Figure 5.1.

When viewed from the pipeline perspective, development at all levels becomes natural and necessary. The pipeline model provided Ecolab with a framework that could focus people on developing the skills and competencies required to perform best at their current levels in the organization, while helping them prepare to transition to the next. This model was particularly attractive because so many of Ecolab's associates occupied sales and service (individual contributor) roles. Movement from an individual contributor role to managing others represents the first and one of the most troublesome leadership passages for many. However, transition through this passage creates the base of leaders an organization most likely needs in the future. Ecolab leaders knew that any new model or framework would fail if it ignored or was irrelevant to this essential segment of their workforce.

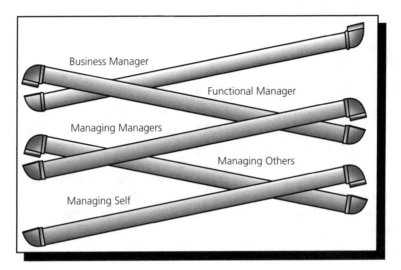

FIGURE 5.1. *Ecolab's Talent Pipeline Model*

With line management as their partners, human resources took the lead to develop and implement a global "pipeline" program that would assure Ecolab could acquire and develop the leadership talent it needed to enable growth and accomplish the goals outlined in its strategic plan.

CULTURE IS CRITICAL

Ecolab has a strong organizational culture that is characterized by an unrelenting drive to achieve results by serving customers' needs. Ecolab's culture has always been a significant strength and source of pride. It helps Ecolab meet its business goals, compels associates to continually perform at their best, and guides how Ecolab associates relate to their customers and to one another. Any new initiative would need to fit with and strengthen the culture, or risk failure and rejection from Ecolab employees. Therefore, the Talent Pipeline effort started here. Ecolab defines six aspects of its culture that provide the foundation for its success:

- **Spirit**. Ecolab associates are the company's heart and soul. They are hungry to succeed and passionate to achieve.

- **Pride**. No matter how big the project or how small the request, Ecolab associates strive for excellence.

- **Determination**. Ecolab associates thrive on challenges, viewing them as an invitation to succeed.

- **Commitment**. Ecolab associates prize dedication and are moved to help each other.

- **Passion**. Ecolab associates wholeheartedly believe in their company. Its goals and objectives are their mission.

- **Integrity**. Ecolab associates set high standards and abide by them.

To shape a more developmentally oriented culture, it was imperative to maintain the spirit and passion for results embraced by individual associates while weaving the expectation of development into the fabric of the organization. Through interviews with Ecolab's best executives and managers, HR gathered input about the critical components for growth *within* the Ecolab cultural setting. This research was analyzed and translated into five key business *drivers*—the critical ways through which Ecolab would achieve consistent, long-term growth and maintain its competitive advantage. These include:

- **Talent Development**. Preparing associates for current and future success.

- **Leadership**. Creating a vision, engaging others, and leading by example.

- **Relationships**. Identifying and building networks to advance business initiatives.

- **Innovation**. Fostering an environment that drives creativity and risk taking.

- **Delivering Results**. Achieving goals by effectively managing resources to get things done.

The drivers are intentionally ordered so that *Talent Development* is first and *Delivering Results* is last. This reflects a shift in focus from a historic emphasis on high performance to a broader leadership growth and development orientation. Ecolab did not abandon its emphasis on results, but sought to be more explicit in specifying the means by which great results are achieved (i.e., through the first four business drivers). The way in which Ecolab visualizes its culture and business drivers is shown in Figure 5.2.

ECOLAB'S TALENT MANAGEMENT PHILOSOPHY

Human resources embraced the challenge of developing the leadership talent required to run a company that would double its size, and began to develop the details, plans, and tactics they needed. Several critical decisions were made to guide planning and crystallize the talent management philosophy they had adopted. Most importantly, Ecolab leaders determined that the company's HR plan would become the third leg (with their five-year strategic plan and the annual operating plan) of a comprehensive organizational blueprint for growth.

The HR plan was grounded in a philosophy that included five key operating principles:

1. Talent is shared. Ecolab's human talent is a company resource, not something that belongs to a particular division or function.

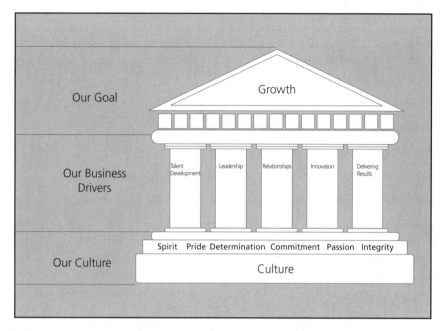

FIGURE 5.2. *Business Drivers and Organizational Culture*

2. Ecolab believes in promoting from within. Development is the key activity that makes transition from one role or level to the next possible.

3. All associates can develop—and it is everyone's responsibility.

4. Performance alone does not equal potential. Readiness to move to the next level can be defined and developed.

5. Talent development should be implemented consistently across the entire organization.

HR's vision was straightforward: ensure the right people are in the right place at the right time to capitalize on the right growth opportunities. The HR vision that was created laid the groundwork for significant organizational change. As a company, Ecolab's goal was to become an organization characterized by considerably greater discipline and rigor directed at ensuring that the right people were identified for the right roles. It would require Ecolab to adhere to more consistent hiring and promotional processes, advocate active development and promotion from within, hold managers accountable for developing their associates, better define the concept of a "high-potential" employee, and refocus their performance management system on *how* things were accomplished (in addition to *what* was accomplished).

THE ECOLAB TALENT PIPELINE

Building on the five business drivers, Ecolab designed and implemented a Talent Pipeline framework that specified the required skills and activities that supported development in and transition through the key passages for each of five organizational pipeline levels:

■ Managing oneself (an individual contributor)

■ Managing others (front-line leaders)

■ Managing managers (mid- to senior-level leaders)

■ Function managers (leaders responsible for an entire function)

■ Business managers (leaders responsible for an entire line of business)

Ecolab's pipeline model is described in detail in their *Talent Pipeline Guidebook*, which it publishes and provides to all employees. The guidebook provides information about all components of Ecolab's pipeline framework. It explains what the Talent Pipeline is and why it was created, as well as how it benefits individual associates and Ecolab as an organization. The guidebook integrates development planning with performance management, clearly outlines expectations for development, and provides tools and resources that can position associates for greater success and potential career advancement. The essence of the *Talent Pipeline Guidebook* is a detailed description of the skills, knowledge, attributes, and success indicators needed at each organizational level in the pipeline for each Ecolab business driver. Figure 5.3 presents a condensed version of the way Ecolab describes expected behaviors and performance at each pipeline level.

The guidebook helps associates better understand what is expected in their *current* roles and also provides a straightforward roadmap through the key passages or transitions associates must make to move through the pipeline from one level to the next. Upward movement in the pipeline requires the addition of the skills required by the next level, a shift in the way a person manages his or her time to meet new and different job responsibilities, and a change in what an associate values or gives priority to in his or her day-to-day approach to work. The key passage points that mark the pipeline transitions for Ecolab are summarized in Figure 5.4. As Figure 5.4 illustrates, moving through the pipeline generally requires learning how to achieve results through increasingly larger numbers of others, gaining a broader and more holistic view of the organization, and developing a more external and strategic perspective on the business.

THE IMPORTANCE OF INDIVIDUAL DEVELOPMENT

One of the most important aspects of Ecolab's approach is the emphasis placed on individual development. The *Talent Pipeline Guidebook* includes the tools, techniques, and templates for identifying development needs and designing individual development plans. To help associates understand where development might be needed, Ecolab created a "180-degree assessment tool"—an assessment based on the

	Managing Self	Managing Others	Managing Managers	Function Manager	Business Manager
Talent Development	• Is motivated to learn through new experiences. • Accepts feedback and uses it to improve self. • Takes actions to develop new talents.	• Ensures that associates are completing a development plan. • Makes staffing decisions that improve the aggregate skill level of the team. • Provides effective coaching and feedback.	• Creates opportunities for managers to gain new skills. • Holds managers accountable for managing and developing others. • Is seen as supplier of quality management talent.	• Holds direct reports accountable for developing leaders. • Develops direct reports who are promotable. • Leverages talent in order to meet function growth goals.	• Fully develops the team's ability to perform. • Holds function managers accountable for developing leaders. • Creates learning opportunities for direct reports and others.
Leadership	• Leads by example—goes the extra mile with associates and customers. • Willingly accepts supervision and work direction. • Is someone others want on their team.	• Instills a sense of identity and purpose in team members. • Articulates the business direction and ensures it is embraced by the team. • Is sought out by others as a mentor or coach.	• Ensures others understand the strategy and how it relates to what they do. • Sets the standard for excellence in teamwork. • Influences effectively upward and across the organization.	• Is viewed with confidence and credibility. • Models leadership and business best practices. • Creates and executes an effective strategy for the function.	• Excels in strategy development and execution. • Drives team performance based on strategic requirements. • Partners effectively across divisions and businesses.
Relationships	• Builds relationships that benefit individual and team success. • Acts as a team player—strives to solidify peer relationships.	• Interacts and communicates effectively with others. • Drives results through relationships with other departments and divisions.	• Maintains an effective external network. • Breaks down communication barriers. • Enhances direct reports' relationship-building skills.	• Supports effective relationship building at all levels in the organization. • Engages in community involvement activities. • Works effectively across organizational boundaries.	• Develops and maintains strong work relationships. • Acts as a persuasive company spokesperson. • Eliminates boundaries between businesses.
Innovation	• Executes new ways of doing things. • Displays curiosity for learning about cross-divisional offerings. • Demonstrates effective problem-solving skills.	• Fosters an environment in which new knowledge and ideas drive growth. • Supports intelligent risk-taking. • Seeks unique solutions that provide a proprietary advantage.	• Identifies new, value-added work to drive growth. • Achieves growth by leveraging other parts of the organization. • Creates a culture where growth is expected.	• Willing to drive change and redirect the function. • Effectively manages risk-taking to achieve large-scale results. • Provides a safety net for direct reports who innovate.	• Designs and executes effective growth strategies. • Continuously improves business processes. • Champions customer investment in new products and applications.
Delivering Results	• Displays technical and professional proficiency—delivers quality work. • Maintains personal plans that reflect yearly objectives. • Ensures commitments are delivered on time.	• Delivers team performance that exceeds targets. • Ensures optimization of resources. • Uses control systems effectively and improves efficiency and productivity.	• Takes strategic action to drive customer retention, account penetration, and new customer acquisition. • Develops and implements long-term plans that create new opportunities and drive growth.	• Delivers results that enable business objectives to be consistently exceeded. • Increases function efficiency year over year. • Uses competitive, market, and industry knowledge to beat the competition.	• Takes actions that gain and sustain a competitive advantage for Ecolab. • Ensures that profits grow faster than revenues. • Executes within optimal cost parameters.

FIGURE 5.3. *Success Indicators for Business Drivers at Each Pipeline Level*

From Managing Self to Managing Others	From Managing Others to Managing Managers	From Managing Managers to Function Managers	From Function Managers to Business Manager
• From achieving results individually through technical or professional skill to achieving results through others. • From teamwork to team building. • From personal planning to planning for the team *and* individual results.	• From achieving results through others to achieving results through managers. • From a top line revenue focus to profitable results. • From team building to organizational building. • From planning for a team to planning for multiple teams' results.	• From achieving results through managers to achieving results for the function. • From profitable results to state-of-the-art results. • From organizational building to functional excellence. • From planning for teams to planning for functional or divisional results.	• From achieving results through functions to achieving results through comprehensive business management. • From state-of-the-art results to competitive advantage. • From functional excellence to customer value. • From planning for function results to creating long-term strategic plans.

FIGURE 5.4. *Key Passage Points in the Talent Pipeline*

success indicators for each business driver appropriate to the associate's level in the pipeline (see Figure 5.5). The 180-degree assessment is completed by the associate as well as by his or her manager. A comparison of results shows the associate and the manager where they agree on the associate's strengths and development needs, and stimulates discussion about areas where their ratings are discrepant.

The development process at Ecolab is designed as an active discussion and planning process between an associate and his or her manager. In the development discussion that follows completion of the 180-degree assessment, an associate and his or her manager explore the associate's career aspirations, desire to move into new roles (either laterally or upwards), and how to differentiate exceptional performance from job proficiency or performance with noticeable gaps. This conversation plays an important role in helping Ecolab associates manage their careers, gain clarity and focus about new opportunities, and calibrate expectations about what these may require.

The 180-degree assessment and development discussion also provide the foundation for creating an Individual Development Plan (Figure 5.5). The *Talent Pipeline Guidebook* provides ideas, activities, and suggested readings for developing skills related to each business driver for each level of the pipeline that the associate can use to complete his or her development plan. As an example, Figure 5.6 shows the kinds of suggestions and recommended development activities that are included in the *Talent Pipeline Guidebook* for associates who need or want help developing themselves to be more effective at building their network of relationships. A similar set of suggestions is included in the guidebook for developing the skills related to each of the other Ecolab business drivers.

At Ecolab, the Talent Pipeline is linked to the performance management system. The *Talent Pipeline Guidebook* fully describes Ecolab's performance management process. It is designed to provide an avenue by which associates and managers can

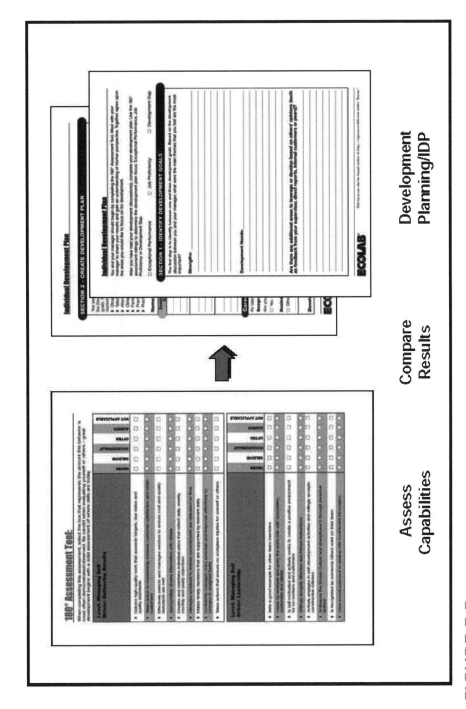

FIGURE 5.5. *180-Degree Assessment and Development Planning*

Assess Capabilities   Compare Results   Development Planning/IDP

Managing Self	Managing Others	Managing Managers	Function Manager	Business Manager
• The next time you are in a meeting, practice using active listening skills.	• Evaluate your internal network. Create a plan for building key relationships and expanding it.	• Identify at the least three individuals from different business units to see whether they view you as a strategic partner. If not, develop a plan to build strategic partnerships with each of these business units.	• Leverage technology to create communication vehicle that keeps people in your function up-to-date and informed.	• Schedule regular meetings with the heads of other businesses. Discuss your key goals and objectives. Look for ways you can support one another.
• Identify someone with whom you disagree. The next time you speak with him/her, listen to understand his or her perspective and paraphrase it before stating your views.	• Once a day, get out of your office and walk around the work environment. Create opportunities to communicate with people throughout the organization.	• Nurture your network. Develop a strategy for staying involved. This can include telephone contact or informal get-togethers with others. Regularly engage in and sponsor activities that bring individuals from different areas together to meet, discuss, and/or socialize.	• Regularly recognize people in lower-level positions to ensure that they feel they are equal and valued members of the function.	• Refuse to tolerate labeling and prejudicial behavior. Speak out if you see such behavior and express your displeasure.
• Evaluate your individual networking system. Identify any gaps, and add someone new to your network every month.	• Set up a formal schedule for keeping in touch with key individuals in your network. Make a list of those in the organization who have both informal and formal power. Compare your network to the list, and identify individuals who need to be added to your network.		• Look for opportunities to use your position power to help your team and direct reports secure needed resources and overcome obstacles that hinder accomplishment of their work goals.	• When you hear good feedback about someone you know, pass along the compliment.
• Volunteer to serve on cross-functional teams, steering committees, or task groups to broaden your perspective and meet peers from other areas.		• Actively strive to be a conduit for information in the organization.	• Schedule regular meetings with the heads of other functions. Discuss your key goals and objectives. Look for ways you can support one another.	• Enhance your working relationship with others by adjusting your style, communication method, energy level, and approach to the person with whom you are working.
• Attend corporate functions with a goal of meeting or reacquainting yourself with at least two employees per month from outside your department.	• Analyze your working relationships with others. Who typically supports you? Who typically blocks you? Who is neutral? Create a plan for enhancing your work relationships.	• Draw a map of your networks—both inside and outside the company. Look for gaps in your network and create plans to fill those gaps.	• Look for opportunities to offer your help and resources to others within the organization—before they ask.	• Analyze relationships that are not collaborative. Change at least one aspect of your behavior to improve your interactions and note the results.

FIGURE 5.6. *Development Actions for Improving Relationships*

work together to define objectives, align them with business goals, provide feedback about results, and clarify expectations. Performance management discussions, including the formal annual performance review, are designed to promote Ecolab's development culture by helping associates realize their potential while fueling the company's success. The guidebook includes Ecolab's performance appraisal form, which evaluates performance against each of the five business drivers and assesses an associate's fit at his or her current pipeline level, as well as readiness for the next passage. Ecolab has found that these development and performance management tools and processes have been successful at creating increasingly transparent, candid, positive, and developmentally oriented performance discussions.

INTRODUCING THE TALENT PIPELINE MODEL AT ECOLAB

The success of the Talent Pipeline Model at Ecolab stems back to the crisp and impactful manner in which the concept and tools were launched at the start. The Talent Pipeline was launched at a global leadership team meeting, where approximately one thousand key leaders were introduced to the Talent Pipeline in a large group session. Following the large group presentation, Ecolab leaders met in small group training sessions to learn more about the concept and the ways in which they would need to support and use it in their units. This approach was critical for Ecolab leaders to fully understand the model, embrace the concept, and internalize the potential benefits.

After the meeting, Ecolab leaders were expected to cascade the program throughout their parts of the company. To aid them, Ecolab provided a toolkit (available in multiple languages) containing the *Talent Pipeline Guidebook* and a variety of presentation materials. This effort was supported with an e-mail campaign and instructional modules. All pipeline materials are available through Ecolab's intranet so that every one of Ecolab's associates can access the model, explanations, and tools. These include the *Talent Pipeline Guidebook*, job profiles, performance management and development planning training, sample performance reviews and development plans, and Ecolab's talent policies and guidelines. As a result, the initiative was spread throughout Ecolab rapidly and with energetic intensity. The model and framework were quickly accepted, primarily because Ecolab associates found it useable and instantly applicable in their day-to-day work.

SUPPORTING SUCCESSFUL IMPLEMENTATION

Ecolab's Talent Pipeline is now well established and continues to support business growth through successful talent acquisition, retention, and leadership development. In part, this can be attributed to the sense of urgency that was created to accelerate its implementation. Creating urgency for implementing Ecolab's Talent Pipeline Model began with an analysis of the numbers of new associates who would be necessary to lead a dramatically expanded Ecolab workforce. Based on a ratio of one manager for about every seven or eight associates, Ecolab calculated the numbers of new associates, managers, and leaders it would need at each pipeline level if the organization doubled in size. To be successful, this translated into the need to add (promote or hire from the outside) one front-line manager per week and two senior leaders each month from 2004 through 2007. Once Ecolab's executives understood the real implications of these plans in practical terms, their commitment to the talent management strategy was solidified. An example of Ecolab's needs analysis is shown in Figure 5.7.

Although Ecolab intended to promote from within, they did not want to place associates in new positions before they were ready—that is, if they appeared unprepared to successfully transition through the next leadership passage. Given the number of new leaders they anticipated they would need, Ecolab substantially expanded their recruiting efforts. Important components of the recruiting function were centralized to standardize processes, take advantage of technology, and better leverage Ecolab's global brand and presence. Traditionally, recruiting and hiring were human resource activities owned by each business. The shift was an opportunity to achieve consistency, implement best practices, and guarantee high-quality new hires across the organization. The approach required significantly greater attention to managing relationships with recruiting partners, developing more precise job profiles for high-incumbent positions, consistent use of improved interviewing and screening protocols, and increased use of new recruiting channels.

Third, Ecolab redefined the concept of "high potential." An associate's potential to advance had traditionally been based primarily on the results an associate delivered. However, Ecolab acknowledged one of the fundamental tenets of the pipeline framework: past performance alone does not guarantee potential for success in future roles. Future roles that are more complex and more senior often require fundamentally new or different skills than a person may use in his or her current position. Based on

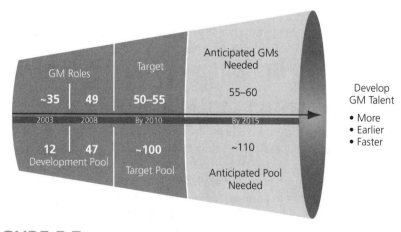

FIGURE 5.7. *Leadership Needs Analysis*

research conducted by the Corporate Leadership Council (2005), Ecolab adopted a model of "potential" that included three interrelated components (see Figure 5.8):

■ **Capability:** The ability to deliver results, think clearly and reason effectively, take on greater responsibility, and demonstrate strong leadership.

■ **Ambition:** The desire for recognition, advancement, influence, and the financial rewards that accompany more senior, more critical roles.

■ **Commitment:** The beliefs and feelings that lead an associate to conclude that remaining with and committing to Ecolab is in his or her best interests.

Fourth, Ecolab established a Talent Council. The Talent Council is composed of ten top Ecolab executives, including the CEO, and represents all key business lines, geographies, and the marketing, finance, and global sales functions. The Talent Council meets monthly to review high-potential talent in the organization, endorse and reinforce the importance of development, manage the promotions and careers of Ecolab's high-potential associates and executive-level leaders, and set priorities and allocate resources to support the Talent Pipeline. The CEO and the Talent Council championed and reinforced Ecolab's Talent Pipeline across the company. The CEO was among the strongest advocates for the pipeline strategy. He spoke to Ecolab associates around the world with an unparalleled enthusiasm for the approach. He challenged and held managers accountable for developing their people and set the expectation that all Ecolab associates would be responsible for developing themselves.

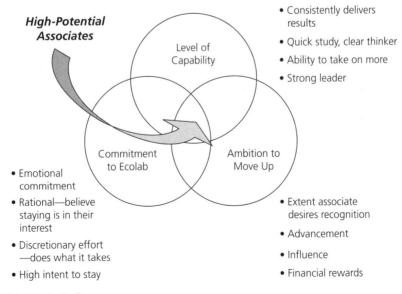

FIGURE 5.8. *Ecolab's Model of High Potential*

KEEPING THE PIPELINE FULL

To keep the pipeline full, Ecolab instituted a number of new organizational practices. One practice has enhanced the way in which Ecolab makes critical talent decisions. Ecolab determined that key promotions and new-hire decisions would be made only with the support of a comprehensive leadership assessment process. The assessment process is provided by an external consulting partner (an I/O psychology firm) and is comprised of a day-long series of personality, motivation, and cognitive ability testing; interviewing; and leadership simulation activities that vary depending on the pipeline level the associate is in or being considered for. The assessment produces an in-depth description of an individual's strengths, work style, and potential limitations.

Because the assessment process is used as part of key hiring and promotion decisions, an expanded set of stakeholders is involved. These include the current manager of the associate being assessed, the prospective future manager, and the appropriate business or function HR generalist. These individuals consult with the assessment firm in advance of the assessment itself so that the assessing psychologist has a specific understanding of the outcomes Ecolab expects. Post-assessment, the group reconvenes to review the assessment results and make a hiring or promotional decision. This discipline has contributed to improved, more objective, and better-supported decisions about critical talent moves.

Ecolab has also recognized the need to be more deliberate in cultivating new associates' commitment to the organization, especially during the first two years of their work at Ecolab. Their new-employee-orientation program was redesigned from a traditional review of policies and procedures to a year-long retention effort called Career-*Start* (see Figure 5.9). After an initial orientation program, new associates are invited to additional programs at three and six months, and then one year after they begin employment. This provides Ecolab with an opportunity to improve retention by helping new employees accelerate their understanding of the organizational culture, other businesses, and functions and to "recommit" to the organization after a year's time.

Finally, all Ecolab business lines and major functions hold an annual "HR Plan Review" with the CEO. The agenda for the HR plan review meetings include discussion of (1) business (or function) performance against the prior year's objectives; (2) the current organization and its key strengths/success factors and challenges/barriers; (3) talent development plans and a discussion of direct-report, high-potential, and executive-level talent using a nine-box method; and (4) succession plans, including the availability of ready-now candidates for the most critical positions in each business or function. These meetings highlight and focus attention on the importance of managing Ecolab's human resources. As many as twenty HR plan review meetings are held annually with the CEO. In addition, business and function leaders hold numerous reviews within their divisions to prepare for their HR plan review meetings with the CEO and dive deeper into their organization.

These (and other) efforts Ecolab has implemented to identify, develop, and accelerate its high-potential talent through the leadership pipeline are illustrated in Figure 5.10. Their programs and resources are organized around five key elements: (1) the performance management and development plan process; (2) leadership assessment;

Pre-Hire	Days 1 & 2 (each 1/2 day)	Weeks 1 & 2	1st Month	3rd Month	6th Month	One Year
Welcome: • Welcome Kit • New Associate "Buddy" • Manager's Checklist	Welcome: • Benefits Kit • New Hire Event – Senior Management – History – Values – Place in Org. – Expectations – Roadmap to Learning – Code of Conduct	Reminder: • Manager Check-in	Check-in: • Manager-associate check-in	Getting Settled: • Applied business information session • Mentor-Associate roadmap check-in	Hitting Stride: • Values in Action session • Manager-associate check-in • New associate survey	Re-recruitment: • Feedback interview • Luncheon with Executives
Candidate Accepts	Associate Starts		Engagement			Re-Recruitment

FIGURE 5.9. *Ecolab's CareerStart Program*

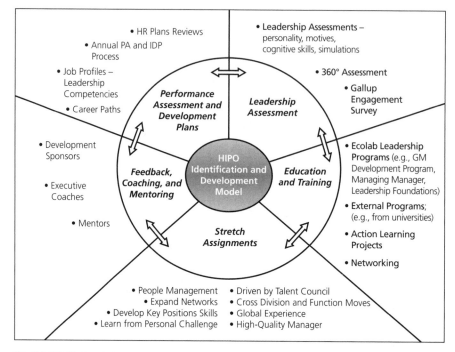

FIGURE 5.10. *High Potential Identification and Development*

(3) education and training; (4) stretch assignments; and (5) feedback, coaching, and mentoring. However, the Talent Pipeline framework has provided the foundation, clarity, and consistency to Ecolab's efforts as a core growth strategy for the company.

RESULTS

The Talent Pipeline strategy has proven successful for Ecolab. In 2008, Ecolab reported net sales of over $6.1 billion, a 265 percent increase over 2001 sales revenue. Ecolab's pipeline approach—emphasizing clarity about the skills needed for success at each level, a focus on development, and the active management of high-potential talent—has been implemented worldwide. Ecolab's top two tiers of executive-level leaders are fully in place and setting new performance standards. Their pool of ready-now business manager candidates has increased three-fold. Ecolab has identified and developed record numbers of high-potential leaders who are ready to assume greater leadership responsibilities, and nearly all of them are in developmental positions. In 2008, Ecolab's Talent Council orchestrated a record number of developmental job rotations and cross-divisional moves and doubled the number of expatriate assignments it made.

At lower levels of the pipeline, all associates regularly complete the 180-degree assessment; discuss development with their managers; and have created practical, realistic, and beneficial development plans. Ecolab has developed a large pool of candidates who are ready to move into critical positions managing others and managing managers. Their Talent Pipeline strategy has taken hold and is becoming ingrained in Ecolab's culture.

CONCLUSION

Ecolab's experience demonstrates that growth in the business requires more and better-prepared leadership talent; that they must promote and hire the best to be the best; and that they must consider how to develop the talent, cultivate the aspirations, and deepen the commitment of all their associates. While they have clearly benefited from a strong senior leadership team, they continue to move their focus further down the pipeline and more fully and consistently meet the challenges that a strong global talent management system presents. They continue to look for ways to accelerate their associates' development and identify potential earlier in associates' careers. Ecolab remains committed to refining its pipeline strategy. They are confident that they have established a firm foundation that will help them continue to drive growth and meet the challenges on the horizon.

REFERENCES

Charan, R., Drotter, S., & Noel, J. (2001). *The leadership pipeline*. San Francisco: Jossey-Bass.

Corporate Leadership Council (2005). *Realizing the full potential of rising talent*. Washington, DC: Corporate Executive Board.

Robert C. Barnett is executive vice president and partner at MDA Leadership Consulting in Minneapolis. Barnett joined MDA in 1985 and has over twenty years of experience consulting in the areas of organizational psychology and organization development. At MDA, he specializes in providing executive selection, leadership development, and organizational change services. He is a graduate of the University of Minnesota, where he received his B.A. and earned his Ph.D. in psychology, and has an M.S. in organizational development from Pepperdine University. Barnett is an adjunct associate professor of management at St. Mary's University of Minnesota, has authored a number of articles and book chapters, and is a frequent presenter at psychological, management, and human resource professional meetings and conferences.

Michael L. Meyer is senior vice president of human resources for Ecolab, Inc. In his current role, Meyer is responsible for human resources globally, with 26,000 associates in more than 160 countries. Prior to joining Ecolab, Meyer was employed at Abbott Laboratories as vice president and general manager, Canada and Latin America, Vascular Products, in Toronto. During his twenty-four years with Abbott, he also held numerous other positions in human resources, including group vice president, Global Human Resources and Medical Products, and vice president, human resources, International Division. Meyer received his B.A. degree in behavioral sciences from Westminster College in Salt Lake City, Utah, and an M.B.A. in international management from Thunderbird, the American Graduate School of International Management in Glendale, Arizona.

Sarah J. Murphy is a principal consultant and partner at MDA Leadership Consulting in Minneapolis. Since joining the firm in 1997, she has worked as part of the core team supporting MDA's talent management and assessment practice, where she consults to executives of MDA's Fortune 500 clients. Murphy specializes in the selection and development of senior leaders. In addition, she provides executive coaching services, is an expert in 360-degree feedback and development of competency models and succession planning systems for her clients. She completed her B.A. at the University of Winnipeg, Canada, and earned her Ph.D. in psychology from the University of Minnesota.

Susan M. Metcalf is vice president, talent acquisition and development, for Ecolab, Inc. Metcalf is responsible for Ecolab's talent pipeline, succession planning, and leadership development initiatives. This assignment enables her to shape the development of all 26,000 of Ecolab's associates. She is a 29-year veteran of Ecolab, and during her tenure has held a number of positions including vice president of talent acquisition, director of planning & development, and a number of human resource business partner positions aligned to various functions and divisions within Ecolab. She received her bachelor's degree from the University of Minnesota, and completed the University of Minnesota Carlson School of Management's Human Resource Executive Program and a University of Saint Thomas Mini-M.B.A.

CHAPTER

6

GE MONEY AMERICAS

TAMMY GRISHAM AND D. ZACHARY MISKO

Developing and sustaining an integrated talent acquisition model utilizing recruitment process outsourcing (RPO), advanced sourcing technology, and process efficiency in conjunction with LEAN methodologies.

- LEAN Methodologies
  - Flexibility Defines the Future
  - Introducing Transactional Lean
  - FS
  - The Lean Journey
  - The Impact
- Expansion
- Conclusion

INTRODUCTION

This chapter introduces the framework, processes, and tools currently used at General Electric, GE Money, for executive talent acquisition. The long-term goals of the strategy and programs GE is currently implementing for talent acquisition include:

- To ensure that an efficient and cost-effective talent acquisition process to provide quality talent and a talent pipeline is identified.

- To provide robust metrics reporting to ensure analysis and measurement of process (efficiencies, waste, quality, time, and satisfaction) are reviewed regularly.

- To maximize performance of recruitment process and HR professionals through utilization of LEAN methodologies.

COMPANY BACKGROUND AND ENVIRONMENT

General Electric is a diversified technology, media, and financial services company dedicated to creating products that make life better. From jet engines to power generation, financial services to plastics, and medical imaging to news and information, GE people worldwide are dedicated to turning imaginative ideas into leading products and services that help solve some of the world's toughest problems.

GE Money is the consumer finance brand for GE Consumer Finance worldwide. GE Money combines the trustworthiness of banks and the speed of finance companies to deliver a unique service to our customers and clients. Around the world, our businesses have embodied the values of GE Money and prospered. Customers are drawn by what GE Money represents: speed, value, flexibility, accessibility, and trustworthiness. When you work at GE, you work with people who have a passion for learning and a desire to innovate. Their obsession with finding better ways to do things creates an exhilarating work environment.

With more than $163 billion in assets, GE Money is a leading provider of credit services to consumers, retailers, and auto dealers in fifty countries around the world. GE Money Americas offers a range of financial products, including private-label credit cards, personal loans, bank cards, auto loans and leases, mortgages, corporate travel and purchasing cards, debt consolidation and home equity loans, and credit insurance.

THE CHALLENGE AND APPROACH

Solving the Staffing Dilemma: Two Leaders Team to Get It Right

We often hear the buzz word "sustainability" in reference to environmental resources. At GE Money Americas, we link the term with human resources, too. Our recruiting process delivers sustainable results today, thanks mostly to our partnership with Kelly's Outsourcing & Consulting Group (Kelly OCG), Recruitment Process Outsourcing (RPO) practice. This recruitment process outsourcing provider helped us get the "people" part right, which can make all the difference in the global scramble for talent.

A True Partner Steps Up

In 2000, GE Money Americas (formerly GE Consumer Finance) wasn't getting it right, and we knew it. Our company, a leading provider of banking and credit services, had staffing challenges common to many large organizations: a decentralized staffing process, inconsistent interview practices, and variable candidate quality from a small number of colleges. Moreover, the cost per hire averaged more than $8,000 and the time to fill a position typically exceeded three months. In short, our process was unsustainable.

A parade of vendors told us they had just what we needed to reform our troubled staffing function. In the end, however, the clear choice was Kelly OCG, which had the competitive advantage in employing experienced, caring people. No surprise that, in selecting a partner to be an extension of GE Money Americas' HR team, the difference came down to people! (See Figure 6.1.)

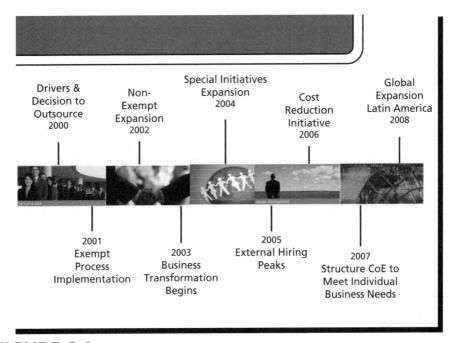

FIGURE 6.1. *The Evolution of Our Partnership*

Kelly OCG launched a revamped outsourcing model in early 2001. Key to the solution were a centralized staffing process and a dedicated team. This shift to centralization included a customized candidate application website and standardized, more thorough screening methods to enhance candidate quality and service level.

The solution also incorporated:

- A hiring logistics strategy to ensure consistency, standardization, and efficiency from interview to offer;

- Management of an Internet-based applicant tracking system;

- Automation of processes once done manually;

- Measurement of staffing and activity costs; and

- Establishment of new benchmarks and goals.

The ability to sustaining a process with year-over-year process improvement given an ever-changing landscape of our business, the economy, and sourcing strategy development are critical.

Results Chart a Success Story

Kelly OCG helped GE Money Americas realize significant savings at virtually every level of the staffing process. In addition, they streamlined a time-intensive prescreening process, enabling more interviews of well-qualified candidates during fewer recruiting visits to a diverse range of campuses in a shorter time frame.

Numbers tell the bottom-line story:

- Our total staffing costs decreased 54 percent. The savings were attributable largely to a halving of sourcing expenditures and an 80 percent reduction in travel and relocation costs. The average cost per hire fell to $4,900 from $8,300.

- Indirect savings included a cycle time reduction to 47 days from 115 days.

In the course of an eight-year relationship, Kelly OCG has helped GE Money Americas obtain year-over-year cost reductions ($2 million in 2007), while continuing to manage a best-in-class staffing process. With a focus on operating more efficiently and sharing best practices, they have improved both candidate quality and our interview-to-hire ratio. They measure their progress in both quantitative and qualitative terms (see Figure 6.2).

The process shown in Figure 6.2 combines both GE managers and the RPO provider team throughout the candidate life cycle.

THE TECHNOLOGY

The Challenge

With the right process defined and in place to attract candidates, we were now experiencing difficulty in managing the high volume of applicants, which negatively

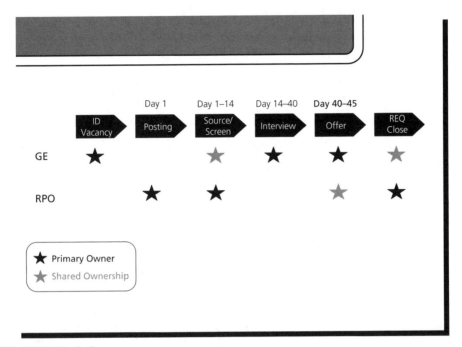

FIGURE 6.2. *The Process Model*

impacted the effectiveness of our staffing function. Additionally, existing technologies did not enable them to execute a highly successful, high-volume recruiting program with the ability to produce metrics on demand.

The company faced these difficulties:

■ Lack of an effective applicant tracking tool designed for high volume, nonexempt hiring;

■ Limited outlets for candidates to apply;

■ A narrow scope of reporting capabilities;

■ Complexities of dynamic recruiting needs in more than twenty locations;

■ Management of the day-to-day functions of a technology provider; and

■ Successful management of phone interview and onsite interview scheduling.

The Solution

Together GE Money and Kelly OCG sought a technology vendor to address the challenges. Kelly OCG selected My Staffing Pro (HR Services Inc.), which offered an applicant tracking and recruiting software system with advanced applicant screening capabilities. Next, Kelly OCG stepped in to manage the implementation and the ongoing day-to-day activities of the applicant tracking system (ATS). This included system, end-user, and reporting functionality. As a result, a variety of improvements were made to the process.

The solution incorporated:

- An interactive voice response system (IVR), which serves as an automated applicant screening and scheduling tool;

- An integrated online and telephone application accessible twenty-four hours a day;

- Automation of candidate prescreening and scheduling previously done manually;

- A custom candidate portal specific to the client;

- Standardized EEO data collection and reporting;

- Advanced statistical reporting capabilities;

- Strategic initiatives that maximized the use of available resources; and

- Automated communication (including confirmation and regrets letters).

The Results

By strategically integrating the right technology partner, Kelly OCG was able to optimize the recruiting process and achieve significant results for GE Money. In the first year 15,332 new applicants were tracked and managed through the hiring process. In the following years the number of new applicants continued to grow and exceeds 80,000 annually. As the client hiring demands and processes have continually changed, the flexibility provided by My Staffing Pro (HR Services) and its technology have helped to seamlessly accommodate their requirements and enable better hiring decisions. Recent successful implementations include the addition of four new call centers, increasing the total number of Kelly OCG recruited call centers to eighteen.

STRATEGY FOR SOURCING

We also refined our sourcing strategy. The Internet, for example, remains an important weapon in our recruiting arsenal, but qualified candidates who are working successfully for our competitors may not be checking web postings. This truth calls for fresh thinking about a model that blends both contemporary approaches and traditional recruiting tactics such as cold calling, all but abandoned during the rise of the web.

Our candidate funnel (Figure 6.3) is streamlined due to an efficient process. Through this process only qualified candidates are invited to an on-site interview, which means Hiring Managers are spending quality interview time and have higher interview to offer ratios.

The Challenge

Dissatisfied with their current methods of generating and implementing an effective method for research and advertising, a world-renowned consumer financial services

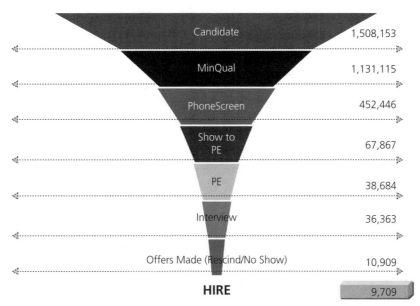

Candidate	1,508,153
MinQual	1,131,115
PhoneScreen	452,446
Show to PE	67,867
PE	38,684
Interview	36,363
Offers Made (Rescind/No Show)	10,909
HIRE	9,709

FIGURE 6.3. *The Candidate Funnel*

company requested assistance in finding a more successful channel of advertising media to increase the flow of candidates. Additionally, the company wanted to improve the way in which they tracked their advertising spending in order to accurately calculate cost-per-hire and manage their annual budget.

The relationship is managed by the Kelly OCG–RPO talent acquisition team, and it is uniform across all locations. Prior to the endeavor to merge the process of ad placement into a single, proficient entity, nearly two dozen client locations were actively placing their own advertisements separately—using limited time and resources.

The company faced the following challenges:

■ Lack of advertising budget management and tracking of spending;

■ Inconsistent process across all client locations;

■ Lack of resources to research best ways to advertise and reach target candidates, including cutting-edge technology and emerging trends; and

■ No cost-per-hire nor ROI tracking.

The Solution

The client needed to hire talent for call centers across the country but did not have a comprehensive or long-term solution in place. Together, TMP Worldwide and Kelly OCG–RPO developed a nationwide annual media plan. With the plan in hand, the client could reference the overall strategy and implement the best tactics for the specific market within a two-week lead time. Included in the plan were specific strategies for search engine marketing, job boards, direct email advertising, mobile marketing, and outdoor advertising.

Since the media plan included strategies throughout the year, in addition to covering all of the client-specific geographic areas, it was easy to implement. As a result, the client took advantage of both traditional and non-traditional media to achieve success in staffing the call center locations. The client is now competitive for hiring for positions across the country—no matter the regional location. The well-received advertising campaign promoted the collaborative and unique company culture and captured the essence of joining a successful team. In fact, the client requested two additional executions promoting the benefits of employment.

The solutions for the client included (but were not limited to) the following:

- Budget management for advertising spending;

- A consultative relationship between TMP and the client managed by the Kelly OCG–RPO talent acquisition team;

- Demographic research provided by TMP Worldwide;

- TMP Worldwide working specifically within company branding guidelines;

- Introduction of new and cutting-edge products/technologies;

- All requests handled by one to two direct points of contact; and

- Cost-per-hire tracking from the Kelly OCG–RPO talent acquisition team to better manage resources.

The Results

Through a partnership with Kelly OCG–RPO, the company's respective locations no longer need to place or research their advertising. All research, recommendations, placement, spend tracking, and budget management are taken care of through this business relationship, thus helping to reduce overlapping advertisements, unnecessary or ineffective advertisements, and unnecessary spending. TMP Worldwide and Kelly OCG–RPO worked together to maintain the distinguished image and reputation of the client company.

> "Partnering with TMP as an ad vendor, and having that relationship and budget managed by Kelly OCG, has allowed us to have one centralized point of contact for advertising needs, research, and staying up-to-date on developments in the market(s). Additionally, this centralized approach has helped us reduce overall advertising/recruiting costs while reducing cycle time and increasing position fill rates."

Effective sourcing strategies have reduced agency spending by over 70 percent (see Figure 6.4).

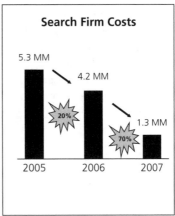

Features:

- ✓ Shared service recruiters
- ✓ Offsite sourcing engine
- ✓ Leveraged sourcing tools and expert sourcing knowledge
- ✓ Sourcing subject-matter experts
- ✓ Accountability to metrics/SLAs
- ✓ Reduced reliance on Search Firms

Provides for dedicated "Headhunters" at a reduced cost.

Search Firm Costs

5.3 MM
4.2 MM
20%
1.3 MM
70%

2005   2006   2007

FIGURE 6.4. *Sourcing Model*

LEAN METHODOLOGIES

Flexibility Defines the Future

Like all successful programs, this one is evolving to meet the needs of our ever-changing organization. Over the past year, we embarked on a Lean quality review. Through value stream mapping, we reviewed opportunities to improve our processes and defined our ideal process state. Working closely with Kelly OCG, we formed *kaizen* teams to effect positive change. Our challenge was to enhance the applicant experience through reduction in process delays and redundancies. In the end, we were able to meet more stringent federal compliance standards while maintaining cycle times and quality of service.

We are most familiar with "Lean Manufacturing" as introduced by Toyota® to improve production manufacturing. In such an environment, it is used to reduce waste, increase quality, and improve production. Could this "Lean" approach be used to improve a transaction-based service operation—like staffing? GE Healthcare thought so. With help from Kelly Outsourcing and Consulting Group (Kelly OCG), "Transactional Lean" has been successfully integrated into their solid business partnership with great results.

Introducing Transactional Lean

In 2006, the relationship was being challenged with increasing hiring volume and heightened requirements from U.S. Department of Labor Office of Federal Contract Compliance Programs (OFCCP). GE Money needed more and more staff to combat these issues, which added more and more cost to the staffing budget. Something had to change. We decided to apply the Lean approach to the staffing process to create efficiencies, improve performance, and generate cost savings.

A team of Kelly OCG managers and recruiters and GE Money human resources managers created a value stream map (VSM) of the current staffing process. The VSM revealed areas of low-quality output to target as kaizen improvement opportunities. But before anything could be set in place, a fundamental culture change had to occur.

5S

To initiate the required culture shift, a Lean principle, 5S, was introduced as the foundation for all improvements. The 5S consists of:

- **Sort**—separation of necessary items from unnecessary items;

- **Set in Order**—arrange items according to how they will be used;

- **Shine**—maintain work area for sorted and set in order items;

- **Standardize**—ensure sort, set in order, and shine are consistently followed; and

- **Sustain**—maintain and improve sort, set in order, shine, and standardize.

5S was first applied to the physical environment, eliminating unneeded storage and files. It soon became evident the discipline to sustain 5S was necessary to sustain a change in the staffing culture to one of continuous improvement.

The Lean Journey

Following the VSM and 5S, the staffing team focused on the kaizen opportunities. Initially, the team led and participated in more than thirty-two efforts to standardize processes and improve quality. Early efforts included:

- Creating application instructions;

- Standardizing the initial candidate phone screening;

- Creating a compliant process for documenting search strings;

- Standardizing the hiring manager call for newly posted positions; and

- Documenting the employee referral process.

The Impact

Staffing continued to improve, with plans to institute visual management practices to capture performance and adopt better process controls with internal audits. With the Lean improvements in place, staffing processes became more consistent. Defects decreased, and the quality of service continues to improve. For the first time, vacations, absences, and peaks in hiring volume do not disrupt customer service. The standards of excellence and defined processes also allow new team members to more easily learn their roles and integrate into the team.

EXPANSION

In 2008 our process and abilities were challenged again to provide our process in Latin America (Guatemala, Central America). This would mark the first site in Guatemala, as well as the first opportunity for Kelly OCG to staff there.

Process Efficiency and Successes

1. Implemented technology and process used for North American staffing and began processing candidates on March 10, 2008.

2. The first hiring date for the new Guatemala site was April 28, 2008 (six weeks to process candidates).

3. In managing vendor relationships, Kelly OCG worked with an advertising vendor to conduct market research on trends and avenues for advertising in a new market and in a different culture. By managing ad vendor relationships and monitoring effectiveness of ad avenues, cost per hire is at $603.12 as of September 30, 2008. The client averages forty-two hires per month since project inception.

4. We streamlined the hiring process to better customize for the client site: removal of redundancies in the process (preliminary English test), reducing total number of interviews down from three to two by combining competencies covered in two on-site interviews to reduce redundancy. HRF also created and adjusted the phone interview used. Through this process improvement, time to process a candidate was shorter and the number of trips a candidate had to make to the recruitment site was reduced. We adjusted the final English assessment (CEDS) schedule to accommodate most candidates.

5. Kelly OCG hired and trained a local team to represent the RPO onsite RPO team.

The Kelly OCG team was entirely responsible for establishing the process, providing/maintaining resources, and processing of candidates. Once the Guatemala team was hired and trained, the U.S. team maintained daily communication, weekly calls, and occasional trips to Guatemala to ensure questions were answered and issues were resolved. The U.S. team co-managed the advertising and participated in weekly update calls with the entire client project management team to discuss updates and resolve issues.

CONCLUSION

We will continue to demand more from our outsourcing provider as new challenges surface. With the RPO practice of Kelly OCG as our strong right arm, we look forward to the future because, through flexibility, scalability, and strategic thinking, we have proved we can successfully manage our talent acquisition within GE Money.

Tammy Grisham is the Staffing Center of Excellence Leader for GE Money Americas. Grisham has over fifteen years of recruitment, operations, and management expertise. She leads the talent acquisition for the Americas and ensures proper implementation and management of the tools aligned to recruitment (employee referral program, leadership development program), as well as temporary and contingent workforce management. Based in Stamford, Connecticut, GE Money is the consumer and small business financial services unit for General Electric. Grisham is based in the Kettering, Ohio, office.

D. Zachary Misko is the global RPO director and member of the leadership team at Kelly Services, Inc., Outsourcing & Consulting Group (Kelly OCG), Recruitment Process Outsourcing (RPO) practice area. Kelly OCG–RPO provides outsourced hiring process management and human resource skills to a variety of different companies. As the global RPO director, Misko works with Fortune 500 clients throughout the world to develop and implement processes that improve and drive the hiring process, recruitment, on-boarding, retention, and selection functions within a company. Misko is based out of the Milwaukee, Wisconsin, office. Prior to joining Kelly OCG, he managed human resource functions at a world-wide leader in biotechnology and life sciences, Promega Corporation, Madison, Wisconsin, and was employed as the senior training manager for Lands' End, Dodgeville, Wisconsin.

Misko has over fifteen years of broad human resource and management expertise in the direct merchant arena, retail, finance, biotechnology, and professional services. Additionally, he has held various positions in the areas of recruitment, employment law, employee relations, consulting, strategic HR planning, performance management programs, training/development, and compensation. He has completed advanced certification from DILHR and is certified in affirmative action and diversity hiring. Additionally, Misko has been a member of SHRM for the past fourteen years and is the past president of the Metro Milwaukee chapter.

CHAPTER

7

INTERNAL REVENUE SERVICE

SUSAN CLAYTON, VICTORIA BAUGH, MATHEW J. FERRERO

An integrated leadership development and succession planning system for front-line to senior leaders that includes executive involvement, a four-step structured process, and web-based assessment and support.

- Results
  - Results for Competencies
  - Results for Bench Strength
- Indicators of Success
- Evaluation
- Next Steps
- Conclusion

INTRODUCTION

This chapter introduces the framework, processes, and tools currently used at the Internal Revenue Service (IRS) for succession planning and development. The long-term goals of the strategy and programs IRS currently uses and others being implemented are to:

- Ensure that there are sufficient "ready now" candidates to address current and future leadership vacancies; and

- Provide the necessary processes to identify and develop individual leaders to ensure our long-term success.

COMPANY BACKGROUND AND CURRENT LEADERSHIP ENVIRONMENT

The Internal Revenue Service was established in 1862 by President Lincoln and Congress to help pay for the Civil War. It is the largest tax administration agency in the world with the following stats:

- 2007 total federal tax receipts: $2.7 trillion;

- 79,000 full-time employees (101,000 during "filing season");

- 8,760 managers in 2008;

- 260 executives;

- 1,897 senior and department managers; and

- 6,603 front-line managers

The IRS operates in a fast-paced, highly regulated environment as it collects the nation's revenue. For example, in 2008 an unprecedented economic stimulus package impacting nearly every taxpayer was passed by Congress. This occurred in the middle of tax filing season and required a tremendous effort by the IRS to implement it prior to the end of the season. Prior to the Revenue Reform Act of 1998, the IRS placed significant emphasis on civil and criminal enforcement actions to collect delinquent taxes and encourage voluntary compliance. The reform act fostered an emphasis on balancing enforcement actions with programs that promoted taxpayer education and outreach and enhanced the way the IRS serves the taxpaying public. Additional funding was provided for technology modernization projects and for promoting and supporting electronic filing of tax returns. Moreover, the IRS totally realigned its business structures and processes. For example, the prior structure was comprised of regional and district offices that served all types of taxpayer entities within a geographic area. This was transformed into a structure comprised of four separate business operating divisions, each focused on serving a specific taxpayer segment, supporting the new emphasis on service and education, while maintaining appropriate traditional enforcement mechanisms, such as liens, seizures, and offers in compromise. Leadership development, which had been largely managed by the regional offices, was one of several significant business processes affected by modernization.

IRS Mission:

Provide America's

taxpayers top

quality service by

helping them

understand and

meet their tax

responsibilities

and by applying

the tax law with

integrity and

fairness to all.

Recognizing that the "new" IRS would require new and different leadership skills and behaviors, Commissioner Charles Rossotti directed a review of IRS leadership competencies. The competency model designed was implemented in June 2001 and has helped leaders to foster a business culture that uses service, education, and enforcement to help promote voluntary tax compliance and support the IRS mission.

The IRS cannot achieve this mission without a highly skilled workforce. The purpose of the IRS Human Capital Office (HCO) is to provide corporate human capital strategies and tools for recruiting, developing, retaining, and transitioning a highly skilled and high-performing workforce. In addition, Commissioner Douglas Shulman, in the fall of 2008, created the "Workforce of Tomorrow" (WoT) Task Force. He stated that:

"The goals of this task force are straightforward: to make the IRS the best place to work in government, and to ensure that five years from now we have the leadership and workforce ready for the next fifteen years at the IRS."

The WoT is focusing on:

- Recruitment strategies;

- A streamlined hiring process;

- Strategies for valuing and retaining employees;

- Enhancing the role of managers;

- A dynamic people strategy; and

- Identifying and growing future leaders.

This chapter describes how the IRS Leadership Succession Planning program, developed in 2006, has become the foundation for many of the new recommendations emanating from the Workforce of Tomorrow Task Force.

THE 21ST CENTURY IRS

Leadership development represents a critical component of modernization, equipping leaders with the knowledge, skills, and abilities necessary to lead the changes required to accomplish the new IRS mission and achieve its far-reaching strategic business goals.

In the 21st Century IRS, effective leadership is much more than expertise in managing a budget, reviewing work for technical accuracy, and analyzing programs. Now, to ensure success, a leader must also communicate with others to instill a commitment to realize the organization's vision, support its values, lead change, build high-performing work teams, and coach/mentor employees to transform the IRS into an organization that continuously improves. In designing and developing its leadership development framework, the IRS incorporated proven best practices in both the private and public sectors. Leadership development and succession planning are based on the IRS Leadership Competency Model.

Leadership Competencies

A vital aspect of the modernization effort was establishing a consistent leadership process designed to support the Service's mission, vision, values, and strategic goals. Assisted by Booze Allen & Hamilton, the IRS developed its competency model based on behavioral event interviews of thirty-five top IRS executives that identified five leadership core responsibilities and twenty-one competencies to establish and sustain the behaviors required to transform both the people and the organization into an effective "engine" to achieve business success.

The Hay Group is a global management consulting firm renowned for the quality of its research and the intellectual rigor of its work. Hay, which has longstanding expertise in competency development, validated the competencies against its voluminous database and described the behavioral characteristics demonstrating each competency. The Department of the Treasury and Office of Personnel Management (OPM) were closely involved in this process, providing input and support as the new competency model was constructed. Ultimately, OPM approved the IRS proposal to link competencies directly to the performance plan used to evaluate all managers.

IRS Core Leadership Responsibilities and Competency Model

The IRS was the first federal government agency to directly link leadership competencies to the core responsibilities contained in a manager's annual performance agreement. Thus, IRS managers establish their accountability by developing their annual performance commitments (what) based on both desired business results and the competency-based behaviors (how) required for achieving them. Figures 7.1 and 7.2 depict the core responsibilities and their linkage with the competencies.

Core Responsibilities

IRS has defined 21 leadership Competencies as essential to organizational success. They are grouped under the Performance Agreement Core Responsibility categories common to all IRS managers. The five Core Responsibilities are defined below. Some Core Responsibilities will relate more to your position than others. They are:

Leadership	Employee Satisfaction
• Demonstrates integrity, sound judgement, and the highest ethical standards of public service • Successfully leads organizational change, effectively communicating the Service's mission, core values, and strategic goals to employees and other critical stakeholders and engaging them in the development of objectives that contribute to those goals. • Motivate employees to achieve high performance by facilitating a positive workplace that fosters diversity, innovation, and initiative; open and honest communication; and teamwork among employees and peers.	• Demonstrates the importance of employee satisfaction in successfully accomplishing the Service's mission. • Promotes cooperation, flexibility, and teamwork among employees. • Ensures that, to the extent possible, employees have the tools and training to do their jobs. • Provides continuous, constructive feedback to employees concerning individual and group performance including timely evaluations of performance. • Coaches and develops employees so that they realize their full potential as members of the Service. • Supports labor-management partnership, responding to employee concerns, promptly identifying trends, and taking corrective action to maintain a safe, high-quality work environment in which everyone is treated with respect.
Customer Satisfaction	**Business Results**
• Demonstrates the importance of customer focus as a critical component of the Service's mission. • Listens to customers, constantly gathering their feedback, actively seeking to identify their needs and expectations, and effectively communicating those needs and expectations to employees. • Insures that employees do the same, and that they are prompt, professional, fair, and responsive to the circumstances of individual customers, to the extent permitted by law and regulation. • Continuously evaluates organizational performance from a customer's point of view.	• Effectively develops and executes plan to accomplish strategic goals and organizational objectives, setting clear priorities and acquiring, organizing, and leveraging available resources (human, financial, etc.) to efficiently produce high-quality results. • Constantly reviews and analyzes performance measures, consults and collaborates with stakeholders, and takes decisive action, in accordance with law. • Continuously seeks to improve business processes, sharing those efforts with other units to better overall Service performance.

Equal Employment Opportunity
• Takes steps to implement the EEO and affirmative goals established by the bureau. • Supports staff participation in special emphasis programs. • Promptly responds to allegations of discrimination and/or harassment and initiates appropriate action to address the situation. • Cooperates with EEO counselors, EEO investigators, and other officials who are responsible for conducting inquiries into EEO complaints. • Assigns work and makes employment decisions in areas such as hiring, promotion, training and developmental assignments without regard to sex, race, color, national origin, religion, age, disability, sexual orientation or prior participation in the EEO process. • Monitors work environment to prevent instances of prohibited discrimination and/or harassment.

FIGURE 7.1. *IRS Leadership Core Responsibilities*

LEADERSHIP	EMPLOYEE SATISFACTION	CUSTOMER SATISFACTION	BUSINESS RESULTS	EEO/DIVERSITY
Adaptability	Continual Learning	Customer Focus	Achievement Orientation	*indicates supporting competencies
Communication*	Developing Others*	Entrepreneurship	Business Acumen	
Decisiveness	Diversity Awareness*	External Awareness	Political Savvy	
Integrity/Honesty*	Group Leadership*	Influencing/Negotiating*	Problem Solving*	
Service Motivation	Teamwork	Partnering*	Technical Creditability	
Strategic Thinking				

FIGURE 7.2. *IRS Leadership Competency Model*

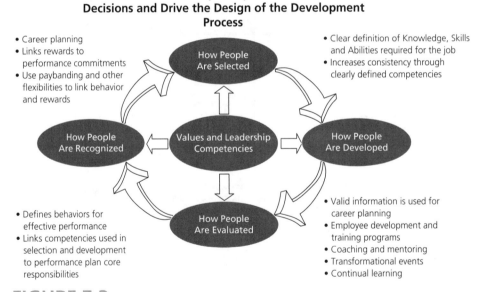

Values and Leadership Competencies Inform HR Decisions and Drive the Design of the Development Process

- Career planning
- Links rewards to performance commitments
- Use paybanding and other flexibilities to link behavior and rewards

- Clear definition of Knowledge, Skills and Abilities required for the job
- Increases consistency through clearly defined competencies

- Defines behaviors for effective performance
- Links competencies used in selection and development to performance plan core responsibilities

- Valid information is used for career planning
- Employee development and training programs
- Coaching and mentoring
- Transformational events
- Continual learning

How People Are Selected

How People Are Recognized

Values and Leadership Competencies

How People Are Developed

How People Are Evaluated

FIGURE 7.3. *Values and Leadership Competencies Inform HR Decisions and Drive the Design of the Development Process*

This link between core responsibilities and competencies ensures that the service can assess results-based performance commitments against the competency-based behaviors consistent within a specific core responsibility. A manager's annual performance appraisal includes an evaluation of those commitments in light of the associated competencies and thus forms the basis for recognition and awards. In addition, the IRS designed a new management selection process that assesses both past performance and future potential in applying the IRS leadership philosophy and competencies on the job. Thus, effective reinforcement of the competency model occurs by integrating processes for how IRS leaders are selected, developed, evaluated, and recognized as illustrated in Figure 7.3.

Planned Changes to the Competency Model

As this article is being written, IRS is in the midst of streamlining its competency model. The current plan is to identify the most vital skills and behaviors that support high effectiveness in the areas of Leading Self, Leading Others, and Leading Improvement. The new competency model will be implemented on or about October 1, 2009.

LEADERSHIP SUCCESSION PLANNING—THE CHALLENGES

Succession planning is defined as the ability to identify qualified candidates for a position prior to the position becoming vacant. By creating a leadership succession environment, organizations are better able to maintain internal continuity and sustainability of operations.

The IRS projects that almost 56 percent of its executives and managers will be eligible to retire by the end of 2010.

Leadership succession is crucial for the federal government and the IRS for two reasons. First, many of the federal government's leaders will soon be eligible to retire. The Office of Personnel Management (OPM) projects that more than 550,000 federal employees—almost one-third of the entire full-time permanent workforce—will leave the federal government by the end of 2012. Although the majority of attrition is expected to occur through retirement, the current economic situation will likely impact this projection.

The IRS faces concerns similar to those of the rest of the federal government as it contends with the potential loss of a significant number of its current leaders by the end of 2010. The IRS estimates that an ever-increasing number of its leaders will be eligible to retire over the next few years. Projections indicate that almost 56 percent of IRS executives and managers will be eligible to retire by the end of 2010. This means that between now and 2018, IRS faces a shortfall of 3,400 leaders—with a need to hire about one manager per day during this timeframe to contend with this shortfall.

As indicated earlier, another reason that leadership succession is critical to the IRS is that leaders in the future will need to (1) be more proactive, (2) embrace change, (3) create and motivate employees around a vision, and (4) think more strategically. All of this will need to be accomplished in less time and with fewer resources than in the past.

Additionally, the IRS faces the following challenges:

- Growing gaps in leadership competencies;

- Increasing difficulty in attracting and retaining talent; turnover percentage for mission-critical occupations has significantly increased over the past three years; and

■ Maintaining a highly skilled leadership cadre to sustain continued technology modernization efforts and significant organizational improvements.

In short, the potential loss of a large number of its leaders within the next several years increases the importance of the IRS having a process in place to fill anticipated vacancies quickly and effectively.

How Is the IRS Addressing the Projected Gaps and Challenges?

The leadership situations described above have contributed to a significant culture shift in the IRS—one that fully recognizes the need for succession planning. Initially, the IRS focused almost solely on developing leaders. In 2001 "readiness training programs" were designed and implemented to develop senior, department, and front-line managers for the next leader level. However, leadership succession was primarily ad hoc and placements were largely uncoordinated. Information on succession risk was unavailable across the service and competency gaps were unknown. Recent efforts, beginning in 2006, have expanded to a formal and more comprehensive succession planning process that includes senior, department, front-line managers, and in some instances non-managers and bargaining unit employees. The remainder of this chapter describes how this was accomplished and the crucial next steps moving forward.

The Approach: Creating a Leadership Succession Planning Environment

After a successful pilot, the IRS implemented the leadership succession review (LSR) process in FY 2007. This process was developed in collaboration with Pricewater-houseCoopers, LLC (PwC). PwC is the world's largest professional services firm specializing in accounting and management consulting. PwC consulted to the IRS on developing a succession planning model and process, the outcome of which is the LSR. LSR provides a highly structured approach described in detail in this chapter. LSR enables each IRS business unit to assess its current and future leadership needs and identify the pools of individuals who are ready now or ready with development for the next leadership level. One major goal of the LSR process is to integrate the LSR assessment process and data on leadership readiness and competency gaps into the existing readiness programs and general leadership curriculum. For readiness programs this is accomplished through using the LSR ratings to identify participants. To address competency gaps identified by the LSR data, both at the service-wide and business unit level, the leadership curricula are being reviewed.

The list below provides a closer look at the LSR methodology, describing its purpose and benefits, as well as the four-stage process.

The Purpose and Benefits of LSR

■ Provides an accurate, current picture of leadership bench strength and capability at every level of the organization, including potential leadership gaps;

■ Identifies individuals who want to become leaders and assesses their potential and readiness;

- Highlights competency gaps at specific leader levels that pose risks for leader effectiveness; and

- Supports planning for recruiting, training, and developing leaders, ensuring the IRS has a "bench" of highly qualified people available for current and future leadership positions.

As in every other part of the IRS leadership structure, the succession planning process is based on the twenty-one leadership competencies described in Figure 7.2. Each of the competencies is segmented into four levels (employee, front-line manager, department/senior manager, and executive) with behaviors that describe effective performance for each level. Each level is hierarchal and assumes that if a person is rated a "4," she or he has demonstrated the three preceding levels. An example of the business acumen competency is shown below in Exhibit 7.1.

EXHIBIT 7.1. Business Acumen

Applies core management area (financial, human resources, and technology) principles and approaches to increase program and workplace effectiveness. Takes steps to prevent waste, fraud, and abuse. Manages available resources, makes cost-benefit decisions, and develops and implements strategies to make sound business management decisions in a manner which instills public trust.

Levels

1. **Understands Core Management Areas:** Demonstrates a fundamental understanding of the principles of financial management, marketing, human resources management, and technology applications in day-to-day activities.

2. **Uses Knowledge of Core Management Areas to Increase Workplace Effectiveness:** Assesses current and future resource (financial and human resource) requirements and uses cost-benefit approaches to set priorities and identify ways to effectively and efficiently satisfy anticipated needs. Considers and uses technology appropriately to increase workplace productivity. Manages programs and budgets in a cost-effective manner.

3. **Understands and Addresses the Most Current Thinking and Practices in Core Management Areas:** Uses a broad perspective of the dynamic shifts in the fields of financial management, human resources management, and technology applications to identify opportunities for new programs or services.

4. **Anticipates Future Trends and Appropriate Applications of Core Management Areas:** Uses in-depth knowledge of the organization and the core management areas to identify and design new strategies for the organization. Determines how the organization can best position itself to add value to the public over the long term.

The numbers in Table 7.1 identify the target level designated for each leadership level for each competency. The four levels provide the framework for assessment of potential for the next step in an individual's career path, along with an analysis of competency strengths and areas for improvement.

The Four Stages of LSR[1]

Stage 1: Data Gathering Stage 1 specifically places emphasis on the individual. Participants in the LSR assessment website complete their demographic information that provides a wealth of background and information for reports. Both a self-assessment and a managerial assessment are completed based on the twenty-one competencies and four levels. Once the manager has done the competency assessment, she or he assesses the person's readiness for the individual's target leadership level, typically the next leadership step in one's career path. A person can be assessed as "not ready," "ready with

TABLE 7.1. IRS Twenty-One Leadership Competency Targets by Leadership Level

Leadership Competency	Executives	Senior Managers	Department Managers	Frontline Managers	Employees
Leadership					
Adaptability	4	4	4	3	2
Communication	4	3	3	3	2
Decisiveness	4	3	3	2	1
Integrity/Honesty	4	4	4	4	3
Service Motivation	4	3	2	2	1
Strategic Thinking	4	3	2	2	1
Customer Satisfaction					
Customer Focus	4	3	3	3	2
Entrepreneurship	4	3	2	2	1
External Awareness	4	3	2	2	1
Influencing/Negotiating	4	3	3	2	1
Partnering	4	3	3	2	1
Employee Satisfaction					
Continual Learning	4	4	4	3	2
Developing Others	4	3	3	3	2
Group Leadership	4	3	3	2	1
Teamwork	4	4	4	4	3
Diversity Awareness	4	3	3	3	2
Business Results					
Achievement Orientation		3	3	3	2
Business Acumen	4	3	3	2	1
Political Savvy	4	3	2	2	2
Problem Solving	4	4	4	3	3
Technical Credibility	4	3	3	2	1

development," or "ready now" for the target leadership level. The manager then completes a succession planning matrix (see Stage 1 in Figure 7.4) on his or her people to take into the Stage 2: Talent Review Discussion.

Stage 2: Talent Review Discussion Stage 2 shifts the focus to the organization. The talent review discussions roll up the organization hierarchically. First-level managers meet with their next level managers in a meeting to discuss the employees on their matrices. In this discussion all of the people assessed are reviewed, and management comes to agreement on final readiness ratings. Management also identifies developmental activities/opportunities for the people discussed in the context of the competencies. Readiness ratings are then compiled into a consolidated Stage 2 matrix for that part of the organization. The information from the Stage 2 meetings flows up the organization to the executive level in the Stage 3 meeting.

Stage 3: Roll-Up of LSR Information to Senior Leaders Stage 3 remains focused on the organization. Stage 3 meetings involve executives only. The discussion focuses on those managers who have targeted executive-level positions as their next step. Additionally, the executives discuss overall business unit bench strength and competency gaps by leadership level for organizational planning and training and development. The Stage 3 meeting information is shared with the executive head of the business unit.

Stage 4: Provide Individual Feedback and Development Ideas Stage 4 shifts the focus back to the individual and is crucial for individual development. Stage 4

Status	Position Title	
	Available	*Not available*
Ready Now This individual possesses the skills, competencies, and experiences necessary to advance to the next level of management at this time.		
Ready with Development With the proper mix of training, education, and experiences, this individual can be prepared for the qualifications necessary for advancement to the next level of management within a 24-month timeframe.	*Available* — *Not available*	
Not Ready This individual will require in excess of 24 months of additional training, education, and experience before he or she possesses the skills, competencies, and qualifications necessary to advance to the next level of management.		
Individuals to Watch Long Term Refers to promising future candidates who are *not* currently eligible for selection. Exhibits excellent performance in their current role. However, lacks many experiences and accomplishments to typically be considered a viable candidate. Due to positive performance trends, the individual should be considered for accelerated development.		

FIGURE 7.4. *Stage 1 Matrix*

meetings are for managers to provide feedback to each direct report on his/her readiness rating and competency assessment. Managers meet with each employee to discuss the readiness rating, competency assessments, career goals, and developmental opportunities. Together, the manager and employee create a career learning plan (CLP).

A summary of the four stages is displayed in Table 7.2.

LSR WEBSITE AND INFRASTRUCTURE

The four stages above are supported by an online user-friendly LSR website that was developed in-house by the Rapid Applications & Technology Group (RA&T) in the human capital office. RA&T is responsible for programming, maintaining, and enhancing the website. RA&T also creates a variety of ad-hoc reports upon request.

The website provides the assessment tool, captures the data, and generates a variety of reports at the individual, group, area, organization, and service-wide levels.

TABLE 7.2. Summary of LSR Four Stages

Stage	Purpose	Participants	Activities
Stage 1	Gather Data	Front-Line Managers, Department Managers, Senior Managers, Executives	(1) Complete the Assessment of Leadership Competencies. (2) Create an LSR Matrix.
Stage 2	Conduct Talent Review Discussions	Department Managers, Senior Managers, Executives	(1) Create a Consolidated LSR Matrix. (2) Create a Chart of Organizational Strengths and Areas for Development.
Stage 3	Roll-Up LSR Information to Senior Leaders	Executives	(1) Discuss Senior Managers' Readiness to Become Executives. (2) Create a Chart of Overall Organization Strengths and Weaknesses. (3) Make Revisions to the Consolidated LSR Matrices.
Stage 4	Provide Individual Feedback and Development Ideas	Front-Line Managers, Department Managers, Senior Managers, Executives	(1) Review and Discuss Self-Assessment Ratings and Managerial Ratings. (2) Identify Approaches to Address Development. (3) Develop a CLP for Individual Development.

More specifically, the website contains information on all stages of the process and includes the process to gather demographic information from the participants, as well as walk them through the self-assessment on the twenty-one leadership competencies. Included on the website are a number of tools and resources available to assist the users through the process. A variety of reports are available to various levels of management, as well as to those who are designated by the business units to have administrator proxy access. Access to reports varies based on the level of management and permissions assigned. Those with administrator proxy access are able to download the entire database for their business unit in order to complete analyses, perform monitoring, and create ad-hoc reports. The Office of Leadership Succession Planning (OLSP) has access to the service-wide database and can pull reports for the entire organization.

In addition to the website, the LSR is supported service-wide by the Office of Leadership Succession Planning (OLSP). OLSP provides planning, support, direction, and consultation on the roll-out and maintenance of the process. Below are a number of written materials developed by the Office of Leadership Succession Planning and located on the Human Capital Office website.

- LSR User Guide

- Competency Target Matrix

- Leadership Competency Booklet, including developmental activities for each competency

- Competency Discussion Guide, with activities to help organizations define the competencies in terms that reflect their work

- LSR Overview PowerPoint

- Frequently Asked Questions

- Leadership Succession Review Process Post-Stage 4 Document, targeted to how to use the LSR data from the individual to the organizational level

- A synopsis for each LSR stage for quick reference

- What LSR means to managers

- List of business unit LSR points of contact

- LSR DVD, a DVD that demonstrates, with professional actors, the entire four-stage process and models providing feedback. (This was provided to every manager via both DVD and online streaming video.[2])

Essential to the success of the process was creating a succession planning point of contact for each business unit. This person's role is to manage the implementation of the LSR for the organization and interface with OLSP. In addition to the points of contact each business unit designated a person with Excel or Access skills to support data collection and reporting for the business unit.

RESULTS

The LSR has provided a wide variety of very useful information and reports, including but not limited to:

- Interest in advancement by leadership level;

- Willingness to relocate at every target level—executive, senior manager, department manager, and front-line manager;

- Statistics on numbers of people "ready now" for advancement (bench strength);

- Statistics on numbers of people "ready with development" for advancement;

- Proportion of management population at or above competency targets (for current level of management); and

- Percentage of managers who meet or exceed the target levels for current level of management.

Results for Competencies

LSR results from Stages 3 (data roll-up to senior leaders) and 4 (feedback sessions) are used at three different levels:

- At the corporate level, the competency proficiencies and gaps are used to focus and refine the service-wide leadership training and development by leadership level.

- At the business unit level, LSR results from Stages 3 and 4 are used to target leadership training and development to the unique functional needs of each business unit. For example, one business unit identified gaps in strategic thinking and problem solving and arranged for contractor-delivered training tailored to their needs.

- At the individual level, LSR results are used in Stage 4 to provide specific feedback on competencies to be strengthened and improved. Results are also used to identify developmental opportunities.

Figure 7.5 provides examples of LSR reports that show competency ratings for a sample of IRS senior managers, comparing current performance with the target level for the senior level manager position. The figure shows two bar charts. The first chart illustrates an example of competencies that are closest to the target and the second indicates the competencies that are farthest from the target for sample group of senior managers.

Figure 7.6 shows the comparison of senior managers' average rating on selected competencies (business acumen, influencing/negotiation, continual learning, developing others, decisiveness, and achievement orientation) with the target level.

Reports like these can be used to identify organizational strengths and improvement areas. The data in the report can be used to appropriately design training and developmental assignments for employees.

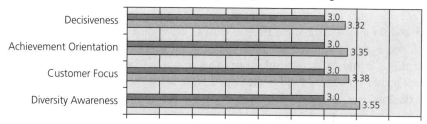

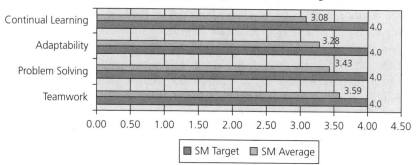

FIGURE 7.5. *Competency Ratings Closest and Farthest from Target—Senior Managers*

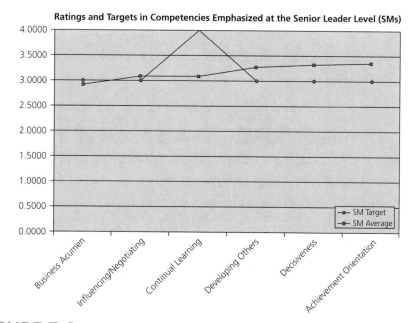

FIGURE 7.6. *Ratings and Targets for Competencies Emphasized at Senior Manager Level*

Results for Bench Strength

At the service-wide level, IRS is exploring the use of 2:1 ratio for bench strength for current and predicted vacancies. People with LSR readiness ratings of "ready now" were plotted against projected attrition data to identify where IRS has leadership risks and surpluses corporately by leadership level. Figure 7.7 shows service-wide data. This data is then compared to projected attrition data to determine the ratio.

At the business unit level, bench strength for each managerial position is identified. A matrix listing positions and people identified as "ready now" or "ready with development" for each position is generated; this identifies gaps in bench strength and where there are surpluses for at-risk positions. The business unit matrix consists of names across the business unit, and is not portrayed as the ratio being used at the service-wide level. The 2:1 ratio is a corporate aggregate indicator: each business unit is identifying its business specific requirements on a more granular level.

At the individual manager level, each manager has identified his or her potential successors within the work group. If there are no potential successors, the manager has looked at his or her talent pool available and identified those who need development.

Senior Managers Assessed = 1214			
	Readiness Level # and %	# Interested in Advancing and % of Readiness Level	# Mobile and % of Those Who Are Interested in Advancing
Ready Now	415 / 34%	249 / 60%	164 / 67%
Ready with Development	579 / 45%	365 / 63%	274 / 75%
Not Ready	220 / 18%	132 / 60%	101 / 76%
Department Managers Assessed = 359			
Ready Now	126 / 35%	109 / 86%	49 / 45%
Ready with Development	193 / 54%	167 / 86%	83 / 50%
Not Ready	40 / 11%	30 / 75%	21 / 70%
Front-Line Managers Assessed = 4,891			
Ready Now	1362 / 28%	1050 / 77%	549 / 52%
Ready with Development	2157 / 44%	1602 / 74%	915 / 57%
Not Ready	1382 / 28%	962 / 70%	592 / 61%
Non-Managers Assessed = 1,271)			
Ready Now	550 / 43%	462 / 84%	269 / 56%
Ready with Development	560 / 44%	444 / 79%	282 / 63%
Not Ready	161 / 13%	109 / 68%	73 / 67%

FIGURE 7.7. *Sample Service-Wide Bench Strength Report*

INDICATORS OF SUCCESS

The success of the LSR process is measured by using the data gathered to help to answer some of the questions below and to develop a corporate process that will address cross-functional and service-wide issues.

- How can bench strength be built and sustained?

- Where are the critical positions that require recruitment/selection?

- Where and what are the competency gaps? At what level, in what function, and/or geographic location?

- What are the competency gaps across the service?

- What are the common needs that can be developed through the IRS leadership curricula, out-service offerings, or cross-functional details or acting assignments?

The IRS is using the LSR data in a number of ways to address competencies, bench strength development, and strategy, as described below.

Competency Proficiency

- Identifying core competencies and competency requirements;

- Planning strategies to close competency gaps;

- Determining talents needed for the long term; and

- Developing a comprehensive picture of where gaps exist between competencies the workforce currently possesses and future competency requirements.

Bench Strength

- Determining current supply and anticipated demand; and

- Developing a business strategy based on long-term talent needs, not just on position replacement.

Development

- Setting up a pool of managers who rotate among various departments or outside of a business unit; and

- Creating organizational learning opportunities by assigning teams of managers from various departments to conduct ongoing or special projects of organizational significance.

Strategy

- Aligning workforce requirements directly with the IRS's strategic and annual business plans;

- Identifying and implementing gap reduction strategies;

- Establishing a formal succession plan for the organization; and

- Utilizing LSR data for strategic and workforce planning.

EVALUATION

There have been a number of forms of evaluation of the LSR process and website since it was implemented.

Lessons Learned The OLSP has held a number of lessons learned meetings and collects data during monthly conference calls with the business unit points of contact (POCs). One of the key learnings was that it is critically important for managers and subordinates to have a common understanding of the meaning and behaviors related to each competency in their specific work environments. The Competency Discussion Guide was a direct output of this learning. Additionally, daily communication with POCs provides direct feedback to OLSP, and a number of teams have been created to address issues and improvements to the process. For example, an LSR System User Group was formed that evaluates and prioritizes requested system enhancements and identifies issues for resolution.

Online LSR User Survey At the time this article was written, an extensive survey exploring every stage of the LSR process was developed and has been administered to a randomly selected group of 1,869 senior, department, and front-line managers and to all IRS executives. The response rate was 71 percent, showing a tremendous interest in the process. The results of the survey will be used to make further improvements to the LSR and the website.

Focus Groups Knowledge Bank (KB), a contractor collaborating with OLSP in writing the IRS Strategic Leadership Succession Management Plan, has done a benchmarking study and a gap analysis on the IRS succession planning process. As part of the gap analysis, KB has conducted focus groups with users and is currently in the process of compiling and analyzing the data. The results will be combined with the information from the survey to improve the system and process.

Lean Six Sigma Workforce of Tomorrow (WoT) has recommended and OLSP and the business units are going to be participating in a Lean Six Sigma exercise designed to determine whether there are process efficiencies to be gained. Lean Six Sigma will assess the LSR process overall, including the four stages and the website. The data from the LSR User Survey and KB focus group findings will be included in this analysis.

LSR Participation One measure of success for a process is the level of participation. Currently the LSR has been used in every business unit to assess managerial potential, and there are more than nine thousand records in the database. A number of the business units have completed one full cycle, defined as assessing all levels of leadership below executive, and most have either started or are preparing to start their second cycle. Furthermore, the majority of the business units have begun or are getting ready to assess specific non-manager populations.

NEXT STEPS

There are a number of next steps planned, including the implementation in late calendar year 2009 of the IRS Strategic Leadership Succession Management Plan, currently under development. The plan addresses and integrates all components of succession planning from recruiting through performance management.

The WoT "Growing Future Leaders" team has been working closely with the Human Capital Office to review and enhance the IRS succession planning strategy and process. Included are proposals for:

- An integrating mechanism called the "Geographic Talent Board" (GTB), described below;

- Developing high-potential employees using the GTB;

- Reducing the number of leadership competencies;

- Streamlining the LSR process (Lean Six Sigma);

- Enhancing the LSR website; and

- Using the GTB to foster a coaching and mentoring approach for development.

A pilot of the GTB is being planned. The pilot will test the concept and functionality of the board. The GTB will consist of executives in a geographic area who meet regularly to:

- Identify high-potential employees (based on the nine-box matrix described below), oversee their development, mentoring/coaching, and feedback and follow-up;

- Coordinate developmental assignments for front-line, department, and senior managers both within and among the business units in the geographic area; and

- Identify mentors and protégés for enhancing development.

To facilitate identifying high-potential employees, the GTB will use a nine-box model based on readiness information from the LSR (potential) and performance data from the last three performance appraisals (performance). This matrix will result in a plot combining potential and performance, assigning individuals to specific blocks which will identify those who are the "stars," demonstrating both high potential and high performance.

The current IRS career learning plan (CLP) is paper-based. With the paper CLP there is no real aggregation of information and there is no efficient method of gathering developmental needs individually, organizationally, or cross-organizationally. Thus, the IRS initiated a project group to design, develop, and implement a web-based career learning plan. The web CLP will automate the process and generate a variety of reports that may be used at all leadership levels. The data will also provide a wealth of information that will be used to plan and budget for training and development. The piloting of the Web CLP will occur in early 2009 with one IRS business unit. WoT expects to pilot it in support of the GTB shortly thereafter.

CONCLUSION

With the leadership succession planning process, the IRS embarked on a journey that has provided vital and important information for managing talent. The LSR process has exceeded expectations. The system is not perfect (no system is). However, the IRS process and technology have been recognized as a best practice in government. With the advent of the WoT Initiative, the succession planning process will move to the next level, providing the information required for identifying and developing our leadership talent, and helping to fulfill Commissioner Shulman's goal of making the IRS "a best place to work."

NOTES

1. The IRS LSR process was designed and implemented in collaboration with *PricewaterhouseCoopers LLP* through an exclusive contractual arrangement to address specific IRS organizational needs. The PwC firm does not accept responsibility to any other third party.
2. The IRS has shared many of these resources and continues to be willing to do so.

Susan Clayton, Ph.D., is assigned to the Office of Leadership Succession Planning in the IRS. Dr. Clayton was a manager of organization development in the IRS; manager of organization and management development at Sun Gas Company. She held a visiting professorship in the Cox School of Business at Southern Methodist University and taught in the business school of the University of Texas at Dallas. Clayton consulted with several Fortune 500 companies regarding their strategic change initiatives. She is a Phi Beta Kappa who holds a master's degree in psychology and a master's in business from Southern Methodist University. Her Ph.D. in behavioral management science is from the University of Texas at Dallas.

Victoria Baugh, M.A., M.Ed., is assigned to the Office of Leadership Succession Planning in the IRS. She played a key role in the implementation of the LSR and the establishment of a service-wide succession planning program in the IRS. During her tenure with the IRS, Baugh has been an organization development consultant, an instructional systems designer, and a training manager. She formerly worked for the Department of Navy as a senior education specialist in a training command and for Escambia County Public Schools as a curriculum coordinator for a self-contained school for severely emotionally handicapped children. Baugh has a M.Ed. in education, training, and management systems and an M.A. focused on learning psychology from the University of West Florida. She also has professional certifications in organization development and process management.

Mathew J. Ferrero is director, Office of Leadership Succession Planning, in the IRS. He and his team support business unit executives in identifying and developing leadership talent for current and future vacancies at all leadership levels. Previously, Ferrero was director of the IRS Leadership Development Center, where he and his team helped create leadership development and succession planning programs that have become the benchmark in the federal government, receiving "best practice" recognition from the American Society for Training and Development, American Productivity and Quality Center, and Linkage, Incorporated. Ferrero was team leader for the IRS Western Region Organization Development Consulting Group and he has held front-line and senior manager positions in the IRS field collection operation. He received his bachelor's and master's degrees in American history from the University of California, Riverside.

CHAPTER

8

KAISER PERMANENTE COLORADO REGION

MARGARET TURNER

A leadership succession management strategy that creates a pipeline of talent to drive current and future organizational performance. Executed through a fully supported system process to develop leadership talent.

- Introduction
  - Company Background
  - The Business Case
- Design
- Process
- Implementation
- Support and Reinforce
- Evaluation
- Next Steps
- Conclusion

INTRODUCTION

This case study introduces the systematic process and tools that are currently used to develop leaders in the Colorado region at Kaiser Permanente. This process and tools, specific to Colorado, were built upon the national review process. Using the national review and the Colorado systematic process and tools helps to create a pipeline of national leaders through the identification of leaders' ability, aspirations, and readiness for their next roles.

Company Background

Founded in 1945, Kaiser Permanente is the nation's largest not-for-profit health plan, serving 8.6 million members, with headquarters in Oakland, California. It comprises:

- Kaiser Foundation Health Plan, Inc.;
- Kaiser Foundation Hospitals and their subsidiaries; and
- The Permanente Medical Groups.

At Kaiser Permanente, physicians are responsible for medical decisions. The Permanente Medical Groups, which provide care for Kaiser Permanente members, continuously develop and refine medical practices to help ensure that care is delivered in the most efficient and effective manner possible.

Kaiser Permanente's creation resulted from the challenge of providing Americans with medical care during the Great Depression and World War II, when most people could not afford to go to a doctor. Among the innovations it has brought to U.S. health care are

- Prepaid insurance, which spreads the cost to make it more affordable;
- Physician group practice to maximize their abilities to care for patients;
- A focus on preventing illness as much as on caring for the sick; and
- An organized delivery system, putting as many services as possible under one roof.

Organization-wide, Kaiser Permanente has 8,663,543 members, 159,766 employees, and 14,087 doctors to serve its regions. Kaiser Permanente is comprised of the following regions:

- Northern California
- Southern California
- Colorado
- Georgia
- Hawaii

- Mid-Atlantic

- Ohio

- Oregon/Washington

Kaiser Permanente Colorado is driven by a social mission. Its mission is to exist to provide high-quality, affordable health care services to improve the health of our members and the communities we serve. We promise to consistently provide high-quality affordable health care in an easy and convenient manner with a personal touch. This case study will focus on the work in leadership succession management in Kaiser Permanente's Colorado Region.

Kaiser Permanente Colorado is a non-profit integrated health care delivery system operated by Kaiser Foundation Health Plan of Colorado and the Colorado Permanente Medical Group. Together they have provided comprehensive health care to Kaiser Permanente Colorado members since July 1, 1969. Kaiser Permanente is Colorado's oldest and largest group-practice health care organization, with 490,000 members in the six-county Denver/Boulder metropolitan area and the Colorado Springs service area. The region has more than 5,400 employees and 2008 revenues of $2.3 billion.

Kaiser Permanente Colorado owns and operates seventeen medical offices and three behavioral health and chemical dependency offices throughout the Denver/Boulder area. In Denver/Boulder, members receive care from more than 300 primary care and 530 specialty physicians. Kaiser Permanente Colorado provides health care in the Colorado Springs service area through a network of 219 primary care physicians and 534 specialists. Additionally, the organization is affiliated with Memorial Hospital in Colorado Springs and Parkview Medical Center in Pueblo.

In 2008, Kaiser Permanente Colorado was awarded the JD Powers award for the highest customer satisfaction. Each year, J.D. Power and Associates surveys millions of consumers around the world to gather their opinions and expectations about the products and services they purchase. This information is used to compile rankings based on product quality, customer satisfaction, or other industry-specific metrics that gauge company performance. Kaiser Permanente Colorado in 2008–2009 is also a top-ranked commercial health plan and top-ranked Medicare plan, according to ranking by U.S. News World Report (Camarow, 2008) and the National Committee for Quality Assurance (NCQA).

The Business Case

The Kaiser Permanente executive recruiting department conducted an analysis of past executive-level hires, internally as well as externally, and realized that 65 percent of its executives were recruited externally. The information from the analysis helped the organization realize that there was a gap in the way leaders were being developed in the organization. Due to this information, the organization set a goal to hire 60 percent internally and 40 percent externally to create opportunities for current leaders to grow with the organization, and still bring in new talents and perspectives to the leadership ranks. The importance of this is for the regions to use and build on the national approach for developing leaders to reach our national internal/external hiring goal. Kaiser Permanente is a matrixed organization. Using a common national framework and region-specific processes to support the growth and development of its leaders serves to create synergies between the national organization and its regions. Because of this, Kaiser Permanente can create a robust national pipeline of leaders, consisting of proven leaders across our multiple regions.

This case study will showcase the systematic approach that Kaiser Permanente's Colorado Region developed to create a regional pipeline comprised of the senior director/director leadership. This systematic approach builds on national processes and feeds into the national pipeline.

The high-potential leadership attrition rate in Kaiser Permanente Colorado is less than *5 percent since 2005*. Sixty percent of the high-potential population has either been promoted to their aspired roles or had job role expansions. These statistics are due to the fact that the Colorado executive team identified a need for a systematic approach to build leadership bench strength for the region in 2005. The executive team is responsible for setting short-term and long-term strategic direction for the region. The strategic direction is focused around affordability, service, quality, membership growth, community benefit, and people. The executive team is also responsible for monitoring the execution of the strategic plan and ensuring that we have the talent in place to deliver on its promise.

The executive team strongly believes that leadership development must be aligned with the organization's business strategy, so that Kaiser Permanente Colorado can execute against its top critical business strategies now and in the future. Leadership development is not seen as a program, but rather as *part of the organizational strategy that creates leadership capability.*

When the leadership review process was first introduced in the Colorado region, it was the beginning process for identification of high-potential talent. This was a great initial step in the process of developing leaders. The review process was implemented from the Leadership Development Department at Program Office (corporate office), since there was not capacity within the region to execute on the process. The beginning of the leadership review process (Figure 8.1) had the executive leaders fill out an assessment on the incumbent based on the incumbent's competencies, interest, and potential. This information was gathered and presented in an all-day forum with the Colorado executive team. The incumbents were discussed as to their potential, aspired roles, and level of readiness. This process was not transparent, and there was not a clear process for communicating the results or resources to follow through on the suggested actions. Also, the review process was designed to have the executives be accountable for the development of their high-potential leaders. As the executives started to work on the development of their high-potential talent, they realized that they needed support to develop these future leaders. The Colorado executive team realized that without those resources the process was incomplete and not driving the needed business results.

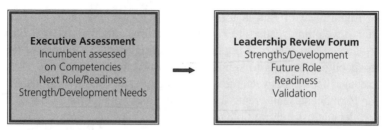

FIGURE 8.1. *Beginning Leadership Review Process*

In 2005, Kaiser Permanente Colorado created a systematic approach to the development of their leaders. First and foremost, the process of leadership development needed to become transparent. It was also agreed by the executive team that all leaders reviewed would be afforded the opportunity to develop not just the high-potential talent. In this systematic approach, different levels of development and resources are identified based on the leader's level of readiness.

The approach for a systematic process involved the following components:

■   Identification of high-potential talent and behavior gaps;

■   Management of talent;

■   Development of talent; and

■   Creation of a leadership pipeline for regional and national roles.

Building leadership capacity in the Colorado region (Figure 8.2) feeds the national pipeline for leadership succession management. The national talent pipeline is comprised of high-potential talent from all regions. Each region conducts a leadership review process and then feeds the information of high-potential talent who aspire to a vice president and/or executive director role to the national leaders. Once validated by the national functional leaders, the incumbents are placed in the national pipeline for development. National and regional resources are used to accelerate the pipeline candidates' development. The Colorado region helps not only to identify incumbents with a high level of readiness for the region, but also for the national organization.

As this case study proceeds, it will outline the systematic process that has been built and the integrated approach to Kaiser Permanente Colorado's leadership succession management.

DESIGN

The purpose of the leadership succession management process folds into the Kaiser Permanente People Strategy for Colorado, which has a clear line of sight to the organizational strategy. Developing leaders is a significant component of the Colorado

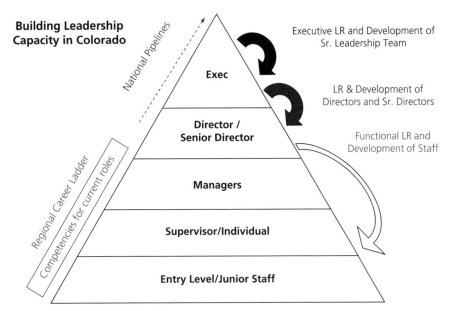

Building Leadership Capacity in Colorado

National Pipelines

Executive LR and Development of Sr. Leadership Team

Exec

LR & Development of Directors and Sr. Directors

Director / Senior Director

Functional LR and Development of Staff

Regional Career Ladder

Competencies for current roles

Managers

Supervisor/Individual

Entry Level/Junior Staff

FIGURE 8.2. *Capacity Building in Colorado*

Region's People Strategy, which acknowledges that our people drive business results. Increasing employee engagement and accountability to execute the region's strategic priorities requires highly skilled leaders and a plan to sustain those skills through succession management. The People Strategy enables organizational performance through people.

One of the outcomes of the People Strategy is to have the leadership talent in place to effectively lead the current business and transform the organization to meet future business challenges. Out of the People Strategy, the framework for building leaders emerged. This framework keeps the customer as the center of focus for leaders to drive business outcomes. Each of the buckets in Figure 8.3 represents areas in which leaders need focus to be successful in driving optimal results for the organization.

The organization's competency model was aligned with this framework. In this way, the development of the organization's leaders is focused on what is most important to drive results.

Another outcome of the People Strategy and the leadership framework was for the executive team to agree to be accountable to the development of the high-potential population as a group. In other words, there was team ownership of

The overarching focus is "To select, retain, and engage talented and accountable team-oriented individuals to execute the region's key strategic initiatives."

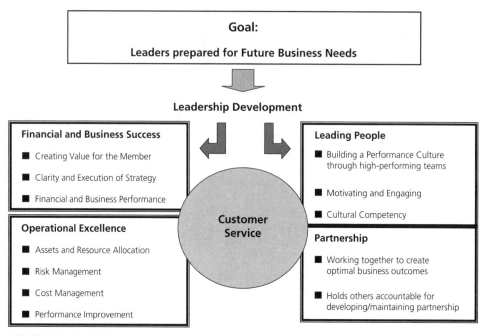

FIGURE 8.3. *Leadership Framework*

identified talent by the executive team. Together the executive team holds itself accountable by:

- Conducting two yearly review processes to update current high-potential talent and to identify new talent (approximately fifty-five incumbents). This also includes leadership diversity talent;

- Providing feedback to the incumbents from the review process as a first step in developing them for their aspired roles;

- Continually working together to identify experience management opportunities that will accelerate the high-potentials' growth toward their next aspired role (approximately thirteen high-potentials, on average);

- Sponsoring and supporting development processes for the high-potential talent as a group; and

- Coaching and mentoring, based on best practices and best-fit principles.

PROCESS

Kaiser Permanente Colorado leadership succession management is a systematic approach to development that starts with the national talent assessment. The national talent assessment process that is used in Colorado is based on a behavioral competency model that measures behaviors that are observable, demonstrated, and critical to successful leaders (Figure 8.4).

The leadership success factors (LSF) were developed after a comprehensive analysis of the leadership competencies that managers must exemplify for Kaiser Permanente to be successful, both now and in the future. These competencies are recognized as applying to Kaiser Permanente managers in all entities and at all management levels of the organization. The LSFs provide a framework for Kaiser Permanente managers to identify and communicate critical leadership behaviors, assess individual manager capabilities (360-degree feedback), and focus developmental and learning efforts. Each LSF is associated with a leadership competency cluster. The clusters provide an overall view of what a leader needs to be successful. The clusters and themes are outlined in Figure 8.4.

Research has shown that emotional intelligence has a positive impact on successful leadership and organizational performance (Goleman, 2002). In order to successfully demonstrate the LSF, one must have emotional intelligence as a baseline competency. For example, to demonstrate effective influence behaviors requires that one be effective in managing one's emotions and understanding the needs of others.

The LSFs are a part of the national talent assessment process which is designed to:

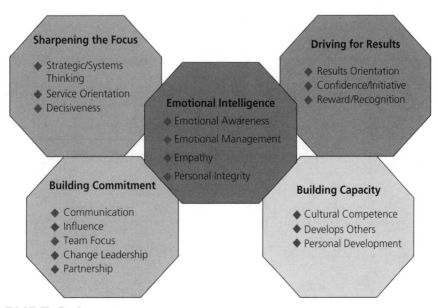

FIGURE 8.4. *Leadership Success Factors*

- Foster objectivity;

- Assess performance and potential, and

- Distinguish between "high potential" and "high performers."

In the national talent assessment process, objectivity is achieved by evaluating the incumbent against the organization's competency model and the Colorado executive team leadership review. The outcomes of the leadership review include:

- Collective understanding and agreement of the high-potential population;

- Peer feedback/input on the performance, strengths/development needs, aspiration, engagement, and willingness to learn;

- Identification of future role, readiness, and mobility; and

- Collective agreement to map high-potential talent to key experiences for their development.

The national model shown in Figure 8.5 clarifies an incumbent's picture of a high-potential candidate. This national model creates a common framework for the regions to identify leadership talent.

The leadership talent review is the first step in the development process, working in partnership with the National Office of Leadership Development. Kaiser Perman-

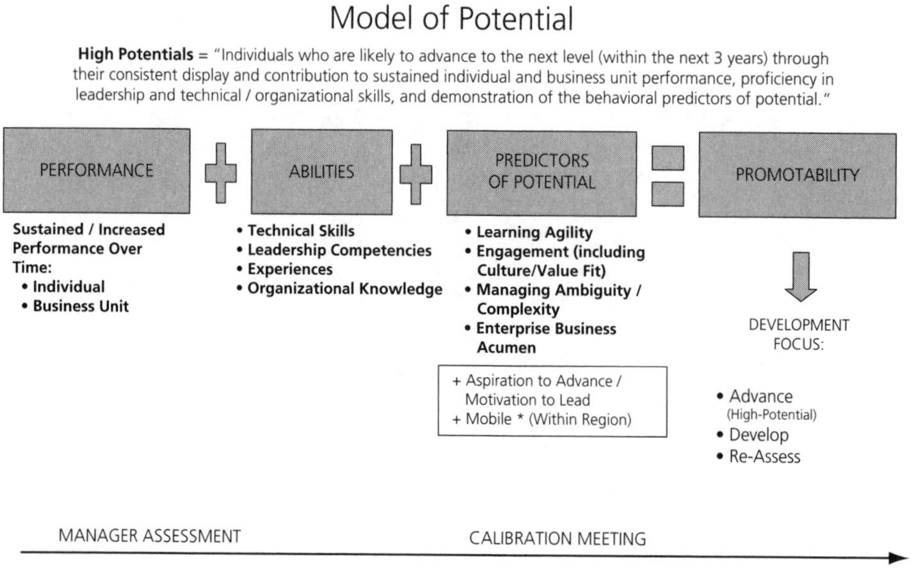

Model of Potential

High Potentials = "Individuals who are likely to advance to the next level (within the next 3 years) through their consistent display and contribution to sustained individual and business unit performance, proficiency in leadership and technical / organizational skills, and demonstration of the behavioral predictors of potential."

PERFORMANCE	ABILITIES	PREDICTORS OF POTENTIAL	PROMOTABILITY
Sustained / Increased Performance Over Time: • Individual • Business Unit	• Technical Skills • Leadership Competencies • Experiences • Organizational Knowledge	• Learning Agility • Engagement (including Culture/Value Fit) • Managing Ambiguity / Complexity • Enterprise Business Acumen	DEVELOPMENT FOCUS:
		+ Aspiration to Advance / Motivation to Lead + Mobile * (Within Region)	• Advance (High-Potential) • Develop • Re-Assess

MANAGER ASSESSMENT   CALIBRATION MEETING

FIGURE 8.5. *National Model of Potential*

ente Colorado has built upon the national review process (Figure 8.6). To further clarify high-potential status in the review process, additional components were developed in the Colorado region, which include preliminary incumbent self-rating, calibration meetings in which the incumbent is discussed with his or her leader to identify several factors, and measurement of engagement and learning. These processes help to give the organization a more informed picture of the incumbent and lead to a transparent talent management process.

The talent review process in Kaiser Permanente Colorado is transparent, in that the incumbent is aware of the expectations of the process. The incumbent fills out a survey with the following information:

- Resume;

- Aspirations;

- Willingness to relocate and time frame; and

- Vice-president-level experiences.

The leader will fill out an assessment on the incumbent based on the leadership success factors, performance (both personal and business unit), future role, and level

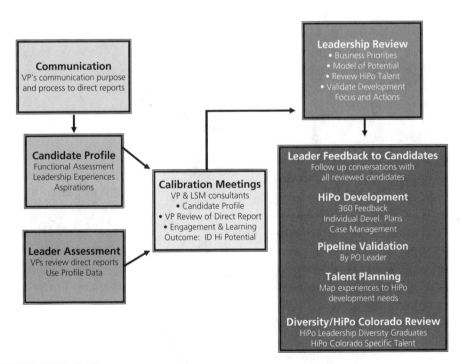

FIGURE 8.6. *Colorado Leadership Review Process*

of readiness. Both sets of information are then brought together and the Leadership Succession Management Consultant meets with the leader to conduct a calibration meeting. In this meeting the following is discussed for each incumbent:

- Strengths—for both current and future role;

- Development needs— for both current and future role;

- Aspiration for future role;

- Derailing behaviors;

- Learning agility;

- Engagement;

- Level of readiness; and

- Development actions.

As a result of the calibration meeting, the incumbent is placed on a readiness matrix. Those incumbents who fall into the now-to-one-year, and one-to-three-year levels of readiness and have the ability to relocate (high potential), move onto the leadership review forum. All other incumbents who go through the process are given feedback from the calibration meetings, create individual development plans, and work with their leaders though quarterly development meetings (Figure 8.7).

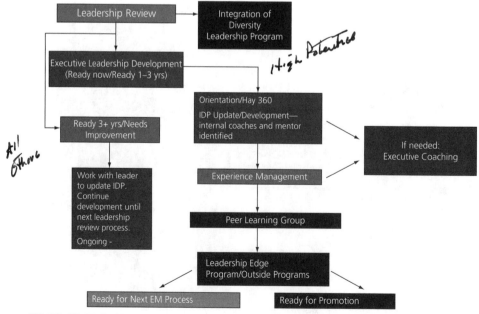

FIGURE 8.7. *Leadership Succession Management Process*

The high-potential candidates are reviewed in a one-day forum with the executive team to validate their level of readiness and aspired, future role. The main results of the leadership review process are the identification, agreement of the talent, and group ownership of the high-potential talent.

Once the high-potential talent has been identified, they start in the systematic process of development. The processes in Figure 8.7 were created in the Colorado region to keep focus and accelerate leaders' development. The process begins with the high-potential orientation and flows into the following processes: peer group activities, individual case management of high-potential leaders, and development opportunities driven by levels of readiness for aspired roles. Each of these processes will be defined in the following section.

Kaiser Permanente Colorado has designed processes, programs, and opportunities for leaders to enhance their development (Figure 8.8). Each of these programs has been strategically aligned to address the development gaps in the organization. Each process, program or experience, inculcates the systematic process for development of the organization's leaders.

Orientation/Assessments Once the high-potential leaders have been identified, they attend an orientation to the systematic process for their development. Accountabilities are outlined and agreed on to continue in the process. Assessments are utilized after the review process is complete to measure the high-potentials' preferences, determine emotional intelligence, and give 360-degree feedback. These assessments help identify current strengths and development needs that inform the individual development plan for each high-potential leader.

Individual Development Plan The individual development plan (IDP) is the road map for a high-potential's development. This plan is focused on the individual's

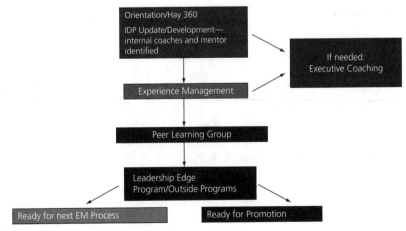

FIGURE 8.8. *Development Process*

business objectives and what behaviors need to be developed to successfully execute those objectives. The IDP process also identifies the high-potentials' future roles, development needs, and experiences for that role.

Case Management   Each high-potential leader is assigned a case manager who works with him or her on the development plan. The high-potential leader and case manager meet quarterly with the high-potential's manager to the review development progress. The executive team, as a group, also receives quarterly updates on each high-potential leader. The case manager, who also partners with National Leadership Development, is the champion for the high-potential leader to help the leader develop toward his or her aspired future role. The outcome of this process:

- Continuous monitoring of the high-potential's development;

- Coaching for development;

- Roadblocks to development addressed; and

- Experiences identified for the high-potential leader.

Peer Network   The Peer Learning Group, composed of our high-potential talent, meets quarterly to discuss development and to provide networking opportunities. The executive team is involved with the group by sharing their experiences of their leadership journey. Expected outcomes of this program include:

- Cross-functional partnerships that help the organization move away from a "silo" orientation—reducing redundant processes;

- Internal/external mentoring support; and

- Peer support network that brings together the high-potential population to work on their development.

Leadership Edge—Senior Director/Director Level   This program was developed by Kaiser Permanente Colorado based on the leadership gaps within the region. It is a thirteen-day learning program extended over a four-month period. The program is based on the core leadership competencies, gaps, and skills critical to the region. What is unique and important about the Leadership Edge program is that executive team members play the role of "color commentators" throughout the curriculum. The color commentator role is designed to have the executive, who is the subject-matter expert, come into the class and interact by challenging participants on current issues that face the organization; listen to solutions to implement; and dialogue on innovation. The Leadership Alumni Group continues working with past graduates on critical business initiatives with the executives. Outcomes of this program have been:

- The first cohort assisted the executive team to define the six key business strategies for the organization;

- Cohorts have made recommendations to focus on two strategic initiatives, down from six initiatives previously; and

- Most importantly, this program is instrumental in breaking down silos for leaders to work effectively across functions.

Experience Management Experience management (EM) is a challenge in a small region. EM is a structured process that identifies the scope of the project, competencies, and resources. High-potential talent is mapped to the following year's key strategic initiatives based on their developmental needs. Risks associated with the project are also identified before assigning a project for the experience. Other sources for developmental experiences are national projects and outside community projects. The outcomes of this program are

- Incumbent gains experience in an area needed for growth for his or her current or future role;

- Incumbents have exposure to executive/national teams; and

- Incumbents receive cross-functional exposure and experience.

Executive Coaching Program The executive coaching program provides a structured approach for individual development. Each high-potential leader has an external executive coach available to him or her. Once the IDP is created, the high-potential leader can request an executive coach through the leadership succession management (LSM) department. Based on their developmental needs, the high-potential leaders receive three bios of coaches and interview questions to help in selecting a coach. Once a coach is selected, the high-potential leader, his or her manager, and the coach meet to agree on the outcome of the coaching, There are mid-course check-ins with these three parties. At the end of the coaching program, there is a final meeting and evaluations are completed. The results have been:

- Increased quality of the individual development plans;

- Noticeable increase in leadership effectiveness; and

- Noticeable increase in commitment to development, at multiple levels.

Outcomes of the System Process Kaiser Permanente Colorado measures high-potentials' satisfaction with their development process with an annual survey. In the 2007 survey, 100 percent of respondents strongly agreed they would stay with the organization. The leadership succession management process has proven to increase the retention of our leaders. As stated earlier, *throughout the three-year process, Kaiser Permanente's attrition rate in the high-potential development program is less than 5 percent.*

IMPLEMENTATION

Sponsorship from the executive team is of paramount importance for successful execution and sustainability. In the Colorado region, the executive team is the sponsoring body for the leadership succession management process.

Two talent review processes are conducted each year with the executive team. One is for overall identification of high-potential talent; the other is for high-potential diverse leaders (supervisor and manager level) and high-potential talent who do not have the ability to relocate within the organization. After the review process, the executive team meets to map the high-potential talent to experiences for the coming year.

Once the high-potentials have been identified, their leader gives them the feedback from the review and they then enter into the case management process. The high-potential talent goes through an orientation process that gives them information on the expectations for being high-potential leaders and the resources available for them. They build their individual development plans, which guide the development actions they will be focusing on for the year.

The training programs discussed below contribute to the development of high-potential leaders:

National Executive Leadership Program—President/Vice President/Executive Leaders The Kaiser Permanente Executive Leadership Program (ELP) is a comprehensive leadership program whereby leaders from across the program gather to concentrate on business focus designed to enhance participants' knowledge, tools, and relationships. This is accomplished through extensive case studies that are designed to help participants examine and refine their leadership points of view. ELP provides participants with a unique opportunity to evaluate their leadership approaches and skills with the expectation that they return to work with their "game up."

The objectives of the program are to:

■ Give leaders a broader perspective;

■ Develop leaders to ensure KP's future;

■ Build a network of organizational relationships that provide current and future value to the participants and to the organization;

■ Deliver customized business content relevant to KP's issues and needs;

■ Build commitment to KP; and

■ Improve participants' effectiveness in their current roles.

ELP participants' behavior change is evidenced by:

■ Taking initiative and leading change more frequently;

■ Exhibiting greater confidence;

- Using a broader perspective to lead more effectively;

- Having higher expectations of themselves and others;

- Having greater energy and delivering better performance;

- Communicating more effectively; and

- Innovating—using newly acquired tools and a network of colleagues to develop new processes.

Diversity Leadership Program The leadership diversity development program for supervisors and managers is a fifteen-month program that includes mentoring, training and development, and case management for leaders of diverse background to increase their leadership skill sets. The program gives the diverse leaders the opportunity to work with mentors and gain exposure and knowledge around organizational issues. It also gives the mentors the opportunity to increase their awareness and skill levels around diverse cultures from the mentees. The outcomes of this program include:

- Identification of high-potential diverse leaders;

- 50 percent promotion rate for individuals who have attended the program;

- Targeted development and support of high-potential diverse leaders; and

- Exposure to senior leaders.

Leadership On-Boarding This program is an introduction for new leaders (both internal and external hires) to create focus and clarity during their first ninety days in their roles. A 30-60-90-day plan of action is the major product of the leadership on-boarding. An executive coach can be attached to this process if needed.

Additional Training Programs Organizational effectiveness (OE) in Kaiser Permanente Colorado believes that the performance management pyramid, as shown in Figure 8.9, is one of the keys in mapping employee development.

OE works with mid-level leaders to achieve the following:

- Set performance objectives linked to organizational objectives;

- Establish standards against which the performance objectives can be measured;

- Identify areas for performance improvement; and

- Provide ongoing feedback.

The paths in Figure 8.9, Explore, Ascent, and Summit, have specific training programs attached that address the developmental needs of that level. The design continuously develops leaders from their first supervisory experiences and empowers leaders in service, change management, and strategic execution.

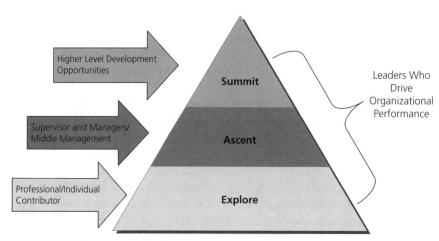

FIGURE 8.9. *Organizational Effectiveness Map*

OE provides various training programs that link to the developmental gaps of leaders in the organization. Kaiser Permanente's program office also has national programs that support the learning of leaders that are used in the development of regional leaders.

All elements of the systematic process are critical, as one builds upon the other. The elements that have had the biggest impact on the development for Kaiser Permanente Colorado are the Leadership Edge Program and individual case management. The success with the Leadership Edge Program is driven by Kaiser Permanente Colorado's executive team involvement. Learners directly interact with the executives and have an impact on the direction of the organization. The case management process gives the high-potential employee personalized one-on-one assistance, which has been instrumental to ensuring development.

SUPPORT AND REINFORCE

Kaiser Permanente Colorado's leadership succession management process is based on sustained commitment to development. The process looks at the leadership talent life cycle from an end-to-end perspective. This starts with the on-boarding of new leaders, identification of top talent, and steps leading to promotion. The manager is ultimately accountable for the high-potential leader's development, with support from the leadership succession management consultants.

Since 2005, we have identified a yearly average of thirteen high-potential leaders. Sixty percent of the high-potential population over the last three years has either been promoted or given expanded roles as an outcome of the systematic process Kaiser Permanente Colorado has developed. To continue executive involvement with the development of our leaders, the Leadership Edge Program has an alumni group that continues to work with the executive team on business solutions.

The executive team models commitment by following through on their actions. They keep development in their daily conversations. When a position becomes open or a project opens up, one of the first places they look is at our high-potential population. This helps to create a culture of development for the organization.

EVALUATION

Kaiser Permanente Colorado measures the success of the leadership succession management process through several different tools. The first is the standard measure around promotion/role expansion per year of our high-potential population. Another is through the leadership development satisfaction survey. In the Leadership Edge Program, the organization is currently reviewing the anecdotal evidence and outcomes of projects to measure ROI. One of the most telling pieces of anecdotal evidence is with the executive team. They are asking the question of development when projects or opportunities arise that might fit an experience for our high-potential population.

Kaiser Permanente Colorado stands out in leadership succession management through the work of creating a systematic process for the identification and development of high-potential leaders. The process has strong executive leadership accountability and support, robust tools, and training, coaching, and mentoring programs in place. Metrics and progress are monitored. All of these elements lead to a successful leadership succession process that retains the organization's top talent and drives organizational performance.

NEXT STEPS

To continue to build on the organization's leadership succession management success, the following is a high-level overview of the work for 2009–2011:

- Drive the leadership review process down to the supervisor level to create a regional pipeline for all levels of leaders;

- Integrate the diversity leadership program into the systematic leadership succession plan to increase the development of diverse leaders;

- Integrate recruiting and pipeline work;

- Generate additional metrics that measure success;

- Conduct a predictive analysis of future leadership needs;

- Deepen the understanding of critical roles;

- Create a peer network for different levels within the organization; and

- Create a formal mentoring process for leaders.

CONCLUSION

The systematic approach used in the Colorado region has provided a consistent framework to identify and develop leaders. It is successful in the fact that it supports the executive team's development of their direct reports, which drives their sponsorship for the leadership succession planning strategy. Success also lies in the partnership with the national leadership development department.

This process is only three years old, and it is still evolving. The systems are continually evaluated and updated for effectiveness. Processes are slated to be incorporated that will enhance leadership development and hopefully increase the velocity with which leaders are moving through their roles. Kaiser Permanente Colorado firmly believes that the development of their leaders will drive creative opportunities and solutions for the organization to execute on its current and future business objectives.

REFERENCES

Camarow, A. (2008). Behind the health insurance ranking. *U.S. News & World Report*. www.usnews.com/healthplan

Goleman, D. (2002). *Primal leadership*. Boston: Harvard Business School Press.

Margaret Turner is currently the internal senior consultant for leadership succession management at Kaiser Permanent Colorado. In her role, Turner is responsible for the strategy and execution of leadership succession planning. She collaborates with her national partners in creating a robust leadership succession process. Because of the success of Kaiser Permanente Colorado's leadership succession process, the body of work is benchmarked throughout the national organization. Turner has over twenty years of experience in organization development, planning, and coaching of leaders. She has a master's degree in organizational management.

CHAPTER

9

MCDONALD'S

JAMES INTAGLIATA AND NEAL KULICK

This chapter describes five separate initiatives that have been introduced in the past eight years to strengthen the areas of performance development, succession planning, and leadership development. For each initiative we describe how and why the changes were introduced, how they have been refined, and the multiple positive impacts they have had on the business over time.

CONTEXT FOR GLOBAL TALENT MANAGEMENT INITIATIVES

The Need for Change

For most of its fifty-four years of existence, McDonald's has been quite successful growing its business while utilizing a decentralized approach to managing its global workforce. As the size, complexity, and global character of the business have continued to grow (to more than thirty-thousand restaurants in 118 countries serving fifty-five million customers per day), however, it became increasingly apparent that sustained success requires the development of more consistent and disciplined approaches to talent management and development. In response to this recognized need, McDonald's has taken a number of steps, starting in 2001, that have enhanced its capabilities for developing local leadership talent and ensuring management continuity throughout its global system. This chapter will provide an overview of how McDonald's system for developing its management talent throughout the world has evolved over the past eight years and will focus on describing the design, roll-out, initial impacts, and continued refinement of five major initiatives that have been introduced to enhance this system since 2001.

A number of factors led the organization to the conclusion that enhancements in its talent management and development system were needed. First, after many years of outstanding business results and growth, business performance began to falter. For the fourth quarter of 2002, in fact, the company declared the first loss in its history. In contrast to the significant problems surfacing in the company's business results, however, the ratings of managers in McDonald's performance management system were incredibly high and suggested that everyone was doing an outstanding job. More specifically, more than 90 percent of the managers were rated either "outstanding" or "excellent," and over 75 percent were assessed as having the potential to advance to take on greater responsibilities. Senior management recognized that "something was wrong with this picture." It was clear that the bias toward inflated ratings of both performance and potential did not align with the overall performance of the business. Furthermore, senior management noted that, despite the very high ratings of employees' potential throughout the system, when key leadership positions actually needed to be filled, the company was frequently having difficulty finding individuals everyone could agree were truly ready for these roles.

These factors led senior management of the company to begin to take significant actions to upgrade the company's talent management systems and processes on a global basis. *(Note:* While the initiatives to enhance talent development that are described in this paper were well under way at the time, the urgency for them was painfully validated when in April of 2004, McDonald's CEO Jim Cantalupo died suddenly and unexpectedly. Fortunately, due to the heightened attention that was being given to talent management at this time, his successor, Charlie Bell, was quickly and smoothly named to step into the CEO role. Tragically, not long after Charlie Bell was named as CEO he was diagnosed with colon cancer and died within a year. Once again McDonald's was challenged to address the succession issue at the very top of the organization and did so by naming Jim Skinner as CEO in January of 2005.)

Business and Global Workforce Strategy

Before launching into an in-depth description of McDonald's talent management system, it is important to make clear how this system fits into McDonald's overall business strategy and aligns with its key values. McDonald's strategy to develop its global workforce is designed to be aligned with and support the execution of its over-arching strategic business goal, which is "to become everyone's favorite place and way to eat." McDonald's has an overall "plan to win" that provides the global business with a common framework for developing tactics to reach this goal. The framework includes five key elements: (1) people, (2) place, (3) product, (4) promotion, and (5) price (see Table 9.1).

The five initiatives that have strengthened the company's talent management system, and that will be described in this chapter, are key elements of the "people" component of the "plan to win." They have been designed and implemented to enhance the organization's global capability to develop and have "at the ready" the quantity and quality of leadership talent needed for effectively executing its "Plan to Win" and ensuring the company's continued growth and success. Further, in order for these talent management initiatives to be successful, it was clear that they also needed to reflect the value that McDonald's places on striking the right global/local balance and customer/employee focus.

Striking the Right Global/Local Balance

In order for McDonald's to successfully execute its business strategy, the company has determined it needs to excel at developing and successfully implementing a balanced

TABLE 9.1. **Framework for "Plan to Win"**

Key Elements	Relevant Measures
People	Well trained Fast and friendly service Delighting customers
Place	Clean Relevant Inviting
Product	Food tastes great Lots of choices Hot and fresh
Promotion	Consistent with the brand Relevant to the customers
Price	Best value to the most people Affordable

global/local approach in managing and developing its global workforce. While global frameworks and parameters can be used to set the stage for success and align the entire business with regard to strategy, essential tactics, and a shared company culture—at the end of the day, the actual execution of the company's "plan to win" depends on the capability of *local talent* to develop and customize the elective tactics to fit their local culture and circumstances. As a business, McDonald's success relies not only on the leverage that comes from its coherent business strategy and focus on standardizing core operations/processes but also on its ability to adapt its tactics to fit the needs and preferences of specific customers in particular regions or countries and to develop a deep connection between McDonald's and the local communities in which it operates. This connection is reflected in McDonald's commitment to local charities; to Ronald McDonald Houses; and, most importantly, to the very people who own, operate, and manage McDonald's stores in any locale, country, or region. Given this, it is deemed highly important that the individuals operating the business come from, understand, and represent the communities and cultures in which the business is located.

All areas of world have freedom to execute in their locales as long as they stick within the basic parameters of the "plan to win" framework by (1) developing an aligned strategy, (2) meeting customer needs within the marketplace, (3) supporting the global brand campaign—"I'm Loving It," and (4) ensuring that their people *develop and demonstrate key competencies that reflect the core elements of the company's common culture and support its "plan to win."* In addition to having the technical skills and expertise to do their specific jobs, staff throughout McDonald's are expected to be attentive not just to getting results but to doing so in a way that is aligned with the company's shared global company culture and values.

Customer and Employee Focus

Whatever is done within McDonald's is routinely assessed and measured against its impact on customers. Customer service and experience levels are key metrics that are embedded within the performance expectations for employees throughout the system. The company's focus on and commitment to quality, service, cleanliness, and value (QSC&V) is strong. These variables have been shown to be strongly linked to customer expectations and loyalty. Any and all efforts to enhance the company's global workforce management system incorporate a focus on key behaviors (customer focus and service orientation) and results-metrics (speed and quality of service, food, and environment) that deliver to customers what they value.

McDonald's has also paid significant attention to its employees and their development throughout its history. The company is well known for the opportunities it has given many of its people to grow with the company and to rise (over time) from working as a member of a store crew to its highest executive ranks. In addition, the company has placed strong emphasis on its managers' ability to create a work climate within which their employees are motivated to excel, give their best, and help to make McDonald's "everyone's favorite place and way to eat." Since 1997, McDonald's has used its commitment survey to assess the extent to which the desired work climate is being created throughout the company. This survey gathers employee feedback on a wide variety of specific management behaviors and practices that have been shown to be linked to employees' personal satisfaction and commitment and to the company's business success. More specifically, the survey assesses employee satisfaction with such factors as the support and recognition they receive, the extent to which their skills are utilized and developed, their workload, the degree of their empowerment, resource availability to get the job done, the quality of supervision/leadership, and their compensation/benefits. A manager's scores on the commitment survey are one of many important factors considered in rating his or her effectiveness and potential for advancement. In addition, turnover and tenure measures are used to evaluate the effectiveness of managers—especially in retaining top talent. The global workforce initiatives described later in this chapter were developed so that they reflect both the customer and employee focus described above.

EVOLUTION OF THE TALENT MANAGEMENT SYSTEM: KEY INITIATIVES AND ENHANCEMENTS

As mentioned earlier, five separate initiatives were developed and have been implemented since 2001 to enhance McDonald's talent management and development processes and support the organization's goal of meeting the global leadership needs of the business. These include: (1) the redesign of the performance development system (PDS) for all staff positions throughout McDonald's; (2) introduction of the talent review process for all officer-level positions; (3) the development and roll-out of a series of accelerated development programs beginning with the Leaders at McDonald's Program (LAMP) launched in 2003 to enhance the development of high-potential individuals for officer level positions; followed by (4) the introduction of the McDonald's Leadership Institute; and (5) the design and launch of the Global Leadership Development Program.

Initiative 1: Performance Development System Redesign

Prior to 2001, McDonald's performance development system was comprised of (1) an "MBO-based" annual performance plan that measured performance against established annual objectives but included no assessment of *how* these results were achieved (that is, leadership behaviors); (2) a 5-point rating scale of overall performance ranging from "outstanding" to "unsatisfactory"; (3) a personal developmental planning element based on a McDonald's-wide competency framework that included nine core competencies and four leadership competencies as well as a menu of "elective" competencies that could be chosen/applied as relevant in specific functional areas (see Table 9.2); (4) a three-level assessment of career potential that combined performance and demonstrated leadership competencies; and (5) an annual compensation system element tied to the results of the annual performance rating.

TABLE 9.2. McDonald's Competency Framework (as of 2003)

Competency Category	Specific Competencies
Core Competencies	
Change Orientation	
Communicates Effectively	
Continuous Learning	
Customer Focus	
Drives to Excel	
Holds Self and Others Accountable	
Problem Solving and Innovation	
Teamwork and Collaboration	
Values and Respects Others	
Leadership Competencies	
Coaches and Develops	
Maximizes Team Effectiveness	
Maximizes Business Performance	
Strategic Perspective	
Functional Competency Menu (elective)	
Job Knowledge	
Leverages Resources	
Decisiveness	
Gathers and Uses Information	
Impact and Influence	
Negotiation and Conflict Resolution	
Uses Technology Appropriately	
Vendor Management	

While the process for rating performance and potential was not unusual in structure and design, the outputs of the system reflected the culture of McDonald's at that time. Specifically, there was *significant rating inflation* for both annual performance (98 percent of managers were rated either "outstanding" or "excellent") and potential (78 percent of managers were rated as having the potential to advance in the business at least one level). Because there was significant inflation in such ratings, there was little meaningful performance and compensation differentiation. Further, since almost everyone was rated not only as being an excellent/outstanding performer but also as having advancement potential, it made differentiation for purposes of realistic succession planning very difficult.

Senior management realized that because the business had been so successful for so long, a *culture of entitlement* may have set in. This was exemplified by many employees believing that their past success and associated rewards would guarantee their future success/rewards rather than their having to earn success each day with every customer. Senior management believed it was important to change the culture in order to help the organization become better able to face the challenging realities of a more competitive global marketplace. As one approach to signaling the need for this change to the organization, the top management team at McDonald's asked human resources to redesign the performance development system in order to (1) place a stronger focus on *accountability for results*, (2) increase performance differentiation, and (3) enhance openness to change and innovation.

The redesign and enhancement of the system (designed for all staff throughout the company—not just officers) rolled out in 2001 included the following changes:

1.   The addition of six key expected leadership behaviors termed "performance drivers" (see Table 9.3) as an element of how annual performance will be assessed so that managers would be measured not just on the "what" of their accomplishments but also on "how" they accomplished them. The performance drivers were very much like "competencies" but were written to measure the actual application of those competencies on the job versus measuring one's level of capability. Further, these "performance drivers" were used as an additional key lever by top management *to signal the importance of needed culture change along certain dimensions identified as critical to enable the organization to compete more effectively in the marketplace* (greater accountability and performance differentiation, more innovation, etc.).

2.   The introduction of a 4-point rating scale ("exceptional performance," "significant performance," "needs improvement," and "unsatisfactory" to replace the 5-point scale) with a rating distribution *guideline* of 20-70-10 percent for each category, respectively (the last category of 10 percent includes both "needs improvement" and "unsatisfactory"). The new 4-point rating scale and distribution guidelines were put in place to help address the rating inflation problem.

3.   A new incentive compensation plan that tied to the improved performance differentiation and ensured that those rated in the "top 20 percent" were receiving *significantly* higher compensation than those who did not.

4.   A revised assessment of potential that utilized a combination of performance, performance drivers, position-specific competencies as criteria supported by a facilitated calibration roundtable process. This revised assessment of potential was also accompanied with a guideline that stated that no more than 20 to 25 percent (this guideline was set based on internal discussions regarding what was realistic as well as some external benchmarking done with outside companies) of managers in any given year were expected to be assessed as "ready" immediately for a promotion to the next-higher level and "ready within two years" for such a promotion.

TABLE 9.3. Performance Drivers

Performance Drivers	Sample Behaviors
Setting Clear Objectives with Results Accountability	Involves establishing high standards for performance, well-defined objectives and targets, and clear priorities for what must be accomplished and taking full personal responsibility for doing what it takes to deliver promised results. For people managers, it includes ensuring that direct reports understand what is expected of them and receive regular feedback on their performance as well as clearly differentiating between top and lower contributors when evaluating performance.
Coaching and Valuing People	Involves treating people with dignity and respect at all times, demonstrating honesty and integrity in all dealings with others; ensuring that the highest quality people are being selected for the organization and are actively provided with opportunities to use their capabilities to contribute to the business as well as grow and develop their potential to do more in the future.
Strategic Focus and Business Planning	Involves being able to develop an effective organizational business vision and strategy that are based on sound facts and that are well thought through, communicating them so that others understand and commit to them, and translating the vision and strategy into a clear overall work plan as well as into the individual goals and priorities that will guide and align the efforts of people at all levels of the organization.
Acting in the Best Interest of the System	Involves demonstrating consistent commitment to work together as a team to achieve the vision and what is in the best interest of the system. Shares information and resources with others to contribute to their success. Acts to break down silos or boundaries in order to help the business maximize the leverage from its combined resources.
Open Communications	Involves demonstrating strong "listening for understanding skills" and valuing diverse opinions. Conveys information and ideas in an open, articulate, and timely manner that enables others to get their jobs done. Communicates in a high-energy, positive way that motivates people to achieve.
Embraces Change/ Innovation	Involves being open to new ideas and innovation and having not only the flexibility to adapt to change but also the energy and drive to initiate and lead it.

New System Roll-Out—Global vs. Local Emphasis How this new system was rolled out globally reflected the balance between the global and local approaches to workforce management. When it was introduced at a global HR meeting in June 2003, it was clear that certain elements of the new system redesign were not suited for the foreign cultures and legal structures that existed in certain countries. As a result, all 119 countries were given latitude (labeled "freedom within the framework") to make certain changes (for example, the labels given to the three rating categories), while they were not permitted to customize other aspects of the process (such as rating distribution guidelines or the use of performance drivers in the ratings). Providing this flexibility made a key difference in how well the new process was accepted by each country and, while many countries would have preferred to continue to use their own performance plans and processes, most willingly began the implementation of the new system and accepted the value of following the framework.

Results of Implementation As with any major change that impacts employees' individual performance ratings and compensation, the introduction of the new performance development system (PDS) was difficult and met some expected resistance. While this resistance was directed, in part, to specific concerns regarding particular changes made in the system (the number and labels for rating categories, changes in format, etc.), people's reactions also reflected the reality that the revisions in the performance management process were designed to help drive what were believed to be some needed changes in the company's management culture (enhanced accountability, greater differentiation in evaluating performance, increased emphasis on openness to change/innovation, etc.). At the same time, leaders of McDonald's wanted to ensure that the focus on people and people development was not diminished.

The introduction of the new PDS system impacted significantly on the distribution of ratings for both performance and advancement potential. For example, in 2000 the vast majority of U.S.-based officers and managing directors received ratings ("outstanding" or "excellent") that were above the mid-point ("good") on the 5-point rating scale. In 2001, however, only 25 percent were given an "exceptional contributor" rating (this rating is for individuals who are judged to have "achieved results that far exceed expectations and requirements of the job in the face of challenging demands during the performance cycle and who have done so while modeling the values and behaviors expected of McDonald's leaders"). Most individuals received a "significant contributor" rating (for "consistently meeting and perhaps exceeding some expectations and planned objectives while demonstrating the McDonald's values and behaviors") that was perceived to be average because it was the mid-point on a 3-point rating scale. For the first time in their careers, many managers (at the corporate officer and managing director levels) had received ratings that were not labeled "exceptional" or "outstanding," and this was a shock and source of discomfort to them. In addition, a relatively small proportion of individuals were actually rated below the mid-point on the scale ("lower contributor/needs improvement" or "unacceptable performer"), which was highly unusual in McDonald's culture. It should be noted, however, that the very year the new PDS was introduced, McDonald's business performance was well below expectations and the stock price hit new lows. This softened the blow a bit, as managers could see that change was necessary and that McDonald's was operating in a different world with new challenges that needed to be met in order to get the business turned around and once again moving in a positive direction.

As the new system has continued to be used, the proportion of individuals in each of the categories described above has stayed in a similar range. We have discovered along the way that it is a challenge to keep the distributions of individuals across performance rating categories consistent across levels of the organization. In other words, ratings creep seems to be a natural tendency as you move, for example, from the VP to the SVP level. What we have done to address this is to emphasize the importance of individuals being compared relative to those in the peer group at their specific level of the organization.

Ratings of Potential Consistent with this more critical differentiation of performance, changes in distributions were also seen in the company's ratings of individual potential for continued advancement. In 2001, approximately three-quarters of U.S.–based officers and managing directors had been rated as having the potential to be promoted at least one more level. With a much more critical and challenging succession planning review process instituted, 2002 ratings of this group's future potential were far more realistic (the proportion evaluated as having clear potential for further advancement from their current officer-level positions was closer to 15 to 20 percent). This proportion has remained in this same relative range since that time.

Lessons Learned While the process was difficult to do, our results would suggest that it's sometimes easier to "bite the bullet" and make a significant change all at once rather than trying to make incremental changes. The PDS change enacted in 2001 effectively lowered the ratings of more than 50 percent of McDonald's managers on a year-over-year basis. This was all done in a single year, but by year two, the organization had adapted to the new process. Other key lessons learned in implementing this initiative included the importance of: soliciting input from around the globe prior to program design finalization (the finalized system has been well accepted and has worked smoothly across widely varying geographic/cultural locations) and keeping the centralized, structured processes as simple as possible. Finally, we have purposefully given the organization time to become familiar with the new system and have resisted any significant "tweaking" of it. Some changes to further streamline the system continue to be made, but they have not been major.

Initiative 2: Global Succession Planning and Development Process

Design of the Global Talent Review Process Prior to the launch of the current global talent review process, succession planning had been conducted at McDonald's for many years. Prior to 2003, this process was less formal, less structured, and less consistent across various areas of the world, yet it probably met the needs of the business, which had an outstanding record of growth of profitability. As business growth slowed and competition increased, however, there was a recognized need to enhance the focus on leadership talent to align better with the new global business challenges.

Beginning in 2003 it was decided that the talent management process at the leadership level needed to be more rigorous and also more transparent. To achieve this rigor and transparency, the presidents of each area of the world (U.S., Europe, Asia/Pacific/Middle East/Africa, and Latin America), along with each corporate staff head (EVP-HR, EVP-Finance/CFO), were given a talent management template that consisted of a series of questions about their leadership talent requirements and the depth and diversity of their talent (see Exhibit 9.1). They were asked to prepare answers to these questions for their respective organizations. It was made clear that these questions would form the basis of the in-depth talent reviews that each of them would have with his or her immediate superior, who at that time was either the vice chair or the chief operating officer.

EXHIBIT 9.1. Talent Review Template Questions

I. Forecast of corporate leadership talent requirements for next three years, including positions, people, and/or competencies

The answers to the following questions should be based on the strategic plan for the business as well as the operational requirements:

- Specify the corporate leadership positions that will be added, eliminated, or changed from the current organization?
- Expected retirements, terminations, promotions, transfers, etc.?
- What, where, when, and how many openings are forecasted for the next three years?
- What, if any, changes in the competencies or roles will be required of the leadership team and how will they be addressed?

II. Assess and develop current talent pool

- Who are your A, B, and C players?
- What actions are you taking to develop and retain your A players? Development plans including development moves? Retention strategy?
- What actions are being taken with your C players to improve or remove them?
- Who represents your next generation of leaders ("ready now/ready future" with higher-level target positions)?
- Development plans including planned development moves?

III. Replacement and/or diversity gaps and associated action plans

- What, if any, significant replacement gaps exist, and what plan is in place to close these gaps?
- What, if any, diversity gaps exist and what plan is in place to close these gaps?

IV. Summary of planned actions

The stated purpose of these executive talent reviews was as follows:

■ Identify executive (officer/managing director) talent requirements for successfully executing their organizational strategy over the next three years and how these requirements will be met.

■ Ensure that plans are in place in each organization to upgrade the executive talent via development, planned movement, strategic hiring, etc.

■ Ensure the "next generation" (the "feeder pool") of leaders has been identified and is being developed to ensure both depth and diversity.

As can be seen from the questions listed in Exhibit 9.1, the talent review covered the broader aspects of talent management, including forecasting needs, assessing current officers/MDs, identifying depth and diversity of replacements pools, and development planning. The premise behind these reviews is that the president and lead staff officer of each area of the world are responsible and accountable for ensuring that they are addressing the leadership talent needs in their area and are doing so within the framework of the template. Transparency was achieved as a result of the in-depth discussions that took place during the actual review meetings.

The talent reviews were held as planned in 2003 and resulted in a much more realistic and rigorous assessment of the "health" of the talent pools in each area of the world and each functional area than had been achieved previously within McDonald's. The increased ownership that leaders were taking for the results of these reviews was reflected in the specific actions that they proactively initiated (such as accelerating the development of high-potential managers, special recruiting initiatives, etc.) to respond to the current and anticipated replacement gaps that had surfaced. The HR support team was able to analyze the overall results of these reviews and look for any organization-wide interventions that would contribute to better addressing talent needs and gaps.

Talent Review Process Impact Results of the one-year follow-up survey with executive management and HR leaders in each of the company's four major regions yielded the following observations regarding improvements in the talent review process: (1) managers and the organization overall became much more aware of the strengths and talent gaps in each area; (2) more candid and more challenging discussions took place on talent and not only focused more crisply on strengths and development needs but also more effectively addressed when it was time to remove individuals from positions in which they are not performing and not developing; (3) more specific actions were being planned and taken to close replacement gaps and development talent in a more focused way; and (4) senior executives were placing greater overall priority on and taking personal ownership for talent management.

Metrics for Assessing Quantitative Impacts In addition to the qualitative feedback described above, a number of quantitative metrics are currently being used to assess the impact of the talent review process. These include tracking:

- The number of officers/managing directors considered to be strong contributors and evidence that those "not meeting expectations" have specific development plans in place and/or have been replaced;

- The number of key leadership positions for which there is at minimum one "ready now" and one "ready future" replacement;

- Improved year-over-year diversity in the talent pool;

- The retention rate for strong performers and high-potentials; and

- The percentage of recommended developmental job moves (these are identified in the talent reviews) that have actually occurred within the planned timeframe.

As the process has continued to be used, the organization has done a better and better job each year of not only building up feeder pools (that are deeper and more diverse) but also with addressing issues with lower performers.

Next Steps for Talent Review While the process has not changed for the most part, it has been done in a more comprehensive manner each year. This includes doing a more in-depth analysis of who needs development, moves to enhance their experience, and a process that facilitates this movement. In 2006 we introduced comprehensive talent management plans at the major country level, which enabled us to roll-up the country plans into areas of the world plans and finally to an overall enterprise talent plan that is presented to our board of directors.

Our current CEO, upon his appointment, declared talent management and leadership development as one of his top three priorities, and the focus on this process has never been greater. Senior management has expressed a strong desire to spend more time in this arena, and they realize that to successfully develop their talent, they must depend on their peers to provide development job opportunities (special assignments, project teams, new jobs) that cannot be provided unless people are able to move more freely across organizational boundaries.

Additional Positive Impacts One additional result of the analysis that was part of the talent review process was the decision to develop a global executive staffing process designed to ensure that when an opening occurred for an officer or managing director role anywhere in the world, potential candidates could be identified on a global rather than a local basis. Prior to 2003, there had been no formal process for identifying talent globally, but rather the organization with the opening would identify candidates based on their own knowledge of qualifications which, more often than not, led to a local candidate being selected. With the new global staffing process, the organization with the opening can come to the talent management organization for a list of candidates who have been identified via the talent reviews described above. As a result of this new process, *there has been more cross-organizational movement that has resulted in better selections and also more development opportunities for those moving to these assignments.*

A second additional impact driven by the results of a more robust global talent review process was the decision to design a program to build up the depth and diversity of the replacement pools for several officer/MD roles and to expedite the development of the highest potentials for these roles. The global Leadership at McDonald's Program (LAMP) was designed and is described below as the third major initiative to enhance McDonald's Global Workforce Management System.

Overall, the executive talent review process introduced in 2003 has not only stepped up the focus on talent management at the leadership level, but has made it more of an ongoing process, versus the episodic process that it had been previously. Our leaders all consider talent management as a high, if not their highest, priority. It's less about a binder being constructed once a year and then put aside for another year and more about working the talent issue on an ongoing basis. It is also clear that by starting the process at the "top of the house" and having it accepted as useful and necessary, the process has been more easily implemented down through the other management layers across the organization and regions.

Initiative 3: Design and Implementation of the LAMP Program

Specific Design Considerations Based on what had been learned in global talent reviews and in earlier training programs directed at developing high-potentials within McDonald's, several particular areas of competency/skill gaps had been identified and were specifically targeted in the design of LAMP content. These included: (1) expanding participants' mindset from local to regional to global; (2) enhancing participants' ability to maximize business performance through strengthening financial acumen; and (3) enhancing participants' innovative, "out of the box" thinking. From an organizational perspective the goals of the program included: (1) building deeper bench strength for key leadership positions; (2) shortening the ramp-up time required for newly promoted officers and obtaining quicker business results; (3) becoming more effective at developing and retaining top talent; and (4) continuing to improve the diversity profile at the officer level.

The Leadership at McDonald's Program (LAMP) was designed to be an integrated approach to developing high-potential talent. Using leadership development as a process to drive results, shape culture, and build leadership depth, the program accelerates the development of future leaders. With a focus on strengthening and building the capabilities of McDonald's future leaders, the program leverages leadership development to improve performance and drive business results by:

- Increasing the ability of participants to improve business results in their current roles as well as prepare them for achieving success at the next level;

- Leveraging participants' on-the-job accountabilities as opportunities to learn and develop;

- Helping participants gain the insight needed to further develop individual leadership capabilities; and

- Providing opportunities to build strong peer networks internally and externally by having them work closely with McDonald's high-potential peers throughout the program and with talented management peers from other companies/industries as part of the Thunderbird Program.

Participation The program was piloted in 2003–2004 with an initial group of twenty high-potential directors who were nominated by their regional, divisional, or functional leadership teams. Selection criteria included:

- Individuals considered "ready now" or "ready future" for positions at the vice-president level or higher based on results from the McDonald's annual talent review process;

- Succession plan gaps (priority for participation given to functions with a shortage of successors or other business priorities, such as improving the diversity profile at the officer level); and

- Participant and boss willingness to fully commit and participate throughout the nine-month-long program.

Group Sessions LAMP was designed to help participants drive results in two ways: vertically (as leaders of their respective departments) and horizontally (as leadership team members). The first LAMP program had five key program components. These included: (1) executive assessment and program orientation; (2) individual development planning and executive dialogues; (3) leadership modules focused on leadership of self, team, and organization with experiential exercises to reinforce the learning; (4) a two-week executive education program with a focus on global business and culture; and (5) business improvement recommendations presented to the chairman's and presidents' councils. These original program components are described in greater detail in Table 9.4. All of the sessions were held at the company's headquarters in Oak Brook, Illinois, with the exception of the two-week executive education component that was held at a university campus.

Individual Learning Opportunities Based on the assessment results, participants consulted with individual coaches to develop a "breakthrough business goal"—one that could truly drive business results in their areas of responsibility. Critical to this process was the linkage of personal developmental objectives to higher levels of business results. The assessment process and feedback to participants helped identify the competencies needed to enhance their contributions to the business. The development needs were then linked to the individual's breakthrough goal. To support and encourage individual learning, the following was made available to participants: (1) individual coaching and development support—each participant was assigned a coach to discuss progress against objectives and receive objective feedback and developmental coaching throughout the program; and (2) LAMP Online!—a web-based tool that

TABLE 9.4. **Leadership at McDonald's Program (LAMP)**

Program Session	Session Description	Length
Program Orientation and Executive Assessment	McDonald's contracted with a leading assessment firm to deliver the assessment process over a three-and-one-half-day period. The assessment process included the following: (1) inventories of thinking skills, personality, work style, and interests; (2) 360-degree feedback; (3) realistic work and business simulations, with immediate feedback provided after the role play or simulation; and (4) background interviews. In addition to the assessment process, participants received detailed information on the LAMP leadership framework, program goals, and key deliverables. They also had the opportunity to dialogue with senior executives. Upon completion of the assessment process, verbal feedback was provided to the participants by their assessors/coaches. A detailed written summary was provided approximately three weeks later.	4 days
Individual Development Planning and Executive Dialogue	During this session, participants received the written summaries from the assessment process. Utilizing these results, participants worked one-on-one with their bosses and coaches to create a development plan focused on driving results in their areas of the business. Utilizing a custom development plan template, participants identified the experiences, coaching, and training required to achieve their goals. In addition, two executive dialogues during this session provided an opportunity to learn more about the business and leadership through direct interaction with senior McDonald's leaders.	2 days
Executive Dialogue and External Thought Leader	LAMP participants had another opportunity to dialogue with senior leaders during this session. A large portion of time during this session was devoted to building knowledge and skills around the critical components of high-performing teams. A number of experiential exercises were utilized to enable the participants to apply and practice their learnings as they began to form their sub-teams responsible for developing and delivering a "business improvement recommendation" to the executive councils.	2.5 days

Executive Education Program	The university consortia program brings together select groups of non-competing, globally focused companies. Each consortium program is two weeks in length and custom developed in consultation with representatives from each member firm. The university offers participants the opportunity to gain a broad understanding of global strategic issues and to strengthen their general management skills. Learning is reinforced through discussions, case studies, exercises, and simulations.	2 weeks
Business Improvement Recommendations	This session focused primarily on a large team review and feedback session for each of the four sub-team's business improvement recommendations. Significant time was devoted to letting the sub-teams continue to develop their recommendations, with feedback, support, and coaching from an external expert in executive communications. An executive dialogue was also incorporated into this session.	2 days
Presenting Team Recommendations and Program Wrap-Up	At the conclusion of LAMP (February 2004), participants presented their business improvement recommendations to the executive leadership councils, comprised of approximately twelve senior-most executives of McDonald's. Teams made presentations to the council members and discussed the overall impact of the program on their personal development and on their individual business results. Support from coaches, dry runs of the presentations, and group dialogue and feedback around each team's presentation helped participants prepare for the presentations.	2.5 days

supports individual learning, facilitates dialogues about the business, and tracks the progress being made against the LAMP goals and key deliverables.

Commitment and Expectations LAMP required a strong commitment from participants and their direct supervisors in terms of time and behaviors. It was clearly communicated to participants and their bosses that participants would be expected to spend approximately 25 percent of their time on LAMP-related activities (attending LAMP group training session, working with their action learning teams, working on their personal development plans, etc.). Recommendations for managing the time commitment included using LAMP as an opportunity to develop the direct reports of the participants—by giving direct reports the opportunity to assume some of their bosses' responsibilities while participating in LAMP.

LAMP Program Evaluation and Impact: Qualitative Feedback and Geographic Program Expansion A survey (shown in Table 9.5) was conducted mid-way through the LAMP pilot program and also at the end of the pilot. It was given to both the participants and their immediate supervisors. It was evident from this survey that the primary goals of the program were met. Both groups surveyed gave the program high ratings and, importantly, reported seeing evidence of significant personal development. The most highly evaluated elements of LAMP included:

TABLE 9.5. LAMP Program Evaluation Survey

Survey Features	Approach and/or Results
Methodology	Online (95 percent response rate)
Evaluation of Program	*Effectiveness of Eleven Key Program Components*
Components	Executive Dialogue Sessions
	LAMP Online!
	Books
	Learning Journal
	Team Building Modules
	Immersive Development Activities
	Classroom Experiential Activities
	Individual Development Plan
	Breakthrough Business Goal
	Overall LAMP Assessment
	LAMP Support Team
	Rating Scale Used
	5-point scale ranging from "not effective to "highly effective"
	Narrative comments solicited as well for each program component
Evaluation of Overall Program	*Questions*
Effectiveness	To what extent has LAMP better prepared you for a significant role at McDonald's?
	The LAMP program has been worth the time and effort required for my development.
	I would recommend LAMP to others in my position.
	Rating Scale Used
	5-point scale ranging from "strongly disagree" to "strongly agree"

■ The opportunity to interact with senior managers during the executive dialogues;

■ The participants' development processes being integrated with the current job and taking place over an extended time period (nine to twelve months), which significantly improved the probability that development would take place; and

■ The experience of going to the university program, where they were exposed to different thinking and best practices from outside of McDonald's via the participation in the program of leaders from several other global companies.

An area identified for improvement was "boss involvement," specifically the need to get the participants' immediate supervisors more directly involved in the process and more directly involved in assisting with their development. This feedback led to enhancements for the subsequent LAMP programs offered—with the level of boss involvement being significantly increased.

Since the successful pilot, the LAMP program has expanded into three parallel programs in order to increase the number of participants needed to meet feeder pool demands more quickly and efficiently. In addition to the LAMP program, which now develops U.S., Latin American, and Canadian high-potentials, European and Asia-Pacific programs were launched beginning in 2004.

Quantitative Impact In addition to the qualitative feedback described above that led to ongoing program design changes, a number of quantitative metrics are currently being used to assess the impact of the LAMP as well as the programs in Europe and Asia-Pacific. A review of these statistics for the 2004–2008 period reflects the kinds of results being achieved. These include: (1) *promotions:* as of 2008, 37 percent of the 249 graduates had been promoted (these graduates came from thirty-four countries, seen in Figure 9.1); (2) *retention:* as of 2008, only 5 percent of the individuals in this highly select and talented group had left the company for other opportunities (it is a key objective of the program for its participants to know they are highly regarded and that the company will continue to invest in their ongoing development); and (3) *boss feedback* has indicated that development is taking place as a result of this experience and being demonstrated in practical ways on the job. In addition to these results, additional measures have been gathered to further evaluate program impact including: 360-degree feedback follow-up (to be compared to the "baseline" 360 results at program start) and self-assessment of personal change as compared to specific targeted change goals.

Evolution of the LAMP Program Changes to the program itself have been relatively minor since it was introduced in 2004. One element of LAMP that has been enhanced is the process for getting into the program. While the overall steps are the same, we have improved the screening of those nominated to improve the overall quality of participants. This is done by making sure the senior team in each area of the world reviews each nominee and concurs with the judgment of the nominee's own manager that he or she is appropriate for the program. This higher-level review has caused more attention

Global Participation

34 Countries Represented

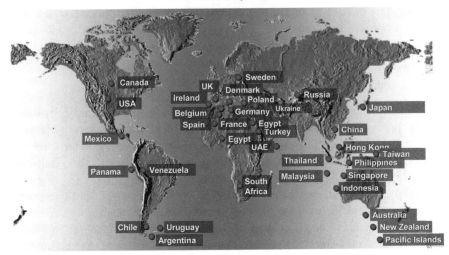

FIGURE 9.1. *LAMP Participants by Country*

on the part of those making nominations to make sure they nominate quality candidates. We have also taken and continue to take further steps to enhance the active involvement of the managers of the participants in the program.

Continued Evidence of Success We have completed four LAMP programs serving participants from the U.S. business, Latin America, Canada, and home office, and now call this program "America's LAMP." We have also completed three sessions of the European leadership development program (ELDP) and three sessions of the ALDP (Asia/Pacific, Middle East, Africa) program. Across these programs there have been a total of 249 graduates, and the number of key leadership positions for which there is now a strong identified back-up has increased from 50 to 80 percent.

One other interesting indication of the success of this program is that it has developed its own strong brand identity and equity within the organization. The value of brand identity is reflected in the differing names for the program in each region, and the brand equity is reflected in the fact that so many employees want to be considered for participation. Overall, the support of the program has increased over time among the senior leaders, who are always asking us when the next program will begin. They also use their talent management plans to identify candidates for LAMP, as this is built into our planning process.

Initiative 4: McDonald's Leadership Development Institute

In 2006, the McDonald's Leadership Institute and the Global Leadership Development Program were introduced as two important additions to McDonald's arsenal to support leadership talent development by attracting and retaining high-performing leaders. The McDonald's Leadership Institute was approved by the company's CEO and funded to provide enhanced development support for all leaders throughout the organization who are positioned at the director level and above (n = 1,200 to 1,500). It was designed to house all of the company's high-potential programs as well as provide development resources to all non-high-potential leaders in the way of an "online development resource center," an in-house leadership curriculum, special learning events, executive coaching, and so forth.

The Institute is a global community that drives McDonald's business by guiding leaders to reach their full potential. Unlike a "brick-and-mortar" approach, the Institute is not a physical place, but a community that provides a culture of learning and development and that can be accessed from any geographic location through our leadership portal and team of Institute guides. Its goal is to be respected as an essential part of McDonald's business and a world-class leadership institute, offering sound guidance as well as challenging, innovative development opportunities and resources to an admired community of leaders. Its offerings include:

- Participation in challenging development experiences at critical career points and transitions;

- Interaction and networking with other leaders globally;

- Individual consulting and tools for development needs assessment, development planning, and key transition activities;

- Exposure to leaders from inside and outside McDonald's; and

- Leading-edge information on McDonald's, the industry, business practices, and leadership.

Initiative 5: The Global Leadership Development Program

The Global Leadership Development Program was developed and introduced in 2006 and focuses exclusively on the company's highest potential officers and managing directors. The initial cohort for this program that was conducted in 2006 included twenty-one individuals from eleven different countries—including North America, Latin America, Europe, Asia/Pacific, and Japan. This program focuses on preparing participants for broader leadership responsibilities. It will also build a strong peer network that will be leveraged going forward as these individuals begin to move into top leadership positions throughout the company. The program was offered again in 2008 and will likely be repeated every two years.

OVERALL SUMMARY

Over the past eight years, McDonald's has taken a number of significant steps to enhance its ability to develop leadership talent and ensure greater management continuity throughout its talent management system. This chapter has described five major initiatives that have been designed and implemented to enhance the system. These included a major re-design of the company's global performance development system, a significant enhancement of the global succession planning and development process, the design and implementation of a customized leadership development program targeted to developing high-potentials at the officer level (LAMP), and, finally, the introduction of the McDonald's Leadership Institute and the Global Leadership Development Program. In addition to the specific positive impacts on internal metrics that have already been described (increased strength and diversity in the leadership team, greater depth/diversity in candidates ready now for advancement, and retention of key performers), as of December 2008, McDonald's had posted sixty-five consecutive months of positive comparable sales—the longest run in McDonald's history—and the stock price hit an all-time high in September 2008. What the overall process described in this chapter has demonstrated is how broad-scale initiatives to develop talent—*when top management owns and drives them and human resources plays the roles of partner/enabler*—can be a powerful lever of culture building and change and make a valuable contribution to business success.

James Intagliata, Ph.D., is president and founder of The NorthStar Group, a management consulting firm that specializes in senior-level executive assessment, individual leadership coaching, and competency-modeling for culture change. Over the past twenty years he has consulted to a diverse group of companies and senior executives and has worked extensively with McDonald's. In addition to his consulting work, he has held faculty positions at the State University of New York at Buffalo and the University of Missouri at Kansas City and taught organizational theory and management at the graduate level. He received his Ph.D. in clinical psychology in 1976 from the State University of New York at Buffalo. His recently published articles include "Leveraging Leadership Competencies to Produce Leadership Brand: Creating Distinctiveness by Focusing on Strategy and Results" (with co-authors Dave Ulrich and Norm Smallwood) in *Human Resources Planning*; "McDonald's Corporation: A Customized Leadership Development Program Targeted to Prepare Future Regional Managers" (with co-author David Small) in *Best Practices in Organization Development and Change* by Louis Carter and Best Practice Institute.

Neal Kulick, Ph.D., has been McDonald's vice president of global talent management since 2001. His responsibilities include executive assessment/development, executive recruitment, and succession management and planning. From 1999 to 2001 Dr. Kulick ran his own organizational consulting practice specializing in the areas of human resource effectiveness and leadership development. Prior to consulting, he served as VP of corporate human resources for Ameritech Corporation in Chicago and as a line operations manager at Michigan Bell Telephone Company in Detroit.

CHAPTER

10

MICROSOFT CORPORATION

SHANNON WALLIS, BRIAN O. UNDERHILL, AND CARTER McNAMARA

Leaders Building Leaders—transforming Microsoft's high-potential development experience that integrates assessment, coaching, mentoring, learning circles, action learning, and business conferences.

- Team Structure and Thought Leaders
- Transition Management Activities
- Coaching as a Primary Development Component for HiPo Development in SMSG
- Learning Circles as a Primary Development Component for HiPo Development in SMSG
  - Circles Process Mirrors How Today's Leaders Work and Learn
  - Unique Principles of Learning Behind Learning Circles
  - Learning Circles Compared to Traditional Forms of Training
  - Life of a Circle
  - Coaching Goals
  - Actions Between Meetings
  - Circle Termination and Renewal
  - How Circles Are Organized
  - Results and Benefits for Circle Members
- Conclusion

INTRODUCTION

The opportunity for ongoing learning and development is a commitment Microsoft makes to all employees. Microsoft invests more than $375 million annually in formal education programs directed at the employee, manager, and leader, offered by the Corporate Learning and Development groups and other profession-specific learning groups throughout the company.

In addition to the development offered to all employees, Microsoft invests in a smaller group of employees who have the potential for, and strong interest in, taking on more senior, critical roles as individual contributors or managers. These individuals are identified and considered for more focused career development, which may include participation in one of several professional development experiences known as high-potential development programs.

In identifying employees as high-potential, it is important to appreciate that natural "gifts" are not sufficient. For an employee, reaching his or her full potential depends on a combination of natural gifts, what he or she does with that talent (hard work, perseverance, courage, etc.), the experiences he or she is given, the support of others along the way, and the context/culture within which he or she operates (McCall & Hollenbeck, 2002; McCall, Lombardo, & Morrison, 1998).

At Microsoft, high-potential development goes beyond traditional management or leadership development. Instead, it focuses on *accelerating* the development of these individuals to advance to the next career stage. The remainder of this chapter will present Microsoft's case for making a significant shift in high-potential development within the Sales Marketing and Services Group (SMSG).

WHAT LED MICROSOFT SMSG TO MAKE THE CHANGE

The Sales Marketing and Services Group is more than 45,000 employees responsible for Microsoft sales, marketing, and service initiatives; customer and partner programs; and product support and consulting services worldwide. Its field sales and marketing professionals delivered $53B in billed revenue in fiscal year 2008 and $34.8B in profit. Additionally, the group is responsible for corporate operations and IT functions that support the work of Microsoft's approximately 91,000 employees around the world.

Recent key accomplishments of the group include:

- Significant increases in customer satisfaction ratings;

- Growing the Windows Client, Server and Tools, Information Worker, Mobility, and Microsoft Business Solutions businesses and winning new customers in a very competitive environment; and

- Building a world-class field infrastructure and streamlining a rhythm-of-the-business, allowing the field to execute in harmony with the business groups on growth planning and the way in which we measure the health of the business.

The organization operates within thirteen geographic "areas" and has more than ten vertical segments, sectors, and functions. In 2004, SMSG had high-potential programs operating in nearly all of them. The individual programs were not aligned to Microsoft's Leadership Career Model and were not easily scalable. Furthermore, consistent criteria for identifying high-potentials did not exist, and areas and segments independently determined the number of "high-potentials" that they wanted to develop. This impacted the larger talent management system and made movement among programs difficult when employees changed areas, segments, sectors, or functions. Given the various objectives of the programs, the experience of high-potentials was inconsistent across SMSG.

To build the pipeline of future leaders, Microsoft SMSG decided to align high-potential development within SMSG to create a consistent experience.

EXPO LEADERS BUILDING LEADERS—THE NEW HIGH-POTENTIAL DEVELOPMENT EXPERIENCE

SMSG began with questions. What is a high-potential? How is high-potential talent identified? How many HiPos are needed to meet future demand? Finally, how is the development of high-potentials accelerated? The answers to these questions led to a new program, ExPo Leaders Building Leaders. ExPo, which stands for "exceptional potential," is a long-term leadership development experience in SMSG for high-potentials. Leaders Building Leaders is a leadership development philosophy that sets up a cascading approach to the investment of time and resources by current leaders into emerging leaders at the next career stage level. Microsoft SMSG would apply this leadership development philosophy across less than 4 percent of the population or more than 1,600 high-potentials in 107 countries. To begin, they needed to identify the high-potentials.

High-Potential Identification

SMSG heavily leveraged the Corporate Leadership Council's 2005 empirical study, "Realizing the Full Potential of Rising Talent." A high-potential at Microsoft is defined as someone with the ability, commitment, and aspiration to advance to and succeed in more senior, critical roles (see Figure 10.1).

These roles include individual contributor, manager, technical and executive leadership. A high-potential differs from a high performer in that a high performer may demonstrate exceptional ability, but may not demonstrate commitment and/or aspiration to advance to more senior roles or to do so in an accelerated timeframe. High-potentials are a subset of high performers and are promotable into the next potential band. In other words, not all strong performers are high-potentials. HiPos must have the ability (skills and competencies), commitment, and aspiration to grow and succeed and be a top performer as a people leader in an accelerated timeframe relative to high performers. The combination of the three is required, and only those employees determined to be highest on all three are selected. As they take on risky jobs, this might

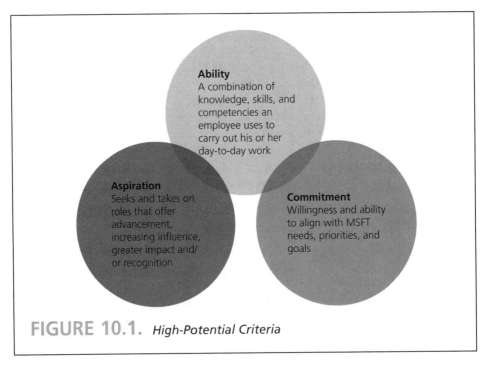

FIGURE 10.1. *High-Potential Criteria*

Source: Adapted from Corporate Leadership Council High-Potential Management Survey, 2005.

slow momentarily as they master new skills, which needs to be accounted for. It is expected that they will catch up and continue on a fast trajectory.

ExPo Tiers

Once the high-potential talent is identified, SMSG sorts them by career stages. Whereas in the former programs, high-potentials were grouped regardless of career stage and received similar development opportunities, ExPo provides differentiated development. ExPo Tiers are the organizing function for offering the development experiences based on the needs of specific career stages. High-potentials are segmented into a three-tier system, as seen in Figure 10.2: junior individual contributors in Tier 3, senior individual contributors and managers in Tier 2, and managers of managers, functional leaders, and business leaders in Tier 1. Each tier has a different focus area based on the unique needs of the particular career stage.

Tier 1's development focus is building leadership capability in priority areas and building a globally diverse network. Tier 2 focuses on building an understanding of the requirements of leadership at Microsoft and broadening the network across time zones. Tier 3 builds commitment and aspiration to leadership through greater self-awareness and understanding of Microsoft SMSG and non-SMSG businesses.

Five Drivers of Accelerated Development for High-Potentials

Once sorted into the appropriate tiers, the high-potentials' development experience begins. Underlying all development are five drivers of accelerated development for high-potentials at Microsoft. The Five Drivers are development activities that *significantly* impact the development of high-potential leaders and are derived from two

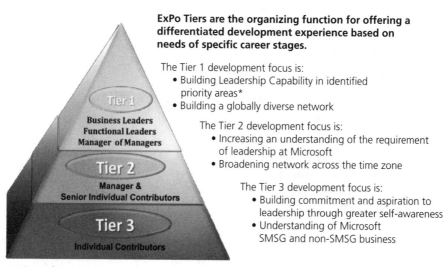

ExPo Tiers are the organizing function for offering a differentiated development experience based on needs of specific career stages.

The Tier 1 development focus is:
- Building Leadership Capability in identified priority areas*
- Building a globally diverse network

The Tier 2 development focus is:
- Increasing an understanding of the requirement of leadership at Microsoft
- Broadening network across the time zone

The Tier 3 development focus is:
- Building commitment and aspiration to leadership through greater self-awareness
- Understanding of Microsoft SMSG and non-SMSG business

Tier 1
Business Leaders
Functional Leaders
Manager of Managers

Tier 2
Manager &
Senior Individual Contributors

Tier 3
Individual Contributors

* Microsoft Leadership Model

FIGURE 10.2. *Key ExPo Tiers*

primary sources, the Corporate Leadership Council (2005) and Morgan McCall (McCall & Hollenbeck, 2002; McCall, Lombardo, & Morrison, 1998).

Research indicates that five key areas, if executed effectively, have the most significant impact on high-potential development (Corporate Leadership Council, 2005):

■ Senior leadership commitment to developing leaders;

■ Manager capability and engagement in the development high-potentials;

■ A professional network that allows for contacts throughout the business;

■ A high-quality, customized stretch development plan with clear objectives; and

■ On-the-job experiences.

These five areas were used as design principles in the design of ExPo. We will consider each one separately.

Senior Leadership Commitment to Developing Leaders Executive ownership in high-potential development is critical to the success of any program. Executives and senior leaders play a key role in modeling the behavior expected of all leaders in developing their high-potentials. They are also responsible for holding managers accountable for developing their high-potentials. For high-potentials to accelerate their development, they must have regular interaction with current leaders in order to build their own capability. Observing executives and senior leaders in action and learning from their stories of successes and failures are a foundational aspect of ExPo.

Executives and senior leaders can demonstrate ownership and engagement by committing to and spending time in activities such as

■ Being accountable for the success of leadership programs, development of their direct reports, and development of their own leadership capabilities;

■ Conducting ongoing reviews of high-potential talent and facilitating cross-company development moves;

■ Acting as mentors and coaches;

■ Speaking at high-potential conferences, teaching in high-potential program sessions, and sponsoring action learning projects; and

■ Spending time with high-potentials in the course of their business travels.

Manager Capability and Engagement in the Development of High-Potentials The research indicates that the most valuable development for any employee is on-the-job learning and key to that learning is the active engagement of the employee's manager (Corporate Leadership Council, 2005).

Partnering with the manager to create access to leadership development opportunities in the current role enables faster development of the high-potential. Managers must be provided with training and coaching on how to develop their high-potentials. In addition to coaching, managers should be made aware of the kinds of experiences that would allow the high-potentials to accelerate their development. When opportunities for those experiences arise, the manager should think first about providing those to their high-potentials.

In addition to being rewarded for business results, managers need to be held accountable through the performance management system for developing their high-potentials. An example would be the inclusion of a measurable objective for developing their high-potentials in their annual performance objectives. It is also necessary to define the accountabilities of the high-potential, the business group, and the organization, as each plays a role in development.

A Professional Network That Allows for Contacts Throughout the Business High-potentials thrive when they have a diverse network of people across the organization that they can draw on to gain access to information, solve complex business problems collaboratively, and achieve business goals. More importantly, the network is most powerful when it consists primarily of other high-potentials. High-potentials develop most quickly when they are managed by high-potentials, participate in a team of high-potentials, and manage high-potentials themselves. Consequently, creating opportunities to build a peer and leadership network across the business is a core aspect of ExPo.

A High-Quality, Customized Stretch Development Plan with Clear Objectives Ensuring each high-potential has a customized, robust, stretch development plan that contains the right mix of learning based on individual development needs is another important aspect of development. A clearly defined career aspiration statement is the most important element of this plan. Without it, the development gap cannot be established, and impactful development activities cannot be selected and executed.

On-the-Job Experiences In ExPo, SMSG has shifted the majority of learning from programmatic to on-the-job development and relationship building. On-the-job development is informed by the experiences that high-potentials have that are related to handling future business challenges and usually includes a cross-business group or international perspective. This type of learning can happen in two ways: placing high-potentials into roles that have been identified as containing key learning experiences or mining current roles for all of the stretch learning opportunities available. Either way, it is critical that learning objectives be defined and that the high-potential is supported in the learning. To gain the most value from development on the job, learning-*from*-the job must be facilitated and made explicit.

In many respects the Five Drivers of Accelerated Development may appear to be common sense. But common sense is not always common practice. For example, it is difficult to ensure that every high-potential reports to a high-potential manager, works on a team of high-potentials, and manages high-potentials. Given that high-potentials represent only 4 percent of the employee population, this is virtually impossible. Thus, ExPo educates high-potentials about the Five Drivers of Accelerated Development and asks them to be conscious about activating them in their development. Additionally, ExPo attempts to simulate the drivers within its development activities. They are imbedded through all aspects of the ExPo experience.

Five Development Components

ExPo allows emerging and experienced leaders to learn from each other through five developmental components that are tied to the five drivers. Each component is executed differently at each tier to provide a unique development experience that builds leader capability over the duration of the ExPo experience. This creates consistency and integrated development for emerging leaders as they move vertically through the ExPo tiers.

The five developmental components, highlighted in the pinwheel (Figure 10.3), provide a leading-edge development experience that builds leadership capability over time.

Orientation Orientation provides the programmatic component of ExPo. It is designed to address learning needs that high-potentials have in common, such as understanding the business strategy at Microsoft, increasing business acumen, and understanding what it means to be a leader at Microsoft. Core content relevant for a high-potential leader at the targeted career stage is provided in a classroom setting and is not meant to duplicate development found in other management or leadership development courses.

Sessions are conducted in peer groups, such as Tier 1, Tier 2, and Tier 3, and:

- Introduce high-potentials to the core elements of ExPo;

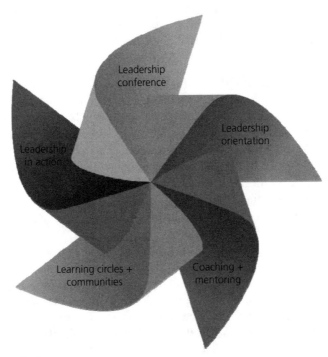

FIGURE 10.3. *ExPo Development Framework*

■ Provide expert instruction—classroom-based education in leadership theory and practice;

■ Include opportunities to network with executives (both internal and external) and peers;

■ Provide a forum for delivering developmental feedback; and

■ Set up executive coaching, mentoring, and "learning circles" (peer coaching groups of five to seven people).

Most importantly, Orientation provides opportunities for leaders who have already demonstrated the targeted competencies (Exhibit 10.1, Microsoft Leadership Competencies) and/or are considered high-potential leaders themselves to teach and share key insights. The program includes and initiates several capability-building activities in order to build individual leadership competencies. Other skill-building activities that are completed in and around orientation include:
Assessment—one of three assessments is used.

■ A Microsoft sponsored 360-degree assessment tool such as the MS Leader 360 instrument created internally and used to assess the eleven Microsoft leadership competencies; or

■ Kouzes and Posner's Leadership Practices Inventory (LPI) 360 instrument, which assesses the leadership behaviors associated with The Five Practices of Exemplary Leaders; or

■ Assessment of psychological preferences in how people perceive the world and make decisions via the Myer Briggs Type Indicator (MBTI) psychometric questionnaire; and

■ Manager/member contracting sessions (a contract is signed to support participation in ExPo).

EXHIBIT 10.1. Microsoft Leadership Competencies (Subset)

Microsoft Leadership Competencies
Executive Maturity
OneMicrosoft
Impact and Influence
Deep Insight
Create Business Value
Customer Commitment and Foresight

A successful development process is a strong partnership between the high-potentials, their managers, skip-level managers, and HR. The partnership is vital for ensuring a concentrated "high touch" and personalized learning experience for each high-potential member. And it is important to highlight that the high-potential development process is *self-managed by the high-potential member* with approval, collaboration, and encouragement from his or her manager, skip-level manager, HR, and POC team. Although the high-potential development process is managed by the high-potential member, without the above-mentioned people contributing time, thought, and effort, the member may still progress, but not at the accelerated rate. The significant expectations on high-potentials and the people involved in ensuring their success rely on each high-potential's level of committed engagement and the people who are supporting their activities.

The manager/member contract is designed to assist high-potentials and their managers in clarifying the purpose, expectations, roles, responsibilities, and commitments of the high-potential development process between these two parties. To ensure clear understanding of the above-mentioned subjects, a contracting guide and session were created to facilitate a robust conversation between the high-potential, his or her manager, and human resources, which concludes with signed contracts ensuring commitment to the high-potential development process.

The signed contracts between the high-potential and the manager pledge the responsibility of personal and professional development with shared partnership necessary to cultivate the high-potential's skills and abilities.

Leadership Conferences Leadership conferences are business conferences, round-table discussions, and live meetings that bring executives (both internal and external) and high-potentials together for mutual benefit and learning. Area Leadership Teams—thirteen geographic leadership teams comprised of the area VP and his or her direct reports who set the direction for and manage the business—commit to a two-day leadership conference that connects the senior leaders of the area with local high-potentials. These conferences create a forum for dialogue and learning around the strategic business issues and challenges of leadership at Microsoft.

Conferences are conducted across tiers, usually Tiers 1 and 2, with occasional participation from Tier 3. They are designed to facilitate reflection, build critical relationships from one level to the next, and provide an additional forum for sharing learning *from* the job that is discussed throughout the year in other components (particularly "leadership in action" and "learning circles"). Smaller leadership conferences, such as leader roundtables, are also held within business units or areas as appropriate and provide opportunities for substantial networking.

Most importantly, leadership conferences are designed and led by the area leaders in cooperation with local leadership and organization development consultants. Each area is able to choose a conference design that is appropriate to its cultural needs and business challenges, so there are differences in design and format.

Conferences enable high-potentials to:

- Work collaboratively with peers and leadership teams on strategic business challenges;

- Gain insight into the requirements of being a broad business leader and the transition required from functional expertise;

- Develop relationships and raise their profile as high-potentials with members of their leadership team; and

- Build and extend their networks.

Leadership in Action Research demonstrates that emerging leaders develop new leadership capability when their learning is linked to real business impact. Development that maximizes this type of learning is called "action learning." It develops leadership qualities, analytical skills, and strategic thinking by way of experience-based exercises. By including the Leaders Building Leaders dimension so that all participants—Tiers 1, 2, and 3—are engaged in one integrated experience, Microsoft SMSG created Leadership in Action (LIA), which benefits SMSG by:

- Building and promoting a common leadership culture as exemplified by the leadership competencies;

- Developing leaders for the future, while establishing a strategic link between senior and rising leaders; and

- Identifying recommendations and action plans to address top business challenges.

The LIA practicum provides the opportunity for small groups of high-potentials to work on finding new solutions to real and tough business challenges. At the same time they are encouraged to reflect on their thinking and action to maximize their development as leaders. At the LIA practicum, tough business challenges are presented to each small group by a selected team leader, a Tier 1 member. Projects are real business challenges from Tier 1 team leaders and are rigorously selected as appropriate action learning projects. Each team leader works with his or her group throughout the event on a solution that he or she is expected to use in solving the challenge during the next six months.

While LIA is centered on action-learning projects, the program is integrated to leverage other capability-building activities such as assessment, executive coaching, and career-focused coaching, which benefit high-potentials by:

- Providing the opportunity to practice thinking systemically;

- Developing their mastery of listening and coaching through use of action learning methodology;

- Building deep relationships with peers across Microsoft and extending their senior networks; and

- Increasing their strategic perspectives on Microsoft.

In addition, Tier 1 team leaders gain fresh perspectives on their business challenges from the high-potential population.

Learning Circles Building leadership networks and collaborative working relationships are two of the most significant leadership needs at Microsoft SMSG. Learning circles are small peer-based learning groups designed to connect diverse groups of high-potentials, both functionally and geographically, to mutually support each other in developing themselves as leaders. Comprised of five to seven high-potentials who meet either face-to-face or virtually, learning circles integrate the learning from current role experiences with development priorities to provide a more impactful learning experience.

Members form close, confidential networks in which they feel free to share support, feedback, and materials to help each other address current priorities and to progress in their careers. Utilizing coaching and feedback as the primary developmental tools, high-potentials surface their learning and identify realistic actions to move their development forward between meetings. In addition, the learning circles enable them to reflect on the actions that they took, which in turn cultivates skills in learning how to learn from their own experiences.

Learning circles enable high-potentials to:

- Drive personal development as a future leader by:
    - Enhancing their proficiency at cross-business collaboration;
    - Increasing their learning agility from their current roles;
    - Customizing action and learning plans;
    - Linking formal learning with on-the-job experiences; and
    - Deepening their insight and understanding of the Microsoft business.
- Create greater business impact by:
    - Creating more effective and diverse organizational networks across Microsoft's emerging leadership talent pools;
    - Sharing support and accountability for results;
    - Increasing performance levels against current performance objectives; and
    - Delivering innovation and execution against key strategic business issues.

Coaching and Mentoring In addition to learning circles, Microsoft offers one-to-one partnerships through coaching and mentoring that involve a thought-provoking process that inspires the individual to maximize his or her personal and professional potential. Through individualized follow-up, coaching, and mentoring, they integrate learning from a variety of sources such as assessment feedback, current role experiences, and development priorities to provide a more impactful learning experience.

Coaching and mentoring enable high-potentials to:

■ Build skills and close development gaps;

■ Develop "big picture" understanding of Microsoft and our industry through cross-boundary and cross-role exposure; and

■ Become more accountable for their own development since the coaching and mentoring process is a self-directed one.

Microsoft has a well-developed mentoring program that automatically matches high-potential mentors with high-potential mentees. The coaching process will be described in greater detail later in the chapter.

THE PROCESS OF REDESIGNING THE HIGH-POTENTIAL DEVELOPMENT EXPERIENCE

Creating ExPo was a classic change management project with three phases.

Key Steps and Timeline

First, Microsoft analyzed the current state—understanding what was working and not working, studying the best practices that existed, and reviewing the research related to high-potential development. Next, the Microsoft team envisioned the future state—considering both internal and external best practices, adopting or adapting them, and creating some new ones. Finally, they implemented the changes. Although this initially began in 2004 with a desire to bring more consistency to the high-potential development experience, the majority of the work took place between August 2006 and August 2007 and was mostly completed by a small team of internal leadership development consultants. It is important to highlight this, as it demonstrates that a change of this magnitude can be completed internally when the right resources are applied. The current state analysis and initial research related to the drivers of development were completed between mid-August and mid-October 2006. A high-level vision was then crafted, refined, and socialized between mid-October and mid-December 2006. Once approved, more research was conducted on best practices in leadership development between January and March 2007 and implementation guides were crafted along the way. The detailed design was communicated in April 2007, and program content was built through the summer in preparation for the launch in October 2007.

Research Activities

To develop the ExPo program, Microsoft began by asking the question, "How is the development of a high-potential accelerated?" The team was guided to the Corporate Leadership Council's 2005 empirical study, "Realizing the Full Potential of Rising Talent" (Volume 1), which provided a strong basis for the rationale and drivers underlying ExPo. After analyzing that research and drawing conclusions appropriate for Microsoft's environment, the team looked at additional research by McCall and Hollenbeck (2002) and McCall, Lombardo, and Morrison (1998).

Once the five drivers were established, the team researched the ways to embed them in the development activities. An extensive literature search for best practices in leadership development was conducted. The team mapped these development activities to the drivers and landed on the five primary development components. With this, the team was able to move from a high-level vision to a more detailed vision. Several months were dedicated to crystallizing the detailed vision and writing implementation guides that would enable HR professionals to comprehensively understand the program so that they could effectively communicate it to business leaders in the field.

Team Structure and Thought Leaders

Core to design and implementing ExPo was a diverse group of professionals who enabled the change to take place. The team structure evolved over time. Initially in 2004, it began with a group of eight individuals who worked virtually and volunteered their time to the initiative. (By August 2006, three full-time positions were created, which expanded to four by August 2007.) Known internally as the POC Hippies (People and Organization Capability High-Potential Team—with High-Potential eventually shortened to "HP," which later evolved to "Hippies"), they isolated the five drivers and created the high-level and detailed drafts of the vision. By February 2007, it was clear that, for the change to be implemented globally, more stakeholders would need to be engaged around the world. The team was expanded to approximately twenty members, who represented different segments, sectors, functions, and geographies. As more responsibilities were added, it was clear that the structure to support ExPo also needed to evolve. Today, three teams exist:

POC Hippies: A group of nearly twenty organization development, leadership development, and business professionals who share a passion for high-potential development; contribute to the overall design and development of the ExPo experience; and work closely with the ExPo core design team. They meet monthly via two international conference calls and twice annually face-to-face in April (Microsoft Headquarters) and August (international location).

ExPo Execution Excellence Team: A group of nine program managers who ensure the execution of ExPo in the thirteen areas worldwide. They meet once monthly at a minimum via conference call and once annually face-to-face in June (location to rotate). They meet virtually and frequently during the pre-launch period (August through September).

ExPo Core Design Team: A group of five full-time leadership development consultants responsible for the overall HiPo strategy and experience for Microsoft SMSG and act as the primary thought leaders for the ExPo components. They meet once per year face-to-face in early February and virtually as needed ongoing.

These three teams were the primary owners of the change management plan and transition management activities.

Transition Management Activities

A change of this magnitude requires leadership commitment, stakeholder involvement, and appropriate phasing. It begins with leadership. Kevin Turner, COO of Microsoft, was unwavering in his desire for one consistent program worldwide. When areas and segments suggested that they were unique and somehow exempt from making the change, Turner did not yield. Instead, he continually asked for one program and one name, ExPo, which was symbolic of the change. In addition, Sue Bevington, CVP HR for Microsoft SMSG, and Jeff McHenry, senior POC director at that time, were equally committed to a common approach to high-potential identification and development, globally.

Critical to making the change was the expanded Hippies team, which met for the first time in April 2007 in Tokyo, Japan, to evaluate the viability of the detailed vision and implementation plan and to provide feedback on how to improve both. Energized by the possibility of change, the team contributed many hours to taking the thinking to all potential HR and business leader populations in order to increase their engagement and the probability of implementation success. In addition, sorting the responsibilities of the team and understanding that three primary team roles were required enabled the team to divide and conquer as the program expanded.

Finally, implementation was phased in over a two-year period. Only four of the five development components were introduced in October 2007. Leadership in Action was held until October 2008 to allow more time for research and testing prior to launch. Likewise, new content is introduced annually as each tier progresses through each year of the program.

Although the program is relatively new, the feedback from the business has been substantial and positive. ExPo has been highlighted as an example of what Kevin Turner calls "business excellence," meaning "innovation + operational excellence." The team responsible for the design and implementation has received internal recognition and awards, and the program has been recognized as a best practice by professional associations.

In order to deliver ExPo on the global scale required, partnership with external organizations was critical. As the design and implementation plans were finalized, SMSG began a search for partners who could lend additional subject-matter expertise to a couple of key components, executive coaching and learning circles. More detailed descriptions of the work with these partners, CoachSource and Authenticity Consulting, are provided next.

COACHING AS A PRIMARY DEVELOPMENT COMPONENT FOR HIPO DEVELOPMENT IN SMSG

Executive coaching is offered to Tier 1 ExPo participants (managers of managers, functional leaders, and business leaders) in the first year of their ExPo experience. Microsoft initially met with CoachSource as the potential executive coaching partner because of numerous references to the firm noted in their study of best practices.

They selected CoachSource for the availability and quality of their global coaching pool, use of technology to support the coaching process, and the flexibility they demonstrated in meeting Microsoft's needs. In the first year, approximately 214 of 250 leaders took advantage of the executive coaching program via CoachSource.

Why executive coaching? Microsoft believes that executive coaching provides the most effective ongoing behavioral development for leaders. Participants receive regular, individualized follow-up to help drive behavioral change over time. A coach offers a third-party, objective support for the leader's improvement efforts.

The definition of executive coaching adopted is the "one-to-one development of an organizational leader" (Underhill, McAnally, & Koriath, 2007). While there are different approaches to coaching, ExPo's focus was around the development of leaders in the organizational context. Coaching is focused on changing leadership behavior in the workplace.

Coaching Process The coaching design allows for approximately two sessions per month, mostly via telephone (or all via telephone if participant and coach are not co-located). The coaching timeline is provided in Table 10.1. Coaching sessions are focused on feedback from the Microsoft 360-degree assessment, associated Microsoft leadership competencies, other relevant data points, and the Coaching Action Plan (CAP) crafted from the results of this assessment. (A sample is provided in Exhibit 10.8.)

This coaching process requires clearly defined goals to be created, which are outlined in the Coaching Action Plan. After the plan is created, it is shared with the program managers, allowing an additional audit that *tangible goals* are the central thrust to the coaching work. Goals have to be clearly identifiable and behavioral in nature to allow for the use of metrics to measure improvement at the conclusion of the assignment (see "Measuring Results").

Following the "feed-forward" process (coined by Marshall Goldsmith), participants are encouraged to share their development objectives with their key stakeholders. Thus these stakeholders become involved in the participant's growth by being made aware of the development objectives and are able to offer future-focused suggestions related to these areas for development. Stakeholders are then surveyed at the conclusion to measure progress over time.

Coaching is ten hours spread over a maximum six-month period. After this time, unused coaching hours are lost. This is done purposefully to encourage participants to stay active with their coaches and keep momentum alive. Leaders at Microsoft are often pulled toward multiple priorities simultaneously. Enforcing a coaching deadline, as well as cancellation and no-show policies, actually helps drive greater (and more efficient) use of the service.

All coaching activity is tracked via an online web-based database. Coaches log dates of sessions, time elapsed, and any general notes to the database. Program administrators can then easily monitor progress of the pool and provide monthly reporting.

Participant/Coach Matching While matching is accomplished through a "full choice" process, it is also designed to operate quite efficiently. Leaders need the element of choice, which research shows increases participant satisfaction and reduces the possibility

TABLE 10.1. **Coaching Timeline**

Coaching Month	Suggested Coaching Hours, Format, and Topics	Coaching/Meeting Hours
1	**Session 1 (telephone):** Debrief 360° assessment, goal setting, and action planning	1.5
	Session 2 (in person): Finalize action plan, meet with manager to gain support for action plan	0.5
2	**Session 3 (telephone):** Coaching on goals and action plans	1.0
	Session 4 (telephone): Coaching on goals and action plans	1.0
3	**Session 5 (telephone):** Coaching on goals and action plans	1.5
	Session 6 (telephone or in person): Review post-coaching development plan, meet with manager to gain support for post-coaching development	0.5
4	**Session 7 (telephone):** Coaching on goals and action plans	1.0
	Session 8 (telephone): Coaching on goals and action plans	1.0
5	**Session 9 (telephone):** Coaching on goals and action plans	1.0
	Session 10 (telephone): Coaching on goals and action plans	1.0
	Total Coaching Hours	10.0

of mismatches. Prior to program start, all ExPo coaches indicate which of the MS leadership expectations are their "sweet spots" (coaches are allowed to select up to four of the eleven leadership competencies). Simultaneously, the development needs of the ExPo participants are gathered. Each leader is then matched with two potential coaches based on regional location, development needs, and language requirements (in that order). An automated email is sent to the participant with coach biographies attached.

Participants are encouraged to review biographies and telephone interview the first coach of interest. If this seems like a match, the participant commences with that coach. If not, he or she interviews the second coach. (And if that doesn't work, additional choices are provided, along with a website of all coach bios authorized for ExPo.)

The selection deadline date is enforced, and participants are reminded that coach availability fills up (which it often does). This seems to encourage leaders to make their selections quickly. Nearly all the matching for 214 leaders was complete within about six weeks.

Measuring Results Two key metrics are employed during the ExPo coaching engagement. First, a coach satisfaction survey measures participant satisfaction with their coach. Secondly—and much more importantly—a "mini-survey" measures impact. This coach satisfaction survey is automatically run after four and a half hours of coaching is logged (see Figure 10.4).

The five questions asked are:

"How satisfied are you with your coach in the following areas:

Q1: Identifies clear priorities for my growth and development

Q2: Genuinely listens to me

Q3: Provides specific, actionable suggestions/advice

Q4: Communicates in a direct and concise manner

Q5: Overall satisfaction with your coaching experience"

This graph shows high satisfaction ratings among the five questions surveyed (N = 39). These data are shared with the individual coaches and adjustments/reassignments are made for any poor feedback.

The mini survey measures improvement over time in the eyes of key stakeholders working with the executive. This is the best "impact back on the job" metric currently available. Results can be aggregated over a set of participants to show leadership impact over time. The mini uses a 7-point "less effective" (−3) to "more effective" (+3) scale (Figure 10.5).

In the first year of ExPo, 22 percent of raters felt the participants had improved at a +3 level; 59 percent noted improvement at a +2 or +3 level; and an impressive 89 percent of raters observed improvement to some degree with the participants (+1, +2, +3 levels).

FIGURE 10.4. *Coaching Satisfaction Survey Results*

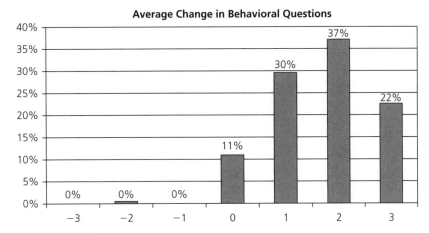

FIGURE 10.5. *Leadership Effectiveness Improvement*

Roles and Responsibilities The participant's boss is an important part of the process. In fact, two of the ten coaching hours are three-way sessions with the participant, his or her manager, and the coach. Managers participate in follow-up metrics to measure improvement over time. Table 10.2 defines the role of the boss (as well as the other key stakeholders).

Roles are clearly delineated for each of the key stakeholders in the coaching process (Table 10.2). Clear responsibilities are defined for not just the participant, coach, and program manager but also for the participant's boss, skip-level boss, and human resources.

Coach Selection and Orientation After a fair amount of research into coach qualifications, the general criteria for ExPo coaches include the following:

- **Business/corporate experience:** Does the coach have specific business or corporate experience and/or background? Has he or she coached executives in organizations of similar size, complexity, industry, etc.?

- **Coach-specific training:** Has the coach had training in a coach-specific process and skill set? How much?

- **Experience in giving feedback on 360-degree or other assessments:** Has the coach had training and/or experience in providing feedback and developing action plans around assessments that will be used?

- **Educational background:** Does the coach have a degree, and in what area?

- **Coach credentials and/or base number of accrued coaching hours:** How long has the coach been coaching? How many accrued coaching hours does the coach have?

TABLE 10.2. **Key Stakeholder Roles for HiPo Coaching Program at Microsoft**

Stakeholder	Role Description
Human Resources	Program approval and general oversight Approval of all communication drafts before they are sent to other stakeholders Approve and sign invoices
Coaching Program Manager (SMSG Program Office)	Decide on coach selection criteria Source interested and qualified coaches Interview and select coaches Manage external coach-client match process Obtain contractual agreements with coaches Train coaches in MS leadership development process and external coaching process Manage and communicate with coaches throughout coaching process Assure surveys (for measurements) are designed, completed, and results reported Assure invoicing and payment to coaches Track themes that surface from clients to coaches and provide updates to HR
Participant's Manager	Meet with coach and client twice during external coaching process: once at the beginning of the engagement, once at the end of the engagement Approve and support client's action plan and post-coaching development plan Provide ongoing support throughout external coaching process (meet monthly with client and include action plan as an agenda item) Look for opportunities to acknowledge and support client Understand confidential nature of coach-client relationship
Participant's Manager's Manager	Hold client's manager responsible to the client's development
Participant ("The Coaching Client")	Review biographies of three coaches and call best-fit coach to make a selection by date indicated Take primary responsibility for the coaching experience, goals, and progress, including all meeting agendas, action plans, and post-coaching development plans

	Schedule/reschedule meetings with coach and manager as appropriate
	Attend and prepare for all coaching sessions
	Request manager's ongoing support throughout coaching process
	Complete co-designed fieldwork between coaching sessions
	Contact program manager if there is any dissatisfaction with the coaching relationship
External Coach	Coach notifies program office when selected by a client and requests they complete an agreement
	Coach client in feedback of 360-degree assessment
	Coach client in qualifying and documenting goals and action plan steps, and in post-coaching development plan
	Support and hold client accountable in movement toward and achievement of goals in progressive sessions
	Co-design appropriate goal-oriented fieldwork for completion between sessions; hold client accountable for completing fieldwork
	Be responsive to client between meetings as needed via telephone or e-mail
	Attend two meetings with client and client's manager
	Hold client information and meetings in the strictest of confidence
	Contact HR or client's manager if client is not attending meetings or is unresponsive to contact to set up meetings (aside from a suspected law being broken, this is the only reason that the coach would contact others regarding the client)
	Collect themes and patterns of issues that Microsoft may need to be aware of (examples: special needs or additional training that may be helpful for group)

- **Willingness to subscribe to International Coach Federation Code of Ethics** (an ethical code in which the coach aspires to conduct him- or herself in a manner that reflects positively on the coaching profession, is respectful of different approaches to coaching, and recognizes that he or she is also bound by applicable laws and regulations): Does the coach subscribe to a code of ethics? If not, would he or she be willing to sign a contract subscribing to the ICF Code of Ethics?

- **Willingness to sign a contract for services:** Is the coach willing to sign a contract or agreement (with all of its organizational specifics) for the coaching?

- **Availability/capacity to take on new clients:** How much space does the coach have in his or her schedule to take on the number of new clients you need to have coached?

- **Specific language requirements:** Is the coach fluent in a specific language needed to coach participants?

- **Location of coach and participant:** Is the coach located in a specific time zone? Although most coaching can be done over the telephone, time-zone proximity will make scheduling easier.

Using the number of ExPo participants and their regions, a forecast is made on how many coaches are needed in each region (based on a 4:1 or 5:1 ratio). In the Americas, a group of Microsoft coaches already met these criteria, and a majority of those were invited to return to ExPo. Outside of the Americas, the worldwide resources of CoachSource were brought to bear to screen and bring this talent on board. Coach-Source screened the coaches according to Microsoft's criteria and brought the international coaches into the pool. Local Microsoft human resources professionals reviewed these biographies and selected coaches for the pool.

Approved coaches then indicated their maximum capacity for ExPo leaders, so SMSG wouldn't overload them. In the end, the ExPo pool numbered fifty-three coaches in thirteen countries, capable of coaching in thirteen languages.

Coaches then attended two virtual teleconference orientations of two hours length, the first focusing on Microsoft and the SMSG business, the second specifically highlighting the details of the ExPo program (coach expectations, the process and timeline, coach-participant matching, manager engagement, coaching success measures, and invoicing process). Coaches already working with Microsoft were exempt from the first orientation, but all coaches were required to join the second session. Microsoft's own LiveMeeting technology was used for these sessions.

International Coaching Forum One of the most rewarding endeavors was the Coaching Forum, held in Microsoft's headquarters in Redmond, Washington. All coaches were invited for the two-day forum. It began the night before the two days with a welcome reception. Day one included presentations by Microsoft executives and coach round-table discussions. The day wrapped up with a special dinner at the Seattle Space Needle. Day two began with joint time between coaches and Microsoft HR, presentations from several executive coaching thought leaders, a tour of the exclusive Home/Office of the Future demo, followed by a visit (and discounts) to the company store.

Coaches were paid a small stipend, and their expenses were covered once they arrived in Seattle. They were not compensated for airfare or professional fees for the two days. Despite this limitation, 70 percent of the pool attended, including coaches from as far away as China, Ireland, England, Peru, and Australia. Feedback from the two days was overwhelmingly positive: the wealth of best-practice sharing, networking, and overall goodwill generated by the event made it worthwhile for all. A sample action plan is shown in Exhibit 10.2 on page 200.

LEARNING CIRCLES AS A PRIMARY DEVELOPMENT COMPONENT FOR HIPO DEVELOPMENT IN SMSG

Circles Process Mirrors How Today's Leaders Work and Learn

As with executive coaching, Microsoft selected a leader in the field of peer learning experiences when it was ready to launch learning circles. Authenticity Consulting demonstrated the expertise necessary to make this component viable and sustainable on a global basis. According to Carter McNamara, co-founder of Authenticity Consulting:

> *"The world of today's typical business leader is very chaotic. In an environment as complex as what Microsoft presents, day-to-day leadership challenges are seldom addressed by carefully chosen, well-structured and highly rational approaches to problem solving. Leaders often don't have time to do that kind of planning for each challenge. Instead, leaders often resort to highly intuitive, real-time approaches that are based on the leaders' learning from their past experiences and on help from others in the organization.*

> *"The most effective leaders have 'learned how to learn,' that is, they've developed the ability to closely examine their own perceptions, conclusions, and actions. They've used that insight to more fully understand their current day-to-day challenges, including what works and what doesn't work to address those challenges. Circles are based on the adult learning and problem-solving process called action learning that very closely matches the real world of today's leaders. As a result, the 'circles' process helps members develop and practice leadership and problem-solving skills that can very quickly be applied in the workplace." (McNamara, 2007)*

Learning for a "circle" member does not occur only when that member is getting help from other circle members. It occurs during the entire meeting when thinking about other members' coaching goals and actions. It occurs when realizing the many interests and challenges of other members in the workplace. Also, it occurs between meetings when taking actions and reflecting on the results of those actions.

Unique Principles of Learning Behind Learning Circles

The circles process is in close conformance with these state-of-the-art principles of adult learning:

- **People learn best when they apply new information to current challenges.** The urgency of current challenges often causes people to be far more interested in using recent learning to address those challenges and, thus, to be far more involved in understanding and benefiting from that learning.

- **People often learn best when they share ongoing feedback with peers.** People often place more value in the help they receive from others in similar situations than from "outside" experts. Continual dependence on outside experts can sometimes cultivate passivity and dependency in people, minimizing their own capabilities.

EXHIBIT 10.2. **Coaching Action Plan**

FY09 ExPo Program: Coaching Action Plan

The purpose of this document is to provide high-potential employees a coaching action plan, agreed on with their managers, which can complement the ExPo development experience.

1. Complete the action plan.

Identify one to three Leadership Competencies you will work on (from your 360-degree results or other feedback items). Full leadership competency descriptions are available on HR Web at http://hrweb/US/CareerModel/Find/Competencies/leadership-comp.htm for assistance with mapping leadership competencies and manager or profession competencies; email "expcoach."

Goals: Identify one to three goals that you are most passionate about working on.	Measures: How will each goal be measured (can be quantitative or qualitative)?	What specific action steps can you take in support of this goal?	Potential Business Impact: What is the value to you and the business if you do not achieve your goal?

What is the value to you and the business if you do?   Target Date: Set a target date for each goal.

2. Schedule the coaching action plan contracting conversation with your manager.

Contracting Conversation: Set up some time to review this document with your manager and coach, ensuring a meaningful conversation and agreement regarding your development plan. Contracting is another form of commitment—commitment to working in a partnership as manager and ExPo member. Think of it as a commitment to maximize your potential; which was identified during nomination; and ensure continued strengthening of the criteria on which a high-potential employee is identified: aspiration, ability, and commitment.

3. Prepare questions that will be used to verify coaching effectiveness.
At the end of coaching, a "mini survey" will be conducted with your stakeholders. List two or three questions that reflect the leadership behaviors you are working on with your coach.

Questions

1) Has this person shared with you in the past six months what she is working on?
2) Do you feel this person has become more effective or less effective as a leader in the past six months?
3) The following improvement area(s) have been specifically selected by this leader. Please rate the extent to which this individual has increased/decreased in effectiveness in the following areas of development in the past six months.
   - Being less specifically directive during project work, versus being inclusive with others ideas and contributions
   - Ability to give feedback in a manner that is genuinely heard and seriously considered by others
   - Able to effectively work with conflict, remaining engaged, without attempting to avoid it or dissolve it at all costs
4) What has this person done in the past six months that you have found particularly effective?
5) What can this person do to become more effective as a leader in the areas of development noted above?

4. ExPo Learning Commitment:
Signoff:
Member:

Manager:

Please take appropriate steps to update and then periodically review your commitments in the Performance @ Microsoft tool and track resulting development activities in your development plan in Career Compass.

- **The person with the problem is the expert on the problem**. The problem presenter is most closely involved in the problem and, therefore, can have the most ability and influence to understand and solve the problem. Quite often, the solution to the problem has to start with that person.

- **Finding the right problem is as important as solving it**. Often, people only see the symptoms of a recurring problem, rather than its real cause. Thus, the problem tends to recur. It is frequently caused more by how the person perceives it versus missing a specific piece of new information. Understanding one's own perceptions and conclusions can enable better learning.

- **Learning involves the whole person**. People cannot learn unless they are ready to learn. Therefore, learning environments must provide opportunities for learners to be involved in that learning. They must be able to fully question new information and materials, to try them out, and to reflect on how that learning best suits how they learn.

Learning Circles Compared to Traditional Forms of Training

Table 10.3 compares traditional training with action learning-based learning circles. The contents of the table do not suggest that one form is always best. Often, both forms together make for very powerful learning and development.

Life of a Circle

Circle Kickoff The "core" circle process, which is common to all tiers, is introduced early in the ExPo experience. Each circle starts with a one-day kickoff session at orientation, during which members learn about the circle process, including the circle agenda and how to select the most appropriate coaching goals to work on in their

TABLE 10.3. Traditional Learning vs. Learning Circles

Traditional Training	Learning Circles
Students are taught by expert instructors.	Learners develop from the inside out.
Students are expected to master subject matter.	Learners focus on actions and learning from those actions.
Instructors pose questions to lead students to discover the existing correct answer.	Learners share questions to increase understanding and develop action plans.
Instructors use simulated exercises to help students master information.	Learners focus on real-life problems to get things done and learn at the same time.
Instructors reinforce the correct answers.	Learners encourage each other to explore their thinking and actions.

meetings. They learn how to coach and receive coaching, how to identify appropriate actions to take between meetings, and how to capture learning during the life of the circle. Members also learn how to self-facilitate their circle meetings.

The kickoff meetings help circle members to be comfortable with the process, develop trust and commitment within the circle, be open to other members, and create a self-facilitated, long-lasting team.

Circle Meetings The power in circle meetings is in their simplicity. Each circle includes five to seven members, ideally six. Members are encouraged to meet four to eight times a year. Circles for Tiers 2 and 3 are self-scheduled, self-facilitated, and usually conducted virtually via teleconference. Circles for Tier 1 might include a mix of externally facilitated and self-facilitated meetings. Meetings are from an hour and a half to three hours long, depending on the number of members per circle and how often members can schedule their meetings. Circles function more effectively when they have frequent and short meetings (for example, eight hour-and-a-half meetings) versus infrequent and longer meetings (for example, only four three-hour meetings). In the meetings, each member addresses a current, real-world priority called a coaching goal that exists in the member's workplace or career. Each member receives equal time in the meeting to get help from other members to address priorities and to identify relevant and realistic actions to take between meetings. Each member learns from the coaching and feedback from the other members and from the reflections on his or her ongoing actions between meetings. Brief, practical evaluations ensure high quality and continuous improvement of the circle process. Ground rules, especially confidentiality, are stressed during each meeting.

Coaching Goals

Each circle member chooses a coaching goal to address in each circle meeting. The goal is considered appropriate if it is in regard to a current, real, and important priority for the member. Usually goals are in regard to matters in the workplace. However, occasionally, a member might take advantage of the trust and confidentiality in the circle to share somewhat personal struggles regarding the goal.

For ExPo Tier 2, members are encouraged to select coaching goals related to enhancing their leadership capabilities in Microsoft. For ExPo Tier 3, members are encouraged to select coaching goals related to learning more about the Microsoft business and/or choosing a career in leadership in Microsoft.

Here are some examples of coaching goals used by members of circles:

1. "I'm really excited about the goals in my career plan. There are so many, I'm not sure where to start."

2. "I don't know how to delegate. All my tasks are in my head. How can I get started?"

3. "I need to manage my time more effectively. I've taken time management courses, but they didn't seem to be helpful."

4. "I'm supposed to convey my department's vision to my employees. What is a logical next step?"

5. "There's a big gap between our five-year vision and what we're doing now. How can I bridge that gap?"

6. "I want to go to the next level of leadership. I'm not sure how to do that."

Actions Between Meetings

During meetings, each member identifies relevant and realistic actions to take to address the coaching goal. Between meetings, the member conducts those actions and records any learnings from those applications. In the next meeting, members choose to report the results of their actions and/or introduce a new coaching goal to work on. Between circle meetings, it's common for members to contact each other to update each other on their actions and learning, to share materials, or to see how others are doing and whether they need any help.

Circle Termination and Renewal

After a full year cycle, circles are formally closed, although circle members may continue their circles on an informal basis. Microsoft does not provide facilities and resources to support the circles continuing beyond one year. Instead, high-potentials join a new circle, with new members, at the beginning of each year in order to expand their network.

How Circles Are Organized

Circles can be used for a variety of results, for example, to solve problems, achieve goals, cultivate close networks and collaborations, deepen and enrich development programs, teach coaching skills, or even provide support groups. Circles are organized differently depending on the desired results. Microsoft uses circles primarily for networking, collaboration, and learning, although the other results are often achieved as well. Therefore, circles are organized according to the following guidelines:

Members with Similar Interests and Responsibilities It's important that members of each circle have somewhat similar interests and levels of responsibility so that they can quickly understand each other's coaching goals and quickly share help and materials that are highly relevant and quickly understood. This guideline ensures that members feel they have enough in common to form a strong team. For example, in ExPo, some Tier 2 circles are comprised of managers and/or senior individual contributors (many of whom have been managers) interested in enhancing a particular management competency in Microsoft.

Members with Somewhat Different Personalities Next, sufficient diversity in the nature of the members of a circle enhances the experience. Diversity of perspectives, ways of learning, and decision-making styles often results in more robust coaching and problem solving among members of the circle. It also expands each member's ability to understand and work with different people in the workplace.

Members with Different Functional Roles Finally, members of each circle should represent different business areas so that members can learn more about all of the other areas and activities within Microsoft. The diversity of roles creates a rich environment for networking and collaboration.

Results and Benefits for Circle Members

Circle members have reported multiple benefits of circle participation, including:

- Substantial cost savings as members share coaching, feedback, and materials;

- Confidential network of peers who respond to a call for help;

- Individualized attention to their needs;

- Leadership skills—skills in establishing priorities and in motivating themselves and others to address those priorities;

- Numerous interpersonal skills, including communicating, consulting, facilitating, and problem solving;

- Resolved real-world issues from using real-world advice and materials; and

- Time to stand back and reflect.

A sample of quotes from circle members follows:

- Accountability—"I feel like I'm letting my circle down when I don't take my actions or help other members."

- Coaching, consulting, mentoring skills—"I've learned to better understand my people's needs and how to help support their own learning."

- Information, materials, and tools—"Additionally, handouts and resources made available on request or in response to a goal have been very good and helpful, targeted and appropriate."

- Knowledge—"I got a fair amount of substantive knowledge about management planning; my other stuff ends up on a bookshelf somewhere."

- Motivation—"What has been most useful is the motivating 'kick in the butt.'"

- Networking—"It is difficult to establish friends and colleagues among organizations who are competitive. This forum allows collegiality to flourish."

- Problem resolution—"I've gotten through several tough issues, even in the first months, with my group."

- Productivity—"The group has spurred me on to getting a lot done."

- Professional development—"This has made a huge difference in my ability to see my role in perspective and my take on leadership; my work, and my comfort with my work have improved considerably from this experience."

- Renewal—"This is the best burnout prevention I can imagine."

- Safe environments—"I can say things here that I can't say anywhere else; I feel safe."

- Self-development—"I am seeing my own experience in a different light and am seeing common issues handled in different ways that I can use—at work and as a volunteer."

- Support—"[I continue to receive a] lot of good support from my circle members."

CONCLUSION

Microsoft has a strong commitment to building leaders at all levels. The ExPo Leaders Building Leaders program is an integrated and comprehensive high-potential development program encompassing multiple learning methodologies, tailored to each leader's level in the organization. The research-based design includes elements of assessment, coaching, mentoring, learning circles, action learning, and business conferences.

As the program progresses into its fourth year, initial ExPo participants are now participating as conference instructors and mentors for new participants. In this way, participants are learning that they are part of a community that continues to grow and develop itself beyond the initial experience. The expectation is that participants will give back to the program over time.

Meanwhile, as the economy continues to challenge the company, Microsoft's investment in ExPo continues unabated. In July 2008, COO Kevin Turner said, "Developing future leaders in the company is one of the most important things we can do as a leadership team." Thus ExPo will continue without any cutbacks, given the critical nature of this development in Microsoft's future.

REFERENCES

Corporate Leadership Council. (2005). Realizing the full potential of rising talent (volume 1). *HR Intelligence Quarterly*.

McCall, M.W., & Hollenbeck, G.P. (2002). *Developing global executives*. Cambridge, MA: Harvard Business School Press.

McCall, M.W., Lombardo, M.M., & Morrison, A.M. (1998). *Lessons of experience: How successful executives develop on the job*. New York: The Free Press.

McNamara, C.M. (2007). *Microsoft learning circles guide*. Minneapolis: Authenticity Consulting.

Underhill, B., McAnally, K., & Koriath, J. (2007). *Executive coaching for results: The definitive guide to developing organizational leaders*. San Francisco: Jossey-Bass.

Shannon Wallis is the director of worldwide leadership programs and responsible for the development of top-tier talent for Microsoft's Sales Marketing and Services Group, a 45,000 employee organization. She is an executive coach, consultant, and teacher with more than twenty years of international work experience in leadership development and organizational change. Prior to her current role, she consulted to and held management positions in Fortune 100 businesses as diverse as Coca-Cola and Universal Studios. Her degrees include an MBA from Duke University and a B.S. in human development and social policy from Northwestern University in the United States. As a speaker, she has addressed Linkage, the Society of Industrial and Organizational Psychology, OD Network, and regional ASTD and industry events, as well as multiple women's conferences throughout the United States. She resides in Fairfax, Virginia, with her family.

Brian O. Underhill, Ph.D., is an industry-recognized expert in the design and management of worldwide executive coaching implementations. Dr. Underhill is the author of *Executive Coaching for Results: The Definitive Guide to Developing Organizational Leaders* (Berrett-Koehler, 2007). He is the founder of CoachSource and the Alexcel Group and previously spent ten years managing executive coaching operations for Marshall Goldsmith. Dr. Underhill is an internationally sought-after speaker, addressing The Conference Board, Linkage, and regional ASTD, SHRM HRPS, and PCMA events. He has a Ph.D. and an M.S. degree in organizational psychology from the California School of Professional Psychology (CSPP) and a B.A. in psychology from the University of Southern California. He holds advanced certification in the Goldsmith Coaching Process. Dr. Underhill resides in Silicon Valley.

Carter McNamara, MBA, Ph.D., is an internationally known expert in organization development and customizing action learning-based, peer coaching programs for a wide variety of applications and results. Dr. McNamara is the author of *Field Guide to Consulting and Organizational Development*, winner of the 2007 Axiom Business Book Award. He is also author of the *Microsoft Learning Circles Guide*, from which much of the materials about learning circles was included in this book. He is co-founder of Authenticity Consulting, LLC, which provides services in action learning, organizational development, and leadership development. He has an MBA from the University of St. Thomas and a Ph.D. in organizational development from the Union Institute. Dr. McNamara resides in Minneapolis.

CHAPTER

MURRAY & ROBERTS LIMITED

ZELIA SOARES

Building a "leadership pipeline" to manage talent through rigorous performance management and development as a lever to deliver sustainable business results.

- Introduction
  - Background
  - The Business Case
  - Analysis and Customization
  - Validation and Communication
- Design and Alignment
  - Rationale: Performance and Development
  - Understanding Performance

The author would like to acknowledge Drotter Human Resources, who provided a sound methodology and language that was user-friendly to implement. She would also like to acknowledge the line managers and individuals who have embraced the Leadership Pipeline philosophy, making it part of their everyday management.

- ■ Performance Management and Development Contract
- ■ Appraisal Process
- ■ Understanding Potential
- ■ Implementation
  - ■ Training
  - ■ Leadership and Succession Review
  - ■ Annual Performance Management and Development Process
- ■ Evaluation
- ■ Summary
  - ■ What Happens Next?

INTRODUCTION

Background

Murray & Roberts is South Africa's leading engineering, contracting, and construction services company. It has created employment, developed skills, installed infrastructure, delivered services, applied technology, and built capacity throughout South and Southern Africa for 106 years, making a significant contribution to sustainable socio-economic development in the region.

Murray & Roberts operates in Southern Africa, the Middle East, Southeast Asia, Australasia, and North America from its home-base in Johannesburg, South Africa, where it has a public listing on the Johannesburg Stock Exchange Limited. It has an international coordinating office in the United Kingdom and principle offices in Australia, Botswana, Canada, Namibia, United Arab Emirates, and Zimbabwe.

Murray & Roberts is primarily focused on resources-driven construction markets in industry and mining, oil and gas, and power and energy, and offers civil, mechanical, electrical, mining, and process engineering; general building and construction; materials supply and services to the construction industry; and management of concession operations.

The Murray & Roberts value proposition is defined through its non-negotiable commitment to sustainable earnings growth and value creation. The Group aspires to world-class fulfillment in everything it does, through its core competence in industrial design, delivering major projects and services primarily to the development of emerging economies and nations.

The Business Case

As the Group's value proposition took shape, came the recognition that people are the cornerstone of sustainability and that a unitary leadership framework was required if the Group was to succeed in delivering on its high-profile order book.

Talent management processes and practices such as performance management, development, and succession were not formalized, and—in some companies—nonexistent. The Group had no centralized talent inventory or succession plan.

In September 2006 after extensive research, Steve Drotter's Leadership Pipeline philosophy was ratified by the Murray & Roberts Holdings Board as the Group's strategic framework for managing talent. This philosophy offered the Group an integrated approach to managing and growing talent using toolkits (performance management and development as well as talent reviews) that line managers and individuals could understand and easily apply. The Leadership Pipeline philosophy allows companies to segment work into various leadership layers and to define what output is required at each layer. This becomes a proven model for identifying future leaders, assessing their competence, planning their development, and measuring the results.

As denoted in outline below, the core architecture of the Leadership Pipeline offered Murray & Roberts a solution which consisted of four drivers. These drivers were implemented in a two-phased approach:

Leadership Pipeline Core Architecture

Phase 1—Analysis and Customization: Build the business case (the destination) and the tailored Murray & Roberts Leadership Pipeline and performance standards (accountability anchor).

Phase 2—Design and Alignment: Design and implement the performance management and development process (the foundation) and introduce the Leadership and Succession review process (the driving mechanism).

Analysis and Customization

Phase 1 took three months to complete. A project team reporting to the enterprise capability director was put together to complete this phase. The project team consisted of both line managers, HR practitioners, and a consultant from Drotter Human Resources. This reinforced the fact that this project was responding to a business need and was not just another human resources initiative.

A clear vision was articulated: The Leadership Pipeline will deliver the leadership the Group requires to deliver on its growth objectives by ensuring that:

■ Every leadership job is filled with a fully performing individual now (high *performance*) and in the future (*succession*) no matter how much Murray & Roberts changes or how fast it grows.

■ Every leadership job in Murray & Roberts is absolutely necessary and adds appropriate value.

■ Murray & Roberts leadership pipeline, as the core leadership delivery system, is effective from top to bottom.

■ Murray & Roberts is able to make high-quality appointment and deployment decisions quickly with high confidence.

This vision resonated with line managers at all levels, as it gave them a working solution to an ongoing business need.

The Leadership Pipeline differentiates and distributes work from the chief executive officer (CEO) to the entry-level individuals. Each layer requires specific skills, mindset, and delivery. The task of the project team was to customize a Murray & Roberts Leadership Pipeline by identifying what work is done in the Group to deliver on the strategy.

The customized Murray & Roberts Leadership Pipeline was designed by conducting sixty structured interviews across both hierarchy and business. These interviews were detailed in nature, and took three to four hours to conduct.

Once all the interviews were completed, a week was set aside to analyze the interview data and design an appropriate leadership pipeline (see Figure 11.1) consisting of eleven different roles.

The next step was to develop generic one-page performance standards that described each pipeline role (see Figure 11.2). These were then benchmarked against global standards kept by Drotter Human Resources.

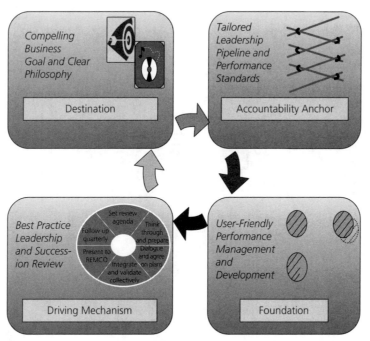

FIGURE 11.1. *Murray & Roberts Leadership Pipeline*

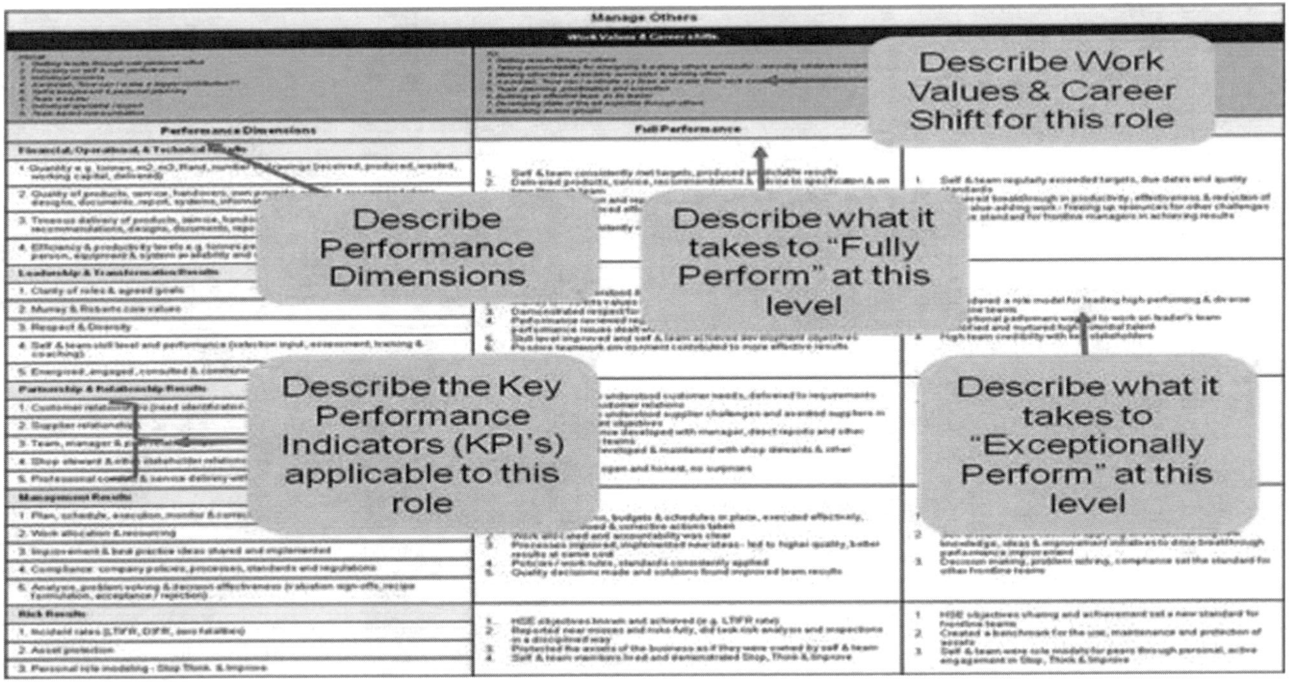

FIGURE 11.2. *An Example of a Typical One-Page Performance Standard*

The eleven performance standards described performance in five performance dimensions:

- Financial/Operational and Technical Results

- Leadership and Transformation Results

- Partnership and Relationship Results

- Management Results

- Risk Results

In the past, individuals were only measured on bottom-line delivery, resulting in a myopic view of performance that did not support sustainability or the Group's growth strategy. Now, the five performance dimensions ensure that individuals are measured and developed on both what they need to deliver as well as how they need to deliver it—results and behaviors. This will support a culture of sustainable results and continuous improvement that is imperative to the Group's growth strategy.

The generic performance standards raise the bar of performance across the Group, and set the standard of what is expected. They are easy to keep updated and are available on the Group's intranet. This transparency encourages individuals to take accountability for their careers as performance requirements are clear and objective. Figure 11.3 is an example of what a typical performance standard looks like: The first column describes

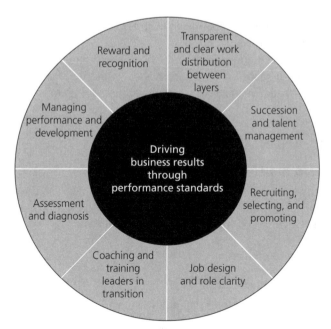

FIGURE 11.3. *Role of Performance Standards*

what performance is required, the middle column describes what full performance looks like, and the last column describes what exceptional performance looks like. The Performance Standards are now the starting point for both line managers and individuals when dealing with any people management issues. They have replaced the need for traditional job descriptions and competency models. (See Figure 11.3.)

Validation and Communication

Once the customized Murray & Roberts Leadership Pipeline and Performance Standards were finalized by the project team, a process of validation began in the Group. Validation was conducted in a structured top-down approach, starting with the chief executive officer and cascading it throughout the Group via sessions with each managing director and the relevant management team. The reason for this was the realization that the implementation of the Leadership Pipeline would require a culture shift in the organization, and that it was not just a process implementation. Visible leadership was critical to the implementation and sustainability of a new way of doing things.

An initial presentation was given at the CEO's monthly forum attended by all the managing directors across the Group. At this meeting the business case, rationale as well as the customized Leadership Pipeline and performance standards were explained. It was agreed that the same presentation would be given to each management team across the Group.

At the business presentations, the relevant managing director was responsible for introducing and endorsing the Leadership Pipeline. Each business was also encouraged to validate the customized pipeline and performance standards and to provide the implementation team with feedback.

These business presentations took three months to complete and gave the implementation team a good sense of which businesses would be ready to move on to the next phase of performance management and development implementation.

DESIGN AND ALIGNMENT

Rationale: Performance and Development

While validation was being done, a performance management and development process was designed in alignment with the Leadership Pipeline. This process is the foundation to the Leadership Pipeline philosophy, as it ensures that:

- A shared purpose is created.
- The work is differentiated and delivered at each layer of the pipeline.
- People are developed to deliver the required work.
- Succession and career management is sustained.
- A common language is used.

The following design criteria were critical:

- Strategic alignment

- Simplicity

- Group solution

- Measurable

- Developmental

- Objectivity

- Transparency

Understanding Performance

To keep the process simple, The Leadership Pipeline philosophy moves away from using a numeric system of describing performance, and opts for a qualitative approach (full, not-yet-full, and exceptional). This requires managers to apply a thinking model supported by evidence as opposed to manipulating and arguing about numbers. (See Figure 11.4.)

Performance is defined through the symbolic use of a circle. The circle depicts the job while the five performance dimensions are each represented by a line in the circle. This simple methodology assists the manager and individuals to keep performance conversations focused and objective:

- *Full performance*—the circle is full, meaning that the individual is delivering the work that is required at this layer of the pipeline in all five performance dimensions.

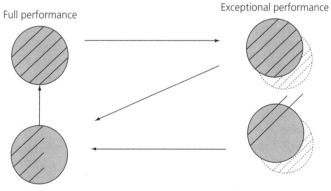

FIGURE 11.4. *Defining Performance*

- *Exceptional performance*—the individual is not only achieving the required results, but is also doing work outside of the circle. This work is typically that of the next layer of the pipeline, showing that the individual has excess capacity.

- *Not-yet-full performance*—one or more gaps identified requiring development interventions.

- *Inappropriate performance*—the individual is only doing some of the work required (possibly what he or she likes or is good at) and the rest of the time doing work at the layer below. This is a typical profile of a micro-manager.

Performance Management and Development Contract

As the Leadership Pipeline and performance standards provide the foundation for performance management, there was no need to design complex templates. An extra column was simply inserted into the performance standard where individuals could capture their job-specific targets, and the exceptional performance column was removed, as individuals contract for full, not exceptional, performance. (See Figure 11.5.)

In the first year of implementation, a paper process was used. Templates were available on the intranet, and the first three layers of leadership were required to complete the process. The focus of the first year was to establish the new language and ensure that the senior leaders of the Group were able to use the new process and adjust their leadership styles to support the process. Leaders had to learn to engage their people and become comfortable in making judgments through observation and evidence.

The automated process was introduced in the second year of implementation. The system was designed for simplicity, and online templates looked exactly the same as the paper templates, avoiding confusion and re-learning of the process. Daily electronic reports were made available to each managing director and HR executive on the status of performance management in the company. Monthly reports were also given at the Group's board meeting to keep the process on the radar screen.

The performance and development contract has two parts:

- The performance contract

- The individual development plan

Once the individual and manager agree on the individual's pipeline role, the individual receives an electronic workflow with a link to the performance management system. In three easy steps, individuals compile their performance contracts and development plans and send them to their managers for discussion. As the template provides a framework for the standard of performance, only job-specific targets need to be formulated. Individuals are encouraged to pick only two to four critical key performance targets per performance dimension. These targets need to be formulated in measurable end-result terms (outputs not inputs). All five performance dimensions have to be considered. This ensures that individuals are measured on both the "what" and the "how" and no longer just on bottom-line results. Once agreement is reached, the individual accepts the contract as final, and the system files the document.

Manage Managers

Key Performance Indicators (Typical Results)	Full Performance	Job Specific Targets/Objectives
Financial, Operational, and Technical Results		
1. Financial results (budget - sales, costs, overheads) 2. Project delivery (design-build, on time, industrially designed & commission effectiveness) 3. Department delivery of services (e.g., tenders; contracts; people; advice; recommendations; standards; intelligence) to client expectations 4. Productivity & efficiency	1. Self & teams consistently met targets, produced predictable results 2. Delivered project results to tendered parameters (cost, time, quality) 3. Delivered services to client expectations	
Leadership & Transformation Results		
1. Functional strategy contribution, translation, & execution 2. Murray & Roberts core values 3. Respect & diversity 4. Selection, coaching, training & development of direct repots & key people 5. Team strength & performance levels 6. Energized, engaged, consulted, & communicated	1. Contributed to development of functional strategy & translated strategy into operational goals & objectives 2. Ensured all department/project/regional members understood, supported & executed the values, vision, and goals of the function 3. Lived, shared, and ensured that everybody in the department/project/region understood the Murray & Roberts core values 4. Achieved diversity targets and ensured respect for people throughout the department / project / region 5. Frontline managers hired, based on demonstrated leadership capabilities rather than only on technical expertise—selected managers of others that "can do & lead" 6. Sought opportunities for growth and development and produced written development plans for self and direct reports	
Partnership & Relationship Results		
1. Clients, suppliers, & partners 2. Team manager & poor relationships 3. Shop steward & other stakeholder relationships 4. Cross-functional team work 5. Professional conduct & service delivery with integrity	1. Client, supplier, & partner relationships delivered predefined department/project/region objectives 2. Trusted and respected by manager, direct reports, peers, & other managers 3. Built & maintained constructive relationships with shop stewards & other stakeholders 4. Self & teams understood challengers facing other departments/projects/regions Self & teams were open and honest, no surprises	

Individuals select 2–4 generic KPIs from the first column and develop customized targets for their specific job in this column. The full performance column guides the thinking.

FIGURE 11.5. *Example of a Performance Contract*

217

The development plan entails three steps:

- The manager and individual agree on the individual's current status of performance by drawing the performance circle. This is supported by work evidence and not opinion.

- Once the circle has been discussed, strengths and development areas are easily identified.

- An appropriate development plan is agreed to. To encourage managers and individuals to consider development more broadly than just educational interventions, the development template breaks down the possible developmental interventions as:

  - On-the-job development

  - Manager coaching

  - Educational intervention

Figure 11.6 shows the one-page individual development template designed to focus on immediate actions that will make a difference to performance.

Appraisal Process

The annual performance cycle comprises three key evaluation activities:

- Informal circle discussions done monthly;

- Interim formal performance and development review done in January, six months into the performance year; and

- Final performance and development evaluation done in June at the end of the financial year.

The informal monthly circle discussions are critical, as it is at these sessions that real performance management happens. The manager identifies both the work that is being done, as well as the work that is not being done, and develops and coaches the individual to do the work.

The two formal reviews should merely be summaries of what has been discussed in the monthly meetings. Managers who do not have the monthly discussions will lack the evidence to make meaningful judgments.

In the final performance and development evaluation, managers will not only be expected to make a call on the individual's performance, but they will also be required to make a call on the individual's potential. This information allows for talent to be segmented and leads into the annual leadership and succession review. As always, judgments must be backed up with evidence.

Understanding Potential

Potential considers the current performance and predicts where the individual is likely to be in two years' time. If there is no evidence of performance, potential cannot be

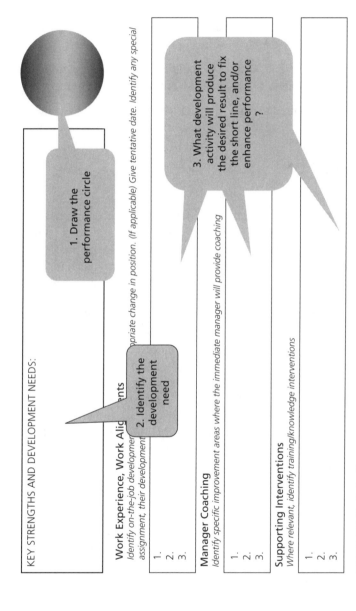

FIGURE 11.6. *Example of an Individual Development Plan*

measured. The Leadership Pipeline philosophy defines potential in three categories to assist line mangers in interpreting the individual's performance against the performance standards:

■ *Turn Potential*: The performance indicates that it is likely that the individual can make a turn to the next pipeline layer.

■ *Growth Potential*: The performance indicates that the individual can transition to a bigger job at the same pipeline layer.

■ *Mastery Potential*: The performance indicates that the individual should continue in the same role, but with continuous learning and improvement.

Managers are required to make this decision in conjunction with the individual. This transparency is fundamental to the retention of skills as well as career management.

IMPLEMENTATION

Training

It was decided to implement the performance management and development process in a phased approach, starting with the top three levels of each company across the Group. Senior managers had to understand and believe in the process (walk their talk) if it was to succeed. Also, as the process starts with each managing director, strategic alignment is achieved and cascaded through the contracting process.

Intensive four-hour interactive training sessions were designed and delivered to not only ensure that managers understood the theory and the tools, but also to help them to develop their performance and development contracts.

Training sessions were facilitated at the different companies by the two project team members who ensured that the same message was being delivered throughout the Group. The managing director (manage business) and his executive team (manage function) were trained first; then training was cascaded to the third level (manage managers). The facilitators were also available to assist the managing directors with their contracts, and to do quality control as required. Supporting material such as relevant articles and "how-to" tactics were placed on the intranet (see Figure 11.7). An e-learning facility was also set up to facilitate system training. The HR executives at the different companies further assisted the implementation process by providing hands-on support to the line managers.

Once the training was completed, it was noticed that some leaders were not implementing the performance and development process as diligently as others. Commitment was lacking, and the main excuse was lack of time. Managing directors needed to drive the process in their businesses by holding their managers accountable for performance management. This could not and should not be done by human resources. It was at this point that the project leader approached the CEO and suggested that he chair a Group leadership and succession review. This required that all the managing directors master the Leadership Pipeline philosophy through the application of the

How to conduct monthly circle discussions:

- Spend a few minutes drawing the circle and lines
- Spend a few minutes discussing the work that is getting done
- Spend a few minutes discussing the work that is not getting done
- Agree on a plan to get the work done
- Capture diary entry online

FIGURE 11.7. *Example of Supporting Material Available Online*

tools and not just intellectual understanding. This created a renewed energy and focus into the system.

Leadership and Succession Review

The annual leadership and succession review is the driving mechanism of the Leadership Pipeline philosophy, as this comprehensive process allows the executive leadership of Murray & Roberts to understand the "bench strength" and related people issues in the Group.

Managing directors were given training in a workshop environment to equip them to prepare for the review. The first leadership and succession review only looked at the "manage function" layer of the pipeline—the managing director's direct reports. The second review, held a year later, included the top three levels of a business: "manage business," "manage function," and "manage managers." This gave the CEO a real-time sense of what talent was available and where the potential risks lay. From a corporate perspective, it is unlikely that the review will include individuals lower in the pipeline. These individuals will be reviewed by the business managing directors. The leadership and succession reviews consist of presentations by each managing director, and cover the strategic triangle which drives competitive advantage. (See Figure 11.8.)

- *Strategic Direction*: What are the major strategic issues, their effects on the organization and consequently on talent management?

- *Organization Capability*: Given the strategy, what are the organizational challenges (structure, values and culture, processes, etc.)?

- *Individual Capability*: Provide a nine-box performance and potential matrix. See Figure 11.9 as well as the necessary supporting data, which includes:

  - Next assignments for individuals who are "exceptional-turn performers"

  - Individual profiles (education, achievements, strengths, and development areas)

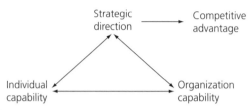

FIGURE 11.8. *Strategic Triangle*

Matrix		Performance		
		Exceptional	Full	Not yet full
Turn Able to do work at next level		John Smith Betty Meyer		
Growth Able to do work of bigger jobs at same level		Josh Govender	Dianne Botha Fred Brown	
Mastery Able to do same kind of work, only better			Peter Brand Stuart Williams	Alan Vorster

(left vertical label: **Potential**)

FIGURE 11.9. *Nine-Box Performance and Potential Matrix*

- Potential successors
- Poor performers
- Employment equity status
- Development expenditure
- Conclusions and plans for improvement

Once the presentations are done, data is collated across the Group and action plans are put in place to manage the most pressing people issues. The managing directors are held accountable for the execution of agreed plans. This process allows managing directors and executive directors an opportunity to review business plans through a people lens.

Annual Performance Management and Development Process

The annual performance management and development process is summarized in Figure 11.10. The process starts annually with the strategy formulation and is positioned as a business process driven by the relevant managing director.

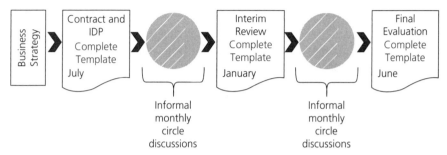

FIGURE 11.10. *Annual Performance and Development Process*

The process drives full performance, ensuring that the right work gets done to deliver the business strategy. Even though the process is there to get the work done, it is fundamentally an engagement tool and is developmental in nature. It embeds the culture of the organization and drives the behaviors critical for sustainable results.

EVALUATION

The Leadership Pipeline language is currently prevalent throughout the Group to the "manage managers" layer. The process has been automated through a workflow system to facilitate roll-out and reporting. Intellectually, line managers understand the need for a leadership framework and the importance of managing performance and development. Many, however, are still battling to make it part of their day-to-day management. The main benefits have been:

- Job clarity

- Identification of successors

- Identification of development areas

- Improved feedback

- Improved engagement

- Cross-company appointments

It is believed that these benefits are likely to lead to improved performance, which should be made tangible post-June when the final performance and development evaluations are conducted.

The three biggest challenges to implementation:

- The line manager's lack of coaching and dialogue skills

- Breaking the culture of measuring only bottom-line results

- Getting line managers to "let go" of work they should not be doing

Corporate leadership programs have been introduced at each layer of the pipeline to provide "just-in-time" development to equip managers with leadership skills to perform at the required standard. These programs have been designed in partnership with the local business school and are in alignment with the relevant leadership pipeline performance standard and the five performance dimensions.

Coaching workshops are also being rolled out in the Group to assist managers to acquire people engagement and feedback skills critical to performance management and having a direct impact on retention. There is an understanding and acceptance in the organization that, with time and practice, the quality of the dialogue and the application of the leadership pipeline tools will improve to the required level of proficiency.

SUMMARY

What Happens Next?

Given the initial success, the following is planned for year three:

- Roll out performance management and development training to the rest of the organization, excluding unionized individuals. Unionized individuals will only be included once discussions take place between the organization and the trade union. This is likely to happen only in year four to five of implementation.

- Align the recruitment process to the Leadership Pipeline. Currently only executive recruitment is being done in accordance with the methodology.

- Roll out the leadership and succession review, per company, to include all individuals.

- Review and align recognition and reward to the process.

- Review the Leadership Pipeline and performance standards to ensure continued relevance.

Zelia Soares, executive: leadership development, is responsible for performance management, talent management, and succession, as well as all corporate leadership programs across the Murray & Roberts Group. Prior to joining Murray & Roberts, she implemented the Leadership Pipeline in two other blue-chip companies. Soares has more than fifteen years of talent management experience, specifically in the engineering and leadership fields. She holds a bachelor's degree specializing in human resources from the University of the Witwatersrand in South Africa.

RESOURCE

Charan, R., Drotter, S., & Noel, J. (2001). *The leadership pipeline: How to build the leadership-powered company.* San Francisco: Jossey-Bass.

CHAPTER

12

PORTER NOVELLI

GREG WALDRON

Applying the Drotter "results-based" Leadership Pipeline approach to create a performance management system in a professional service firm.

INTRODUCTION

The Drotter results-based approach is tailored to a professional services firm structure and applied in the development of a performance management system aligned with the business's strategy. Drotter's Leadership Pipeline approach is implemented, with the full performance definitions for each leadership level in the tailored pipeline becoming the basis for a new organization-wide performance management application. The Drotter full performance definitions subsequently become the "source code" for selection, talent management, and training planning applications. The focus of this paper is the first application, performance management.

Business Diagnosis and Assessment

In 2004, Porter Novelli, a leading global marketing communications firm, undertook a fundamental strategic assessment and visioning process to guide it through the next five years. The firm's CEO, president, and chief strategy officer led this process. The vision focused on a new approach to client account planning, a more client-centric structure, and a greater emphasis on operating interdependence between the globally dispersed offices in the service of multinational clients. It was felt that these three initiatives would dramatically increase the firm's capacity to win and grow large, complex, and geographically dispersed client accounts—the firm's strategic market target.

The senior management group identified the need to upgrade and align human resources management processes to successfully communicate and implement the new business strategy. The firm proceeded to hire a chief talent officer (CTO) to assist in the strategy implementation effort by designing and installing a more systematic, business-focused human resources management process.

In the CTO's opinion, the vision implementation challenge centered on creating the highest possible level of employee engagement with the vision in the short term—by providing people throughout the firm with a clear, specific understanding of what the business strategy meant for them.

His metaphor for engagement was specifying the "four entitlements of all employees." The CTO's experience with corporate change efforts had led him to the conclusion that specific answers to four fundamental questions were a reasonable baseline expectation for every employee, regardless of level or function:

1. What *specifically* do you expect of me?

2. How will you define success (and measure me)?

3. What's in it for me if I deliver the results you expect?

4. Will you provide me the resources I need/eliminate the barriers I face to achieve these results?

Individual role clarity and clear performance expectations are absolute requirements for these questions to be addressed. It was clear that the firm's current approaches, although based on current practice and invested with significant effort, were not meeting these requirements.

The CTO had previously become familiar with Stephen Drotter's Leadership Pipeline work, both as a client and as a consultant working with Drotter Human Resources. Drotter's primary focus has been executive succession and the related processes: executive assessment; organization and job design; succession planning; and tailored individual development plans. However, his core concepts add significant value in broader application, particularly for performance management, selection, and development planning at all levels. The emphasis on specific results required, as well as the positioning of management and leadership results as measurable business outcomes, aligned well with the needs of the firm.

Performance management practice was spotty at best, as the firm's current system—based on generic competencies—was complex and process-heavy. A leadership competency model upon which to base the system was missing. Professional development was considered important, and a full curriculum of professional training was offered. In the absence of a common "source code," the various HR processes did not align well, and therefore opportunities for mutual reinforcement were being missed.

Clearly, there were opportunities for human resources to make a business impact through better practice application.

Management Interviews Discussions with the CEO, president, chief strategy officer, and other senior managers both before and after the CTO commenced employment confirmed the need for a set of management processes that strongly reinforced individual accountability as well as the increasingly interconnected nature of the company's operations. Senior managers in all offices around the world would be asked to place global priorities over individual office considerations as multi-office and multi-region client accounts became the strategic imperative for growth.

The "Vision" Process "Vision 2004" was a combined business planning and senior management team-building exercise that involved detailed reviews of internal and competitive analysis, discussion of strategic alternatives, and development of the new client account planning approach for the company. A small internal team facilitated the process, which involved a global management meeting outside New York City, as well as a number of regional follow-up sessions. It provided the starting point for the strategy implementation effort. There were several significant outputs:

- Agreement on a new core client account planning perspective—that is, a new method for assessing a client's business situation and challenges and for developing solutions for the client;

- Management training in this new methodology;

- Confirmation of an emphasis on acquiring and growing large, complex client relationships;

■ Commitment to a closely coordinated "interdependent" operating approach across the global network; and

■ A project management structure to move these initiatives forward.

This set the stage for the communication and implementation effort. The chief talent officer joined the organization shortly after the first implementation projects had begun and moved quickly to review and recast the talent management portion of the overall plan.

Business Results A key assumption underlying the visioning logic was robust business growth over the strategic plan period. The company was solidly profitable, and the business was growing. The senior management group was confident that the enhanced focus on larger, more complex client relationships would take revenue and margin growth to new, sustainable levels. The bar was set higher.

Climate Measurement The company administers a biannual staff climate survey that measures operating culture along thirteen dimensions: teamwork; organizational culture; strategic planning; leadership; long-term focus; stake in the outcome; quality; client satisfaction; learning orientation; empowerment; communication; morale and loyalty; and survey results implementation. Scores in 2004 were on track with parent organization averages, but management wished to improve these scores on both a trend and relative basis. This would be an important metric for the effectiveness of the leadership and human resource management interventions being developed.

Feedback

As a member of the senior leadership team, the chief talent officer had abundant access to the other members of the group—the CEO, president, and the chief financial officer—to discuss his ongoing findings and developing recommendations. After the first ninety days, he had effectively presented his findings and made overall recommendations regarding priority areas to address and an agenda for the HR and knowledge development and learning functions.

The group's frequent and informal open discussion format facilitated processing of the feedback and gaining consensus on how to move forward. The feedback and recommendations were

■ The business strategy was timely and sound, but it required better aligned human resources processes to successfully implement.

■ Important requirements of the business strategy—higher levels of sustained collaboration between senior managers across offices and geographies; a greater emphasis on leadership and management work; more explicit definition of role expectations and required performance at all levels; and stronger link between individual performance and reward outcomes—would be best achieved through revised role and performance definitions.

- The revised role and performance definitions could be best defined and delivered through an application of the Leadership Pipeline approach to work definition and performance standards development.

- Pipeline-based definitions of senior roles would more explicitly define management and leadership accountabilities for reinforcement with coaching, performance management, and revised incentive compensation plans. This would be effectively the first application of the Pipeline approach.

- The second application of the Pipeline approach would be a complete revision of the firm's performance management system. This was required to buttress reinforcement of individual accountability as well as support the updated performance-based pay and reward programs to be installed.

- The third Pipeline application would be selection practice, as an opportunity would be created with the new work definitions to introduce a more structured and consistent interviewing process.

- Another opportunity for Pipeline application would be to better organize and align the substantial existing training offerings with the company's career structure, as well as guide the prioritization of investments in new and revised offerings.

The general findings and recommendations were also communicated and discussed with the senior manager group over a number of regularly scheduled conference calls. There was broad acceptance of the conclusions and proposed direction, so program work was commenced.

Program Design Considerations

The appeal of the Pipeline model as the foundation for the new human resources systems was based on several opinions shaped by the chief talent officer's experience:

- Drotter's thinking takes us first to work, role, and organization analysis before classic human resource applications such as assessment/performance management, selection, development planning, and training are considered—moving from the "supply side" to the "demand side" for talent. People are ultimately treated better and more engaged if these role definition and organization design issues are addressed first. The approach constituted an ideal basis for specifying and communicating the new personal accountabilities required by the new strategy.

- The Pipeline model does not rely on competencies, but rather required work results by level for its core "source code." These required work results are actually the first element of a classic competency model development; the key notion is that focus is maintained on actual work results rather than abstracting one level to the associated knowledge, skills, and personal values/attributes. The CTO felt this was fundamentally sounder for specific role and full performance definition purposes. Performance management and selection applications would be built on foundation of work results definitions.

- The model focuses on the vertical distribution of work in the organization. Vertical organization and process considerations have frequently been overlooked as organizations have "flattened." The process of de-layering actually places a greater requirement on thoughtful vertical task distribution, communication, and coordination across the enterprise. While recent organization design thinking has been around selecting the optimal horizontal structure (organizing by product, customer set, geography, process, function, or matrix), vertical considerations have been overlooked.

- Drotter requires the same explicit definitions of management and leadership results by level as financial and customer results, making these accountabilities far more specific, measurable, and therefore understandable to employees. The down-to-earth, application-based approach demystifies leadership in particular and facilitates the introduction of simple models to describe and explain both activities.

- The core Leadership Pipeline concept of a job is well suited to the fluid, fast-changing business environment of a professional services firm. A job is considered a collection of results to be delivered, many of which are shared with other employees and therefore requiring cooperation and collaboration to achieve. Required results change as business conditions change, giving the model great dynamism and flexibility. It is a particularly relevant approach for reinforcing an internal collaboration-based strategy.

- Core Leadership Pipeline level, performance dimension, and full performance definitions can be used as the core work architecture—the "source code"—upon which all talent management and development applications are based. As a result of this common basis, the various programs would better align and mutually reinforce each other.

These last two points are contrary to the belief held by some that the Leadership Pipeline model is inflexible and geared primarily to large industrial company applications. The thinking has universal applicability, and the model is actually quite flexible. Frustration has resulted in some cases in which practitioners have attempted to literally apply the generic large company examples in *The Leadership Pipeline* (Charan, Drotter, & Noel, 2001). Drotter has actually been quite explicit in requiring that tailored pipeline level, performance dimension, and full performance definitions be developed for every company application. This development involves structured work content interviewing, analysis, and comparison with a large database of work results definitions across scores of companies.

Therefore, the chief talent officer committed to building a tailored leadership pipeline and installing it by creating results-based role definitions, performance management process, selection and training structure based on its "source code."

PROGRAM IMPLEMENTATION

Tailored leadership pipelines are based on the specific work requirements of the company. Typically, an implementation project plan includes the creation of a trained team of human resource professionals and line managers who conduct structured work content interviews with a sample of full performing employees at different levels across all functions in the organization.

Tailored Leadership Pipeline Development

The generic work content interview format must be reviewed and customized as needed to fit the individual company's operating culture and language—the goal being to make the questions as understandable and familiar as possible to employees unaccustomed to this type of information-gathering method. The customized work interview format was tested with several staff members before being used for project team training and actual information gathering. Several small language adjustments were recommended by the test subjects and subsequently implemented.

A core project team of two senior human resource managers and a senior line operating manager was trained in conducting structured work interviews and recording and analyzing the input data. This training took the form of a session explaining the interview format, question by question, and covering important interviewing techniques. The workshop was followed by two two-on-one interviews per team member with the CTO to practice interviewing and data recording skills and to receive coaching.

As the firm's history was the combination of acquired offices and companies, it was felt important to get a work interview sampling that ensured geography and legacy firm representation as well as level and work function coverage. This resulted in the completion of seventy-five interviews in ten of the firm's twenty-three offices across North America and Europe, with staff members ranging from entry-level professionals and administrative support people to senior partners. Every major legacy company location was covered.

An interesting and quite positive side-effect of the work interview process was the new insight gained by a number of staff members concerning the purpose of their work. When facilitated to first describe the actual results they were responsible for delivering, rather than work activities, tasks, or required competencies, interviewees gained a clearer understanding of their roles' key business purpose. For a number of managers, this produced not only a better understanding of their own work requirements, but also a clearer basis for determining account team capacity requirements by level.

Upon the completion of the interviews, the resulting data was analyzed and integrated by the project in a series of meetings facilitated by the CTO. The CTO then developed a draft work architecture for the firm, specifying both leadership levels and company-specific contribution dimensions that aligned with the business strategy and operating process. Full performance standards were created for each contribution dimension at each leadership level. The first determination was that the tailored leadership pipeline structure for the firm was constituted of five leadership levels, shown in Figure 12.1.

This structure appears to be typical of professional services firms, with the manager of managers level populated by the critically important client account directors who manage the firm's revenue-producing activities on an ongoing basis. The business manager level incorporates functional managers as well as classic P&L owners, and there are no true group managers in what is essentially a one-business model.

This structure works well in capturing both the client service and the support functions of professional services businesses. The client-facing function is supported by the specialty and support functions (research; planning; marketing; finance; human resources; information technology), and this simple two-function structure is represented by this architecture.

The work content analysis involved in the development of the essential pipeline "skeleton" provides the analyst with many rich opportunities for organizational diagnosis and enhancement. The first such opportunity occurred for the CTO when populating the new leadership levels with job titles. An operating complication for the various offices when attempting to create cross-office, cross-geography client teams was understanding and integrating the various title structures that existed in each

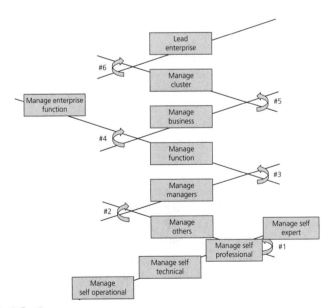

FIGURE 12.1. *Leadership Pipeline for a Professional Services Firm*

TABLE 12.1. **Job Title Rationalization Using the Leadership Pipeline Levels**

Leadership Level	Job Titles
Enterprise Manager	CEO; president; CFO; CTO; other C-level executive committee members
Business Manager	Subsidiary president/CEO; regional director; office managing director; global account director; director
Manager of Managers	EVP; SVP; account director; director; functional/specialty director
Manager of Others	VP; account manager; associate/deputy director; senior consultant; project manager; account supervisor; function/specialty manager
Manages Self	Senior account executive; account executive; assistant account executive; consultant; junior consultant; coordinator; functional/specialty professional

country and in different legacy firm offices in the United States. The mapping of titles onto the enterprise-wide leadership layer architecture created a title rationalization grid that was distributed to all offices providing a global organization translation for team managers, as shown in Table 12.1.

The contribution dimensions identified for the firm were based on a literal analysis of the work content interviews, but also vetted against and aligned with the new client-centric strategy. The contribution dimensions are of critical importance, as they outline the "source code" to be used in developing performance appraisal, assessment, selection, and career development applications. Close alignment with the business strategy facilitates full line of sight for every staff member and powerful process reinforcement of the key strategic and operating cultural elements. The contribution dimensions were:

- Client Results

- Leadership Results

- Management Results

- Relationship Results

- Innovation/Creativity Results

- Business/Financial Results

The order in which the contribution dimensions are displayed and communicated was of primary importance in conveying the firm's full strategic message to its staff at all levels.

■   Clearly, a "client-centric" strategy must place the client as the first strategic priority, so this factor was listed first.

■   Leadership and management had been the great "wild cards" in strategy and performance discussions; everyone realized they were critically important, but everyone struggled to operationalize this importance as neither term was particularly well defined, and therefore not well articulated or measured. Now these dimensions took their appropriate places.

■   Relationships with clients had always been recognized as critical; the new strategy mandated a closer, more selfless "interdependence" between partners and senior managers than ever before, and this dimension captured the new emphasis.

■   Creative thinking and its business-focused application in the development of client strategies had a similarly traditional importance; the new dimension of innovation was added as new approaches to both client business solutions and growing the firm aggressively were viewed as critical for success.

■   Financial results were intentionally placed last. They had previously been so heavily emphasized that they had become the primary strategic goal, to the detriment of factors such as client satisfaction and professional work quality. This perception was confirmed in staff climate surveys that asked respondents to prioritize the importance of a number of key operating factors. Financial results had come in first. The CTO found this a particularly disturbing finding in the case of junior professionals at the firm—people who had no direct impact on the overall financial performance of the enterprise. So financial results were characterized as literally the "bottom line"—the result of excellence in delivering the first five dimensions. The message was that above expectation growth and financial returns would occur if clients, people, and the work were the primary leadership focus.

Finally, the work interview data and strategy input were analyzed against a database of other companies' standards to draft full performance definitions for each leadership level, for both client-facing and specialty/support functions. As the firm had been struggling with the fundamentals of good performance management practice—again, a rather typical professional services situation—it was decided that the first iteration of the performance model would follow the work architecture's simplicity. Therefore, only the full performance benchmarks would be detailed, with consideration of adding exceptional performance definitions left for later versions.

The draft performance standard definitions were presented and discussed with several focus groups of managers and professionals in the New York and London offices, as it was felt these large, central operations would most efficiently capture the full range of client and functional populations. Also, the U.K. groups were a critical test of the portability of the language, and in fact it was necessary to make significant modifications in the text to better reflect proper British English in this major operating location.

The architectural foundation was now established, and application development could commence. The CTO felt that the approach was sufficiently different that managers would first need an introduction and orientation to the core pipeline concepts. A three-hour overview of key concepts, as well as an introduction to the new model of management and leadership the CTO wished to apply, was developed. The title was "Achieving Excellence Through Your People" to reinforce both the business focus as well as the leadership emphasis of the new approach. A four- to five-hour version of the content with some added introductory skill building in goal setting and coaching was also developed for manager and staff member groups across the offices.

The concept orientation for management covered the following topics in an interactive discussion format:

- *A New Talent Management Focus:* Starting from the demand (work and organization design) side rather than from the supply (people acquisition and development) side to build the core architecture for talent management.

- *Understanding Performance as Results Achieved:* As opposed to activities or competencies alone, the key business requirements are every job being necessary and adding appropriate value, and every staff member being a full performer.

- *Understanding Development and Potential:* Potential is no longer defined as "high," "moderate," or "low," but rather is expressed as the assessed ability and readiness to do different work within the planning period.

- *Understanding the Work of Leaders:* A simple definition of leadership and management and how they interact and together create full capability.

- *Understanding the Pipeline Model:* People had to know its origins, its core definition as an application model based on differentiation of required output, and how each business's pipeline was unique (that is, the book cannot literally be applied). The firm's tailored pipeline model was introduced, along with the performance dimensions, and coverage included the definition of each layer as well as the transition points and associated changes in required skills, time applications, and work values.

- *The New Definition of a Job:* Understanding the new dynamic and interdependent definition of roles at the firm and their placement within the pipeline architecture. Jobs were seen as collections of results to be delivered, many of which required close collaboration with other staff members for achievement.

- *Three Key Skill Sets for Leaders of Other Professionals:* Assessment for selection, performance planning, and assessment for developmental appraisal; coaching for current improvement and future development.

Sessions were held in the major offices, and the reception the concepts received was uniformly positive. While human resources people in particular found the emphasis on results rather than competencies a bit unsettling, line managers and professionals found the approach far more in tune with the reality of their work situations and refreshingly free of process complication and jargon. In particular, people found the concepts and language easy to embrace. Initial signs were hopeful.

PERFORMANCE MANAGEMENT SYSTEM DEVELOPMENT

The core element of the new talent management implementation was to be a completely revised performance management system, and this application is therefore our focus. The CTO felt the key business drivers of revised, specific, and reinforced role definition, significantly strengthened operating concepts of personal accountability, and a clear definition of the management and leadership roles were best covered by this first step. In addition, new cash compensation designs being anticipated were more heavily dependent on a robust performance management process. The other executive committee members agreed.

Design Considerations

The existing, competency-based system was not widely used. There were several reasons for this. Generic competencies were applied, creating the challenge of relating each behavioral definition to each staff member's level and role. The process itself was quite complicated, and the formats were long and daunting for busy managers and their staffs to use. Training and reinforcement had not been adequate to overcome these shortcomings.

As a result, the challenge was to re-introduce performance management as a core management discipline with the new approach. Reaction to the announcement that the old system was being discontinued was universally positive. As the new system needed to be as user friendly as possible, the process design needed to simultaneously:

- Align with Leadership Pipeline principles;

- Provide both specificity and flexibility in defining job requirements and personal accountabilities; and

- Be as easy to understand and use as possible, for people new to both goal-setting-based performance management as well as the results-oriented approach. This last requirement proved to be the most difficult to achieve.

Chosen Approach, Format Development, and Introduction

The new system was titled "Results Based Performance Planning and Appraisal." The business context for this approach was made clear: clients paid the firm for results, not for competencies, capabilities, activity, or effort. Therefore, the new "true north" on management's compass would be the results that individuals, teams, and the firm delivered to clients, staff members, and investors. This message had great resonance with people at all levels in the firm.

Instrument development took the CTO in a different direction than previous pipeline-based performance management applications he was familiar with. The results profile for a client-facing manager (Figure 12.1) provides the rich detail a pipeline definition provides for role clarity, but can introduce a significant amount of process burden when literally applied to performance planning and management. Rather than compromise the comprehensiveness and detail of the results profile, the approach the CTO eventually chose used the results profile as a reference document with a separate instrument driving individual performance planning and review discussions. Both formats are for use by client handlers at the manager-of-managers level.

The CTO elected a simple goal-setting approach to provide individual role specificity to the general performance standards by level. A total of fourteen formats, conforming to the pipeline leadership levels for both client-facing and specialty/support functions, were created using the full performance standards as source content. There were multiple formats for several leadership levels, conforming to differentiated job categories within the lower leadership levels:

- The Manages Self or individual contributor level included forms for administrative support positions, junior individual professional, and senior individual professional positions.

- The Manager of Others level included forms for supervisors/project managers as well as managers. The supervisor/project manager position was a particularly important threshold management role and required some differentiation from the full manager position.

While this number of formats could be difficult to navigate the first time around, the introduction was supported with two-hour orientation and training workshops for managers and staff as well as an easy-to-use, step-by-step tutorial posted on the company's intranet. The overriding advantage of multiple, job-type-specific formats was the ability to use general full performance definitions as individual employee guidance, with specific goals being required in only a few results areas. This ease of use factor was considered very important in gaining early adoption.

The objective of the introductory orientation sessions and online support materials was to familiarize people with two fundamentally new concepts for them: first, the focus on results in defining jobs and performance within them, as opposed to competencies or activities, and second, the use of goal setting to further reinforce personal accountability. It was anticipated that two to three years would be required to achieve full adoption with associated skill mastery for the new system. The formats and process would be refined after the first and second performance management cycles were complete and feedback from managers, staff members, and human resources managers was analyzed.

The rating scale used, which followed the Pipeline approach, was also new for the firm. The three-point scale was created for developmental purposes and was comprised of "exceptional performance," "full performance," and "less than full performance."

The preponderance of ratings—75 percent—would be in the "full performance" range, consistent with the philosophy that virtually all staff should be delivering full performance if properly managed and engaged. "Exceptional performance" was defined as not only significantly superior to full performance on an ongoing basis, but unique and different. Exceptional performance was the qualifier for promotion to significantly greater accountability.

This simple rating system avoided much of the "fluffing" of ratings prevalent in most traditional systems that was caused by managers wishing to avoid demotivating good employees by assessing them as merely "average" or "meeting expectations." Lake Woebegone, that place where everyone is above average, was therefore avoided.

The CTO added an additional performance point, establishing two levels in the full performance category, for base salary planning and administration purposes. This was subsequently implemented and worked well in reinforcing the pay-for-performance approach.

The new formats were tested in several large offices, and these pilots provided valuable feedback regarding changes to process instructions and on-line support content. The formats were introduced in early fourth quarter of 2005 for 2006 performance planning. Managers and employees were given the option of using the new formats for 2005 reviews if they had not had any performance discussions for the year. A number took the CTO up on the offer.

Experience and Action Learning

For performance year 2006, formats were posted as downloadable Word documents in a new suite on the company's human resources intranet site. Support tutorials were also posted. Take-up varied from office to office; however, reported participation and completion rates were significantly higher than with the old system.

An early problem that developed was difficulty in understanding and applying goal setting for many managers and staff members. The CTO, having come from environments with long-established performance management practice, had fallen into the trap of assuming too much familiarity with basic performance management concepts. Follow-up remedial workshops addressed the issue, and for performance year 2007 a performance management workshop focused on skills in creating SMART goals and cascading goals from manager to subordinates in a work team was offered ahead of the performance planning period.

The workshop also provided guidance on completing the performance appraisal step by covering the gathering of performance evidence to properly justify and document assessments. It was offered throughout the course of the year as well as at the commencement of the 2007 appraisal preparation season.

2006 was a year of significant change in other areas of human resources and talent management. The CTO had gained management approval to move to a common base salary review date as well as a common appraisal schedule that supported a pay-for-performance approach. The introduction of the new results-based approach was advanced and reinforced with a more disciplined pay-for-performance process; however, more simultaneous change was heaped on managers already under pressure to maximize personal billability. The CTO had hoped to lessen this impact with an employee-initiated planning and review process; however, both planning and appraisal periods were lengthened and made more flexible to accommodate overloaded managers.

Strong positive feedback was received regarding the effectiveness of the process in clarifying and prioritizing job expectations, as well as structuring development discussions on more specific, quantifiable work requirements for different job levels. The previous competency-based approach had been roundly criticized for its ineffectiveness in specifying differences in performance expectations and standards from job level to job level in career hierarchies.

For 2008, the president had led an effort to update and focus the company's strategy. The strategy coalesced into three results areas (the results concept had been thoroughly embraced and was a prominent part of the operating vocabulary): serving and growing clients; developing people; and cultivating new client prospects. The CTO and his staff updated the core results by level definitions and performance standards for client staff, grouping them into these three strategic buckets to map the strategy goals to every staff member's job. For functional and support staff, the three buckets became professional work product; developing people; and integrating the functional work into the business strategy.

In addition, the 2008 performance management process went to a fully online format for enhanced accessibility and ease of use. Training was further evolved to address reported concerns as well as to orient new managers and staff members in the process. The company entered 2008 having attained an over 95 percent appraisal completion rate and a virtually 100 percent on-time salary adjustment administration performance for 2007—unprecedented in the firm's history.

EVALUATION

Business Results

It is frequently difficult to connect talent management practice directly with business results. Intermediate measures such as unwanted turnover, survey trends, and the like provide more credible evidence of efficacy. Overall, the company produced the best two financial performances in its history in 2006 and 2007, no doubt aided by the strong economic environment that existed in the United States and Western Europe through mid-year 2007. The focus on results, as opposed to activity or effort, and the strong emphasis on personal accountability can certainly be cited as contributing factors.

Employee Climate Survey Results

Survey results are considered proprietary and cannot be cited in detail. However, it is notable that a pulse survey administered in late 2006 showed significant positive trends in all thirteen measured organization climate dimensions. Particularly significant improvements were shown in Morale and Loyalty (the key engagement measure); Quality (that includes performance communication and management practice); and Leadership.

Turnover Results

Overall turnover decreased 24 percent from 2005 to 2006, before rising 14 percent in 2007, amidst a particularly competitive labor market. Turnover of identified high-potential managers stood at virtually 0 percent for 2006 and 2007.

Anecdotal Evidence

The professional services audience easily and enthusiastically embraced the Pipeline concepts. While performance management is still no doubt seen as a difficult and time-consuming process, this is in comparison with very little prior subscription to any performance management activity. Leadership feedback is consistent with other feedback that Drotter has received from other companies: that there is a strong connection with business context and a refreshing absence of professional "jargon." It is viewed as conceptually elegant and easy to embrace. The language of results and accountability, as reported earlier, has become a core part of the leadership language.

Beyond the scope of this paper are the additional applications of the Pipeline concepts for selection, talent inventory, and training planning that were put in place, as well as new management variable compensation plans dependent on the results-based performance management system.

REFERENCE

Charan, R., Drotter, S., & Noel, J. (2001) *The leadership pipeline: How to build the leadership-powered company.* San Francisco: Jossey-Bass.

Greg Waldron is a principal and executive consultant with Drotter Human Resources, a consulting firm focusing on executive succession and the critical related processes. His prior industry experience spans marketing communications, travel and hospitality, financial services, investment banking, and logistics/supply chain management. As a corporate human resources executive, Waldron has been an advisor to the CEO and board, an author of corporate organization studies, and a global leader of the HR function. He has created and implemented talent identification and succession planning processes, executive selection and performance management approaches, and total compensation programs. He has significant experience in helping leadership groups address major business change, including acquisitions, divestitures, management transitions, and initial public offerings.

CHAPTER

13

SOUTHERN COMPANY

JIM GREENE

A robust leadership development and succession planning process that uses leadership performance standards and competencies to identify successors and high-potential individuals, and target development.

241

- Evaluation and Lessons Learned
  - Evaluation
  - Lessons Learned

INTRODUCTION

Having a steady supply of leaders with the right skills in the right jobs is critical to the success of an organization. Facing the possibility that a number of long-tenured leaders across all levels would soon retire, Southern Company enhanced its succession planning and leadership development processes to ensure a full leadership pipeline to sustain business success. This chapter details these processes.

BACKGROUND

Southern Company is an electric utility serving 4.4 million customers in the southeastern United States. A leading U.S. producer of electricity, Southern Company owns electric utilities in four states and a growing competitive generation company, as well as fiber optics and wireless communications. Southern Company brands are known for excellent customer service, high reliability, and retail electric prices that are significantly below the national average. Southern Company has been listed as the top ranking U.S. electric service provider in customer satisfaction for nine consecutive years by the American Customer Satisfaction Index (ACSI). Southern Company employs approximately 26,000 people.

In 2003, America's aging workforce began to receive a lot of attention and was viewed as a potential business challenge for Southern Company. A "grow your own" company, Southern Company historically hired at the entry level and relied on internal promotions rather than external hiring to fill leadership positions. In the late 1970s and 1980s, the company hired a large number of people. A low turnover rate resulted in the leadership group being very stable and growing progressively older. In 2003, the average age of executives was fifty-two. The average ages of middle managers and first-line managers were forty-nine and forty-seven, respectively. This age bubble posed a potential succession risk. Southern Company has developed a cadre of leaders who possessed deep business knowledge and fit the organization and culture. Projections showed that, as executives began to retire in greater numbers, their successors would leave soon after. The need to develop a new generation of leaders became the driver for re-looking at the succession and leadership development efforts to ensure a sustainable supply of quality leaders to meet business needs.

In early 2004, Southern Company's CEO initiated an in-depth review of succession planning and leadership development. The goal of the study was to review current practices and determine the steps necessary to advance leadership development to the next level and ensure an adequate supply of leadership talent over the next ten years. The study began by interviewing a cross-section of executives and managers to gain an internal perspective of the strengths and gaps of the succession planning and leadership development systems. An external consultant was engaged to provide an objective third-party view and to provide best practice research.

The review noted several strengths. Senior leaders were engaged and devoted a significant amount of time to leadership development. During the interviews they talked about conducting mentoring groups and spending time getting to know key high-potential individuals in their company or business unit. Southern Company also had basic processes in place to identify and develop leaders. Succession planning was conducted annually, with its primary focus being on replacement planning. Assignments and development moves were used to provide individuals a wide range of experience. A number of decentralized leadership development activities were in place. These programs utilized a variety of activities, including mentoring, group mentoring, business acumen discussions, and education classes. A corporate action learning program for high-potential first-line leaders was conducted annually.

Several gaps were identified. During the interviews, leaders talked about knowing the high-potential talent in their organization very well. However, they did not know talent across Southern Company. Cross-system calibration of talent was difficult for several reasons. A standard set of information was not available for comparing individuals. Southern Company lacked a comprehensive model that identified the key leadership practices necessary to achieve business success. Across Southern Company there were a number of different definitions of leadership, and emphasis was placed on developing different skills and abilities. A person viewed as high-potential at one location may not have been viewed in a similar light at other locations. Managers also tended to promote individuals they knew and had working relationships with. The study also revealed that the assessment process lacked sufficient rigor to support critical talent decisions. Southern Company has had the luxury of multiple people viewing a person's performance over a long period of time in different jobs and situations. This provided a good indication of people's capabilities. However, because people were viewing leaders through different lenses, there were different opinions of people's capabilities and potential to assume expanded roles. More objective measures to help predict potential were needed.

The succession planning process placed too much emphasis on replacement planning and not enough on developing critical talent pools. There was insufficient focus on high-potential talent five to ten years from the executive level. Leaders reported having difficulty targeting development to the most critical areas. A final gap noted information on succession plans and high-potential individuals was kept in a series of separate files located across Southern Company, making consolidated information difficult to obtain and use.

INITIAL IMPROVEMENTS

Following the review, Southern Company took steps to improve leadership development. The initial effort focused on building a common leadership framework across Southern Company, including a common definition and understanding of leadership. Southern Company adopted the leadership framework articulated by Ram Charan, Stephen Drotter, and James Noel in their book *The Leadership Pipeline: How to Build the Leadership-Powered Company*. Central to this framework is understanding that leadership begins with the work leaders perform. Managers go through key transitions in their careers when they move up the organizational ladder. The scope and complexity of work increases at each level, requiring new skills, time applications, and work values. Southern Company began building its leadership framework by identifying the major leadership transitions within the company and their associated requirements. Stephen Drotter was employed to help customize the framework for Southern Company. Selected executives and managers were interviewed, asking them to identify the major results they needed to produce in their jobs to be successful. This information was analyzed and resulted in six levels of leadership being identified within Southern Company:

- *Individual contributor*—leads self.

- *First-line manager*—leads a team of individual contributors. May have first-line supervisors reporting to him or her.

- *Manager of managers*—Leads a large department or organizational entity. Has first-line managers as direct reports.

- *Functional manager*—Leads a single function or organizational entity. Usually an officer.

- *Multi-functional manager*—Leads multiple functional areas.

- *CEO/business unit manager/enterprise functional manager*—Leads a company, major business unit, or a major function at the enterprise level.

For each level, the associated requirements (performance standards) were identified. Performance standards list the complete set of results expected of leaders at that level. For each level of leadership, the identified results were grouped under the following performance dimensions:

- Business (Operational, Technical, Financial)

- Management

- Leadership

- Relationships

- Community/External Involvement

- Customer

A sample set of performance standards for manager of managers is shown in Figure 13.1.

Business Results (Operational, Technical, Functional)
NOTE: Business results are the specific goals stated in the Business Results section of the performance plan. Please use the performance plan form to document business results and progress against them.
Management
Achieve results by directing the work of other managers & the organization
Produce annual operating/business plans which are connected to functional strategy
Create measurement systems for evaluating & monitoring major goals
Build an organizational structure that supports mission/goals & promotes efficient work processes
Optimize resource allocation & trade-offs among teams
Optimize work processes
Build a strong leadership team with noticeable teamwork that produces results
Ensure that self & direct reports conduct performance management & act on poor performers
Make tough, timely decisions
Effectively handle crisis situations
Measure direct reports on introducing innovative processes/programs; that the value added outweighs the cost
Collaborate & integrate across organizational boundaries
Leadership
Establish & communicate vision & direction such that everyone in organization can articulate direction & goals
Communicate essential information to organization in a timely manner; use managers as communication channel when appropriate
Role model Southern Style; hold team accountable for living Southern Style; ensure managers do the same
Ensure that direct reports collaborate & help with trade-off decisions
Select, develop, & retain effective leaders & a successor
Mentor first level management
Leverage appropriately diverse team; create an inclusive work climate where people trust & value one another
Drive change initiatives
Relationships
Build effective working relationships with manager, direct reports, & the next level(s) down
Build effective networks to get things done (peers, cross functional, business partners, contractors)
Build coalitions to accomplish results
Community/External Involvement
Be an active member of at least one appropriate community & external group
Respond appropriately to community requests for assistance
Use every opportunity to be an effective & knowledgeable spokesperson for Southern Company
Customer
Focus organization on delivering exceptional customer service (internally & externally)
Use the results of customer surveys & feedback (internal and/or external) to improve customer service
Look for opportunities to promote the sale of available Southern Company products

FIGURE 13.1. *Manager of Manager Performance Standards*

The identification of specific performance standards helped leaders understand the expectations for a particular level. They also helped build a common definition of leadership across Southern Company. Performance standards enabled more objective discussions of people and facilitated better development plans. Managers reported that their discussions of people became more objective because they were focused on a common set of expectations.

Performance standards were woven into succession and leadership development processes in several ways. A small group of human resource professionals were trained to conduct behavioral interviews to determine an individual's performance relative to the performance standards. The results of these assessments were used in talent review sessions. Managers were trained to use the performance standards in their development discussions with leaders reporting to them. The performance standards were also used during succession planning to help identify high-potential individuals.

The use of performance standards in the succession planning process took hold in pockets of the organization. Overall, the implementation of performance standards was viewed as a human resource initiative rather than coming from line management. Some organizations used the standards in succession planning, while others used them as part of their development planning for leaders. They were not consistently applied in all parts of the organization. The accuracy of the behavioral interviews conducted by HR professionals was questioned by management. To fix these issues, Southern Company took several steps.

THE LEADERSHIP ACTION COUNCIL

In 2005, Southern Company's CEO chartered a group of executives to serve as the steering committee for leadership development. This council was given the responsibility to develop guidelines and facilitate integration of leadership development programs and processes across Southern Company. The council is made up of senior line executives representing each operating company and business unit and the senior VP of HR. The formation of this council moved leadership development from being a human resource initiative to being line-driven. Human resources served in a partnership role with the council. Southern Company is a highly matrixed organization. Having a council that represented all of the parties was essential to gaining traction.

Building on the work done previously, the Leadership Action Council established project teams to research issues and make recommendations. These teams reviewed the areas of succession planning, leadership assessment, leadership development, and leadership education. Each project team was led by Leadership Action Council members, had line management participation, and utilized HR support. These teams reviewed best practices, gathered management input, determined gaps, and made recommendations. The Leadership Action Council made the following recommendations in 2006.

- Create a competency model aligned closely to the performance standards to assess leadership candidate strengths and weaknesses;

- Implement an external, objective assessment process for executives and high-potential individuals;

- Expand the succession process to focus on creating targeted development plans for successors to executive positions;

- Design and implement a leadership database to capture and track talent information and provide key analytics to assess talent gaps;

- Create a multi-event educational experience for high-potential managers of managers who are ready to move into functional manager (officer) roles; and

- Align operating company/business unit leadership development programs to have a common focus.

The creation of the Leadership Action Council helped Southern Company make major progress in advancing leadership development to the next level. The ongoing involvement of senior executives was critical in revising, gaining approval of, and implementing succession planning and leadership development programs and processes. Described below are the initiatives that Southern Company adopted as an outgrowth of the Leadership Action Council recommendations.

COMPETENCY MODEL

The Leadership Action Council noted that leaders were having difficulty identifying the right development actions. There was also a misalignment between feedback individuals were receiving from an external assessment process and the feedback they were receiving internally. To rectify these problems, a core set of leadership competencies was developed.

Performance standards describe the set of results individual contributors and leaders are expected to produce. These standards were used as the basis for identifying critical leadership competencies. Working with an external organizational consulting firm, Blankenship & Seay Consulting Group, leadership competencies were selected that best aligned with and supported the performance standards. The Leadership Action Council validated these competencies to ensure they were critical to achieving business success. The competency work resulted in the adoption of the nine leadership competencies shown below.

Southern Company Leadership Competencies

- Adapting and responding to change

- Critical thinking

- Deciding and initiating action

- Entrepreneurial and commercial thinking

- Formulating strategies and concepts

- Leading and supervising

- Persuading and influencing

- Planning and organizing

- Relating and networking

Two competencies typically found in leadership competency models, ethical behavior and driving results, were not included because they are emphasized in Southern Company's values statement, Southern Style.

The performance standards and associated leadership competencies now serve as the foundation for all succession planning and leadership development work.

LEADERSHIP ASSESSMENT

A gap in the leadership development model described earlier was lack of a rigorous assessment process. Subjective views of people were used to make developmental and succession decisions. Southern Company supplemented internal views with data from assessments done by an external industrial psychology firm. In partnership with this firm, changes were made to increase rigor and alignment. The new process, used for executives and high-potential leaders, measures an individual against the nine core leadership competencies listed above. The process takes half a day and consists of a battery of psychological-related tests, a simulation exercise, and a structured interview. Participants receive ratings on the nine leadership competencies and a report containing their results and development suggestions. Figure 13.2 shows sample results from the competency assessment. Participants also receive direct feedback from the psychologist. This new process increases the rigor and consistency of executive assessments and provides objective data as input into the succession planning, talent review, and development planning processes.

Southern Company has also revised the 360-degree assessment and upward assessment processes to align with the nine core leadership competencies.

NAME: John Sample
LEADERSHIP LEVEL: Manager of Manager

Competencies	Low		Low-Mid		Mid-Range		High-Mid		High	
	1	2	3	4	5	6	7	8	9	10
Adapting & Responding to Change						●				
Critical Thinking						●				
Deciding & Initiating Action							●			
Entrepreneurial & Commercial								●		
Formulating Strategies							●			
Leading & Supervising				●						
Persuading & Influencing							●			
Planning & Organizing					●					
Relating & Networking						●				

The blue shaded areas represent the expected range for a manager of manager at Southern Company. The range was empirically determined by assessing a cross-section of individuals at this level of leadership, and differs for each level of leadership. The black dots are the individual's score for the particular competency.

FIGURE 13.2. *Sample Leadership Competency Assessment Results*

Leaders receive feedback from subordinates, peers, and their managers on each of the nine competencies and Southern Style (values statement).

SUCCESSION PLANNING

Another recommendation made by the Leadership Action council was to expand the succession planning process to focus on identifying and planning the development of people who can take on expanded leadership roles in the future. Succession planning is done annually and consists of three major steps shown in Figure 13.3.

Identification of Potential Successors and High-Potential Individuals

In this step management identifies candidates who are ready now to fill a critical leadership position should it become vacant and candidates who, with additional development, could fill the position. Plans for all executive and director-level positions are developed. Potential successors are classified as:

- *Ready Now*: An individual who could be placed in the position today, without hesitation. There should be a close match between the requirements of the job and the individual's skills, knowledge, and experience

- *1–2*: An individual who needs additional development in a current position or one additional move to become ready

- *Long Term*: An individual in the pipeline for the targeted position and needs two to three additional moves to become ready

Management judgment, along with the assessment information described earlier, is used to identify potential successors. The identification process is generally bottom-up. A leader in a key role suggests potential successors for his or her position. This list is validated or modified as it is discussed by senior management.

A new tool, called a success profile, was developed to help managers identify the right successors. The success profile specifies the key competencies and experiences required to perform a specific leadership role. Success profiles are created by either interviewing the job incumbents and the direct manager or by sending them an Internet-based survey. The results from the interview or survey are combined and validated by

FIGURE 13.3. *Succession Planning Process*

executive management. Requirements are based on future business needs, not just today's world. Specifically, a success profile identifies:

- The leadership competencies most critical for the position;

- Additional business/technical knowledge, skills, and abilities needed for the job; and

- Key experiences that best prepare someone for the position.

See Figure 13.4 for a sample success profile. Success profiles provide specific criteria for managers to use in selecting successors and identifying readiness. Several examples have been noted whereby the list of successors for a particular job changed as a result of using the success profile. To date, success profiles have been completed

POSITION: Manager, Distribution
MANAGERIAL LEVEL: Manager of Managers

	Low		Low-Mid		Mid-Range		High-Mid		High	
Key Competencies	1	2	3	4	5	6	7	8	9	10
Deciding and Initiating Action					▓	▓	▓			
Leading and Supervising					▓	▓	▓			
Planning and Organizing							▓	▓		
Relating and Networking							▓	▓		
Other Competencies										
Adapting and Responding to Change							▓	▓		
Critical Thinking					▓	▓	▓			
Entrepreneurial and Commercial					▓	▓				
Formulating Strategies			▓	▓	▓	▓				
Persuading and Influencing					▓	▓				

Critical Knowledge, Skills, and Abilities
- A knowledge of distribution operations, including field work, applications, and restoration activities
- Solid understanding of budget activities/processes
- General understanding of and familiarity with metering, fleet operations, and distribution planning
- Knowledge of disaster preparation and restoration activities (internal and external)
- A technical knowledge of Distribution Systems and Equipment
- Basic knowledge of Distribution coordination practices
- Basic knowledge of computer systems and programs that are used in Distribution
- Basic knowledge of accounting practices used in Utilities
- Basic knowledge of Distribution Indices like SAIDI, SAIFI, Customer Value
- Broad business knowledge

Experiences
- Committee involvement at the SoCo level would be beneficial since this position represents Distribution at the SoCo level
- Storm restoration experience
- Experience in building consensus among different entities/groups
- Good understanding of how each electric utility department works and their dependencies on each other. This also includes the dependencies of Operating Company to Operating Company

FIGURE 13.4. *Sample Success Profile*

for some executive positions, and plans are to complete them for all executive and director-level jobs.

In addition to successors, management identifies high-potential individuals during the succession process. This is also done using a bottom-up approach. Managers identify individuals within their organization whom they judge to have the potential to take on expanded roles. This list is validated or modified as it is reviewed by managers up the chain.

"Potential" addresses the aptitude to perform work at the next leadership level. Managers rate the promotability of all leaders at the manager-of-manager level and above using the following categories:

- *Promotable:* able to make the turn to the next leadership level within two or three years. These individuals are high-potential.

- *Growth:* able to do additional work, run other functions, or manage a broader organization at the same leadership level.

- *Well placed:* having neither turn nor growth promotability.

The performance standards are the basis for making the judgment on promotability.

Below the manager-of-manager level, leaders list their high-potential individuals, rather than rating the promotability of everyone in their organizations. This is done due to large numbers. The following definition is used to assist managers in identifying high-potential individuals:

- *Sustained high performance.* High-potential individuals have demonstrated sustained high performance over time.

- *Foundation skills.* High-potential individuals possess a set of skills that allows them to grow quickly and adapt to different situations. These include drive/ambition, strong interpersonal skills, presence, ability to learn and apply new skills quickly, strong political/organizational skills, ability to adapt to change, and resilience.

- *Ability to perform future leadership roles.* High-potential individuals demonstrate the aptitude to perform the performance standards at the next level of leadership.

Assessment of the Talent

In this step, successors and high-potential individuals are assessed by the external industrial psychology firm using the process previously discussed. All successors and high-potential individuals are not assessed in a single year. Rather, assessment data is built over time, refreshing the assessment information as needed. Everyone who is being reviewed by one of the executive talent review teams (described below) is assessed. Others are assessed on an as-needed basis.

Review of Individuals

In this step, successors and high-potentials are reviewed by executive management for the purpose of getting to know them and targeting development actions. Generally:

- Successors for senior officer positions are reviewed by the Southern Company CEO and his direct reports.

- Successors for officer positions are reviewed by operating company or business unit CEOs and their direct reports.

- Other high-potentials are reviewed by department management.

Talent reviews are done slightly differently in each operating company, but usually consist of:

- Review of the person's background, education, and major accomplishments;

- Information from the external leadership competency assessment;

- Identification of possible career path(s);

- Identification of major development needs; and

- Identification of development actions needed to accelerate development, such as potential moves or assignments, development actions in current job, coaching/mentoring, education, or participation in a specific leadership development program or activity.

Each management council reviews twelve to sixteen individuals per year. Usually, the candidate being reviewed meets with each council member prior to the review meeting so that each executive can get to know him or her. Following the discussion, the individual is provided feedback by council members, and the development plan is modified as needed. These individuals are tracked over time to make sure they are receiving the development they need to prepare for new roles.

A new tool called a candidate profile was developed to help identify the right development actions. The candidate profile compares an individual's assessment results to the specific job criteria listed on the success profile discussed earlier. The competency assessment is from the external assessment. Critical knowledge, skills, and abilities are rated by people within the organization knowledgeable of the person's performance. Candidate profiles are used after a success profile has been completed and the assessment information is available. See Figure 13.5 for a sample candidate profile.

Succession planning begins during the first quarter in the operating companies and business units. They complete plans for all executive and director-level positions and identify their high-potential individuals. Plans are created for other key roles as needed.

Succession plans for the top sixty-five positions across Southern Company are consolidated and reviewed by the Southern Company CEO and his direct reports. This

POSITION: Manager, Distribution
MANAGERIAL LEVEL: Manager of Managers

Key Job Challenges:

		Low		Low-Mid		Mid-Range		High-Mid		High	
Key Competencies		1	2	3	4	5	6	7	8	9	10
Deciding & Initiating Action							•				
Leading & Supervising									•		
Planning & Organizing						•					
Relating & Networking									•		
Other Competencies											
Adapting & Responding to Change								•			
Critical Thinking						•					
Entrepreneurial & Commercial							•				
Formulating Strategies						•					
Persuading & Influencing										•	

Critical Knowledge, Skills, and Abilities

None	Some	Proficient	
		X	A knowledge of distribution operations, including field work, applications, and restoration activities
	X		Solid understanding of budget activities/processes
		X	General understanding of and familiarity with metering, fleet operations, and distribution planning
	X		Knowledge of disaster preparation and restoration activities (internal and external)
		X	A technical knowledge of Distribution Systems and Equipment
	X		Basic knowledge of Distribution coordination practices
			Basic knowledge of computer systems and programs that are used in Distribution
X			Basic knowledge of accounting practices used in Utilities
		X	Basic knowledge of Distribution Indices like SAIDI, SAIFI, Customer Value
	X		Broad business knowledge

Experiences

None	Some	Proficient	
X			Committee involvement at the SoCo level would be beneficial since this position represents Distribution at the SoCo level
	X		Storm restoration experience
	X		Experience in building consensus among different entities/groups
	X		Good understanding of how each electric utility department works and their dependencies on each other. This also includes the dependencies of Operating Company to Operating Company

FIGURE 13.5. *Sample Candidate Profile*

fosters cross-calibration of talent and a better understanding of the executive bench strength across Southern Company. The Management Council also reviews executive turnover and movement, potential executive retirements, and leadership demographics. Action plans are created to address emerging issues. The Southern Company CEO reviews the succession plans of key executives with the board of directors.

LEADERSHIP DATABASE

All of the information related to succession plans and high-potentials is housed in Oracle's PeopleSoft application. The succession planning and career development modules within PeopleSoft are used. Some modifications to the panels and standard reports were made. This functionality enables us to:

- Create and report succession lists for individual jobs;

- Combine succession lists across companies to create and report system-wide succession slates;

- Track high-potential people identified during the succession process;

- Track and report on individuals nominated for and completing leadership development programs; and

- Create employee profile reports.

Security limits access to the information to specific human resource professionals across Southern Company.

DEVELOPMENT ACTIVITIES

Southern Company uses a variety of methods to develop successors and high-potential individuals. Job assignments, development moves, and special assignments are the primary methods of development. Developmental assignments flow from succession planning and management reviews. Development assignments are monitored at the corporate/operating company/business unit level. As a practice, all open positions below the executive level are posted on an internal job board. Development moves are an exception to this practice and generally require executive approval.

Senior Leader Development Program

A gap in development efforts was that high-potential middle managers were not prepared to move into officer positions. An educational experience to address this need was developed in 2008 jointly by Southern Company human resources and Duke Corporate Education. This program, titled the Senior Leader Development Program, was delivered in 2008 and 2009. The program is grounded by two sessions, four days each. The program content focuses on:

- Understanding how global, environmental, regulatory, and human capital challenges are impacting the future of the energy industry;

- Examining methods to make objective, disciplined decisions in an increasingly uncertain business climate;

- Building strong networks of relationships to drive organizational change;

- Developing capabilities to manage diversity, complexity, and ambiguity;

- Creating a vision of the future for self and the company; and

- Articulating personal commitment to action.

    A variety of learning components are incorporated in the program.

- Presentations and discussions with Southern Company executives, university professors, and external thought leaders;

- Case studies;

- Activities designed to help participants apply learning to current business issues; and

- Networking opportunities with fellow class participants and Southern Company executives.

    Participant feedback about the program was strong. Among the noted highlights were

- Interaction with and insights gained from Southern Company executives;

- Networking and building relationships with peers from around the company;

- Modules on finance, leadership presence, and difficult discussions; and

- Opportunity for personal reflection.

    Later in 2009 each participant will be interviewed to gather feedback about the impact of the program, specifically, how the learning is being applied to real business and leadership issues.

Emerging Leader Programs

Below the corporate level, operating companies and business units have the responsibility for providing development activities and programs for high-potential emerging leaders. These programs increase business acumen and leadership skills, leverage networking opportunities, and increase exposure to senior leaders. These programs typically last twelve to twenty-four months.

These leadership development activities and programs develop the following leadership competencies.

- Critical thinking;

- Persuading and influencing;

- Planning and organizing; and

- Relating and networking.

Emphasis is also placed on the remaining five leadership competencies, as well as career development and business knowledge. The specific activities in these programs vary based on specific business need. Following is a menu of activities that are used.

- *Group mentoring sessions.* Program participants are divided into small groups, and each group is paired with a senior executive. Mentoring groups generally set their own agendas and focus on gaining business knowledge, career development, and leadership knowledge and lessons.

- *Common education.* Participants attend a defined set of educational activities focused at building core competencies.

- *Action learning.* Participants take part in projects aimed at gaining business knowledge and leadership skills. Participants are divided into small groups, and each group researches and makes recommendations on a specific business problem or issue.

- *Forums.* These are large-scale events focused on specific business and leadership topics.

- *Group discussions.* Participants are divided into small groups wherein they discuss common topics. For example, the group may read and discuss a leadership book.

EVALUATION AND LESSONS LEARNED

Evaluation

Metrics to measure the effectiveness of leadership development at Southern Company are evolving. The strength of the leadership bench is evaluated using the following measures that come out of the succession planning process.

- Percent of key roles with at least two ready now successors;

- Average number of successors per key role;

- Demographics of successor pool;

- Percent of key jobs filled from succession list;

- Number of cross-company and cross-functional executive moves; and

- Projections of leader attrition.

Recently, Southern Company began entering information on high-potential individuals into PeopleSoft. At the completion of the current round of succession planning, the following additional metrics will be analyzed:

- The size and demographics of the high-potential pool;

- The number and type of high-potential job moves; and

- Turnover of the high-potential pool compared to the overall pool.

As additional data are collected from external assessments on executives, successors, and high-potential individuals, overall competency strengths and gaps will be identified to better target development programs.

Lessons Learned

Critical to success was the ownership by the Leadership Action Council of leadership development and the improvement of the process. Too often HR had tried to design and implement systems without executive support and buy-in. Once the CEO established the Leadership Action Council, the council members became the drivers of the initiatives. They were able to get input and support from their "home" organizations as well as look at what was best for Southern Company as a whole.

A second lesson learned was the necessity to simplify and integrate the various parts of succession planning and leadership development. Simple things like tying development and succession planning together enabled people to see the big picture. Early in the process leaders said they were creating succession lists in one place, high-potential lists in another, and planning development in a third. They did not see how these activities connected until they were integrated. The language must be consistent and the various tools and processes linked. The output of the external assessment process, the success profile, and the candidate profile all have a similar look and use the same set of competencies.

REFERENCE

Charan, R., Drotter, S., & Noel, J. (2001). *The leadership pipeline: How to build the leadership-powered company.* San Francisco: Jossey-Bass.

Jim Greene is currently assistant to the senior vice president of human resources, diversity and inclusion at Southern Company. Prior to his current assignment, he was director of executive succession and development. In this role he had responsibility for leadership development strategy and processes, succession planning, executive assessment, and executive development. Greene has spent twenty-three years at Southern Company serving in a variety of human resource roles. Prior to Southern Company, he spent three years as a management consultant and ten years in mental health/mental retardation. He holds a master's degree in educational psychology from the University of Florida and completed selected post-graduate work in educational psychology and organizational behavior at West Virginia University.

CHAPTER

14

WHIRLPOOL CORPORATION

KRISTEN WEIRICK

The development and refinement of a customized leadership competency model with robust analytics and integrated assessment training to build deep capability.

Whirlpool Corporation would like to acknowledge Michael Tobin, Ph.D., of Vantage Leadership Consulting. Mr. Tobin's knowledge of leadership development and coaching, combined with his deep and insightful perspective of the company's unique organizational culture, fueled the development of Whirlpool's Leadership Model and resulting tools and resources.

INTRODUCTION

Whirlpool Corporation is the world's leading manufacturer and marketer of major home appliances. Founded in 1911 by Lou Upton, Whirlpool initially produced motor-driven wringer washing machines. Today Whirlpool Corporation realizes annual sales of approximately $19 billion, has 73,000 employees, and maintains approximately seventy manufacturing and technology research centers around the world. Whirlpool Corporation manufactures and markets major brand names that include Whirlpool, Maytag, KitchenAid, Jenn-Air, Amana, Brastemp, Consul, and Bauknecht to consumers in nearly every country around the world.

During its first fifty years, the company grew and expanded manufacturing operations to include a full range of kitchen and home appliances. By the 1970s, company leadership began globalizing with expanded operations in Brazil, Mexico, and India. Whirlpool Corporation accelerated its global expansion in the 1990s, with an expanded presence throughout Europe, Latin America, Asia, and parts of Africa. The company was on its way to becoming the global leader in the home appliance industry.

With the acquisition of Maytag Corporation in 2006, the company drove efficiencies that resulted in an even stronger organization that was able to offer more to consumers in the increasingly competitive global marketplace. Whirlpool Corporation became a more efficient supplier to trade customers while offering a broader portfolio of innovative, high-quality branded products and services to consumers.

THE BUSINESS CHALLENGE

For most of the company's history, the right talent was easily and readily available to help drive the business. However, a number of factors emerged over the past two decades that have impacted how Whirlpool Corporation attracts, engages, and develops talent to ensure it has the level of leadership to succeed in a constantly changing global business environment.

- The growth, size, and scale of the business added a level of complexity that required different skill sets and capabilities to compete in the global marketplace. Those skill sets and capabilities either had to be developed internally or acquired through new hires externally.

- Along with the change in the size and scale of the business, the external consumer marketplace was demanding fast-paced change and innovation in products and services. The development of technology-enabled products to meet the changing needs of consumers was necessary to compete globally. Innovative and technology-savvy talent was needed to meet these demands.

- The new global marketplace drove increased competition for market share and talent. During this time, companies experienced the shift from an employer's market to a candidate's market in which great talent was both highly desired and scarce.

■ In addition to the competition for talent, the nature of the workforce was also changing. Decreasing corporate loyalty, business outsourcing, and the needs of the talent marketplace were creating an environment in which employee tenure declined. Workers more easily changed jobs, companies, and locations in search of better opportunities.

In summary, a "perfect talent storm" was brewing: a more complex and globalized market, demanding better talent to drive greater results and differentiation and an increasing scarcity of the talent that could provide it. It was imperative to have a defined set of leadership competencies and a talent management system in place that would enable the company to:

1. Define the type of leadership it needed to continue to be successful.

2. Assess the company's current leadership competencies and talent and define any gaps.

3. Develop the necessary leadership competencies internally.

4. Assess all future leaders against these competencies for external acquisition and internal talent pool succession planning.

5. Provide a consistent set of tools, resources, and defined process to manage the company's talent on a global scale.

6. Deeply embed the competencies and operationalize the supporting tools and resources.

DESIGN AND APPROACH

Phase I—Leadership Competency Development

In 1999, Whirlpool Corporation began development of its leadership competencies, which became known as the Whirlpool Leadership Model. The model was developed with active leadership participation and input from the company's executive committee and then-chairman David Whitwam.

The goal of the Leadership Model (Figure 14.1) was to provide a common language for leadership around assessing and developing employees, managing talent pool and succession planning, and assessing external talent for acquisition. The model is unique to Whirlpool Corporation as it defines *who* is wanted as a leader, *what* leaders are expected to do, and *how* they are expected to perform. The "who," "what," and "how" of Whirlpool's Leadership Model have been organized in terms of leadership *attributes, practices,* and *performance.*

Leadership Attributes describe the characteristics and behaviors expected of leadership at Whirlpool Corporation. The company expects its leaders to have great *Character* and *Enduring Values.* Long before the demise of many companies due to compromised ethics, such as Enron in the late nineties or the mortgage and banking

Whirlpool's Leadership Model

Leadership Attributes	Leadership Practices	Leadership Performance
1. Character and Enduring Values	1. Vision	1. Extraordinary Results
2. Confidence	2. Strategy	
	3. Communication	2. Driver of Change/ Transformation
3. Diversity and Inclusion	4. Management Skills	
4. Thought Leadership	5. Attracting, Developing, & Engaging Talent	
	6. Customer Champion	

FIGURE 14.1. *Whirlpool Corporation Leadership Model*

industries at the beginning of the 2008 recession, Whirlpool Corporation defined and demanded a high level of character and integrity in its Leadership Model.

In addition to *Character and Enduring Values*, an appropriate level of *Confidence* and forward-looking ideas (*Thought Leadership*) were defined as necessary leadership attributes. Confidence is defined as the ability to take appropriate and decisive actions and develop confidence in people and organizations that lead to responsible risk taking and the ability to win. Thought Leadership is viewed as the ability to consistently challenge and improve thinking and decision-making processes to develop innovative thinking and sophisticated judgments that lead to positive results.

Finally, the model defined the attribute of *Diversity and Inclusion*. Leaders must create an engaging environment that leverages each individual's thoughts, beliefs, and ideas to achieve optimal results for the company and its customers.

Leadership Practices address the company's needs for people who exercise *Vision* and *Strategy*. Great leaders must be able to create a vision and a strategy to support it and persuasively align stakeholders and the organization to achieve the vision. Leaders must exhibit excellent *Communication and Management Skills*, communicating clearly and with candor and engaging in dialogue to enable alignment. They must also demonstrate effective management and delegation skills to drive results through others.

Leaders must be deeply concerned with their ability to *Attract, Develop, and Engage Talent* around them. Each leader must focus on his or her own development needs, as well as the needs of those around them. Finally, leaders must be able to consistently put the customer at the heart of every process (*Customer Champion*).

Leadership Performance focuses on the requirement to generate *Extraordinary Results* and be a *Driver of Change and Transformation* within the company. Great leaders are able to deliver performance and results that are truly extraordinary—beyond what is expected. They must also be able to anticipate future needs of the business and creatively mobilize resources to meet and exceed those needs.

Whirlpool Corporation's Leadership Model was created exclusively for Whirlpool based on what the organization was like at the time and on how the company wanted to succeed in the future. It was also purposely designed to create a very high bar for talent within the organization—against which all current and future leaders would be assessed.

Embedding the Leadership Model required that leaders at all levels and the human resources organization have a clear understanding of the model and its implications. Training and guides were used to educate both leadership and employees. The leadership model was emphasized in assessments of talent potential and annual performance appraisals. Discussion of an employee's potential begins with his or her leadership model assessment, which is also a consideration for their nine-box rating. Performance appraisals include a section on behaviors based on the leadership model and our values, ensuring that *how* an individual achieves accomplishments is as important as the results.

Phase II—Top Talent Indicator and Derailer Definition and Deployment

While the Leadership Model was successfully embedded into the people processes and culture of the organization, it also presented a major challenge: It was cumbersome. With a total of twelve competencies spanning attributes, practices, and performance, the model provided a comprehensive and hefty view of leadership. However, practical ongoing application necessitated further definition of the company's Top Talent Indicators and Derailers.

The Leadership Model continues to be the foundation of leadership competencies at Whirlpool Corporation. However, each of the competencies of the Leadership Model was analyzed to determine which were most indicative of high potential or "top talent" within the organization. Whirlpool Corporation looked at the company's most successful leaders—those who had continuously delivered successful results over time, demonstrating both performance and potential. Through this analysis of performance and potential against the Leadership Model, four competencies, or "top talent indicators," emerged. Specifically, leaders who demonstrated the Leadership Model competencies of *Thought Leadership, Extraordinary Results, Driver of Change*, and *Attracting, Engaging, and Developing Talent* were almost always successful at Whirlpool Corporation. Those competencies were identified as top talent indicators.

In the same analysis, however, it was discovered that either a lack or, in some cases, excess of one of three of the other Leadership Model competencies could derail success—even in the presence of success in the other top talent Indicators. The top talent derailers were identified as a lack of *Character and Values*, a lack of *Management Skills*, or a lack or excess of *Confidence*. For example, a leader who consistently demonstrates all four of the top talent indicators but is also arrogant (excess of confidence) will not be successful over the long haul unless he or she is provided with the right feedback and coaching to better align with the competency of *confidence*.

With the top talent indicators and derailers defined, the challenge centered around developing a global training curriculum that highlighted the indicators and derailer competencies and educated employees across the globe on how to identify them and differentiate levels of competence of an indicator on a five-point scale. The training consisted of four modules delivered over two days and covered:

- **Module 1**: Building a deeper understanding of each of the top talent indicators and derailers and how to discern them at differentiated levels.

- **Module 2:** Recognizing and eliminating biases and traps that may impede the assessment process.

- **Module 3a:** Utilizing the top talent indicators and derailers to assess external talent and appropriately calibrate assessment results.

- **Module 3b:** Utilizing the top talent indicators and derailers to assess internal talent and calibrating results in talent pool and succession planning processes.

The use of simple, yet highly effective tools reinforced learning and provided sustainable reminders for application. The modules were accompanied by a toolkit of resources that included interview guides and reference tools. The "bias card" (Figure 14.2), while simple, provided a handy reminder of different types of biases and how to minimize their effect in the assessment process.

The Top Talent Indicator and Derailer Training Modules and tools were developed and launched globally in 2005. As it was important to drive a top-down approach, the training began with the company's executive committee and senior-most leadership. Over a period of five months, it was delivered to leaders of people in all regions across the globe.

Phase III—Business Acceleration Drives "Next Level" Talent Assessment

In April 2006, Whirlpool Corporation acquired Maytag Corporation, making them the true leader in the global appliance industry. The company's competence in the assessment of "top talent" was stressed through the rapid assessment of all Maytag talent. In order to drive required efficiencies and ensure that the newly acquired employees from Maytag were treated with the respect they deserved, Whirlpool committed to assess and deliver decisions regarding Maytag heritage employees' status within ninety days of the acquisition.

Through a combination of deep assessment- and efficiency-driven decisions, offers were extended, and the new organization began to emerge. While Whirlpool

MINIMIZING THE EFFECTS OF BIASES AND TRAPS

We all interpret new information based on our own filters on the world. Culture, education, attitudes, and beliefs all contribute to our individual perspectives. While such biases are natural, they are not universal. The ability to recognize biases and traps will enable an individual to look beyond them in an assessment.

"Planters" Bias: Assessing an individual with a preconception in mind based on discussion with other colleagues who know or have assessed the individual.	❑ Refrain from asking colleagues for their impressions of a candidate before speaking with him/her personally ❑ Do not offer up information about a candidate before your colleagues speak with him/her personally
First Impression Bias: Making an overall judgment about an individual based on job-irrelevant data or impressions collected during the first few minutes of an interview.	❑ Make note of any impressions you have in the first few minutes, acknowledge them and determine to suspend judgment until the end of the meeting
"Wow" Factor Bias: Judging one candidate more favorably than others based on his/her tremendous accomplishment or other notable fact.	❑ Do not ignore tremendous accomplishments as they can be indicative of the candidate's character (determination, tenacity, competitiveness, drive for performance, etc.) ❑ Be aware of the impression these accomplishments have on your assessment of the individual and determine not to give them more weight than you give to other data you gather
Negative Emphasis Trap: Rejecting a candidate on the basis of a small amount of negative information.	❑ Probe to understand any points that concern you about the candidate and your initial impression ❑ Look for both confirming and disconfirming information ❑ Weight this information in proportion to all other information you have about the candidate
Contrast Effect Trap: Strong candidates interviewed after weak ones may appear more qualified than they actually are because of the contrast.	❑ Document the criteria and performance standard you expect of all candidates in advance – take these into an assessment with you as a reminder ❑ Document statements and examples that appropriately factor into your decision-making and compare candidates on this basis

Module 2 Tool 1 Ver 4 Revised 12.10.05

FIGURE 14.2. *Assessment Bias Card*

received a higher than average rate of acceptances, Whirlpool went from a typical load of sixty-five open requisitions at any one time to more than two hundred. The resulting talent and resource requirements necessitated a rapid growth of the talent acquisition function (300 percent over a twelve-month period) as well as the need to further build and embed the capability to assess external talent.

To address the need, the master assessor program (MAP) was launched in June 2006 to skill and equip targeted individuals—both HR professionals and line managers with frequent hiring needs—with a mastery level of assessing talent to ensure the bar for talent was kept high. Upon successful completion of the training, an individual was certified as a "master assessor of talent." The rigorous training program includes a one-day classroom session followed by months of practical training. Once certified, a master assessor developed the capability to:

- Describe and identify behaviors demonstrated by top talent;

- In real-time assessments, confidently differentiate top talent from competent talent;

- Identify relevant information in resumes; elicit highly relevant information from candidates in fair, productive interviews;

- Write a clear, professional, accurate assessment report;

- Lead and/or participate in calibration meetings with colleagues and contribute substantial insight into final decisions of candidates' assessment, hiring decisions; and

- Once certified, teach and supervise subsequent master assessor program participants.

The rigorous practicum following the classroom session truly differentiated MAP from previous training. It provided participants with actual experience and immediate coaching and feedback on their assessment capabilities. Individuals in the certification process completed three phases of practicum with actual candidates that included (1) observing a certified master assessor conducting candidate assessments, (2) co-conducting candidate assessments with a certified master assessor, and (3) conducting candidate assessments while being observed by a certified master assessor.

Since the program's launch in 2006, close to fifty master assessors have been certified at Whirlpool Corporation. With a goal of having at least one certified assessor on every interview team, the company continues to ensure a high bar for talent and further embedment of the leadership competencies defined in the top talent indicators and derailers.

EVALUATION

A key measure that is directly related to the effectiveness of Whirlpool Corporation's assessment capabilities for defined leadership competencies is its "Quality of Hire Report." The recently launched quality-of-hire metric is designed to provide a measure of the company's ability to assess and hire top-quartile talent. The report is developed through a short survey of a new hire's supervisor at both the six- and twelve-month marks and consists of survey questions targeting four key criteria:

- Satisfaction

- Promotability

■ Leadership (as measured against the top talent indicators and derailers)

■ Performance to date

Whirlpool Corporation's quality of hire report provides a visual snapshot of the company's overall quality of hire metric and can be segmented by function and individual. The resulting reports and dashboards allow for the comparison of functional and individual hiring measures. Figure 14.3 demonstrates an individual report sample and Figure 14.4 depicts a functional dashboard sample.

Whirlpool Corporation's quality of hire metric measures the effectiveness of the company's candidate assessment capabilities and its Master Assessor Program by tracking all hires that were assessed by a MAP-certified interviewer. The company is also planning on correlating the quality of hire results to the effectiveness of various sources. As a source effectiveness measure, the company will be provided with actionable information to make decisions regarding external sourcing strategies.

Initial results from the quality of hire metric indicate that the MAP process has had a very positive impact on quality of hire. The average score on the quality of hire index indicates the company's new hires are being assessed as well above average. The level of leadership attributes displayed by new hires, as measured against the top talent indicators and derailers, shows almost 50 percent were rated consistently at a level of 4 on a 5-point scale, with 5 considered "role model." Assessed on their potential at Whirlpool, 77 percent of new hires were deemed promotable at least one band[1] level in the next three to five years, with 17 percent seen as promotable at least two band levels. Measured on their performance to date, 93 percent of new hires are already producing strong results, with 43 percent achieving very strong or exceptional results. However, one of the most significant measures revealed that almost 100 percent of new hires would be recommended for another role within the organization, showing high levels of satisfaction. In other words, the value that the newly acquired talent is bringing to Whirlpool Corporation is exceptional.

NEXT STEPS

Given the success of the master assessor program (MAP), Whirlpool Corporation is in the process of developing MAP Level II training. The new training program continues to target deeper embedment of the top talent indicators and derailer competencies. However, the focus of MAP Level II is tailored to the internal succession planning and talent pool process. The training and certification will consist of a Level II classroom session reinforcing the leadership competencies and top talent indicators and derailers, providing application guidance to the internal assessment process and building awareness of the differences between internal and external assessment. The certification process following the classroom session will focus on actual participation and calibration in a series of talent pool sessions with a certified Level II MAP assessor.

Quality of Hire – Sample Individual Report

Jane Employee

Position: Financial Analyst Senior
Band: 6

Hiring Manager: Joe Supervisor
Function: Finance

Gender: Female
Education: State College (BA); Harvard (MBA)
Experience: Arthur Andersen; Mercer Consulting;
Procter & Gamble China; Lincoln Financial

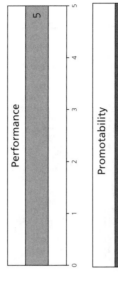

FIGURE 14.3. *Individual Quality of Hire Report*

267

268

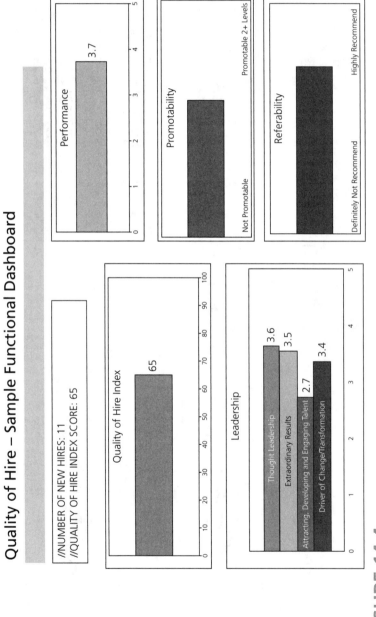

FIGURE 14.4. *Functional Quality of Hire Dashboard*

SUMMARY

Over the past decade, Whirlpool Corporation has defined, implemented, and embedded a leadership competency model and assessment methodology that serves as the foundation for all its critical people and talent management processes, including performance management, talent acquisition, talent pool, and succession planning. All the tools, resources, and training to develop leadership, drive employee engagement, and build capability are deeply embedded and integrated with the strategy for driving the future of the business.

NOTE

1. Whirlpool Corporation has a banded compensation structure with multiple role levels within one band. An example of two-band-level promotability wouldbe moving from a manager to a vice president within three to five years.

Kristen Weirick is the director of talent acquisition at Whirlpool Corporation. She is responsible for directing talent acquisition activities for the global appliance manufacturer, with a strong focus on leading the company's global employer brand strategy and the development and management of systems, tools, and processes that support recruiting and talent management. Weirick began her career with Whirlpool Corporation in 1997 and has held roles of increasing responsibility. She holds a bachelor of arts degree in communications with a specialization in human resource development from Oakland University.

CONCLUSION

Everything should be as simple as it is, but not simpler.

—ALBERT EINSTEIN

The case studies presented in this book provide a detailed picture of how fourteen organizations have successfully responded to challenges in talent management. The tipping points for action were varied, and included declining growth, a lack of qualified external hires, a need for internal succession planning, and the need to align talent strategy with business strategy. While the solutions were uniquely crafted to the needs of each company, each utilized the six-phase strategy advocated by the Best Practice Institute: Business Diagnosis, Assessment, Program Design, Implementation, On-the-Job Support, and Evaluation.

In order to present a fuller and more complete picture of the best practices in talent management, in March 2009 the Best Practice Institute released results from a groundbreaking online survey of some of America's most dynamic companies. The *Talent Management Survey* included twenty questions that addressed the heart of today's talent management challenges. Responses from fifty-one senior management professionals has allowed us to define, in a way not possible before, the best practices of leaders in industries including healthcare, government, financial services, energy, business services, consulting, information technology, the non-profit sector, and others. A sampling of the companies surveyed include the following:

Agilent Technologies

American Family Insurance

American International Group, Inc.

APS Arizona Public Service

Art Gallery of Ontario (AGO)

Baptist St. Anthony's Healthcare System

Baxter Healthcare

BBN Technologies

Best Buy

CalPERS

Cargill

Corning Inc.

Gap Inc.

Intel Corp

Internal Revenue Service

IRS

Johns Hopkins University

JohnsonDiversey

Kaiser Permanente Colorado Region

London Health Sciences Centre

Medtronic

Medtronic China

Motion Picture Industry Pension and Health Plans

Raytheon Missile Systems

Saudi Aramco

The YMCA of Greater Rochester

Trillium Health Centre

Trubion Pharmaceuticals

Tundra Semiconductor

Tyco Electronics

University of Connecticut

Upstate Cerebral Palsy

Whirlpool Corporation

The *Talent Management Survey* results complement the case studies presented in this book. In some instances the results affirm what we have learned through the case studies, and in other ways they provide startling new insights that could only have been revealed through a personal response survey.

AN OVERVIEW OF TALENT MANAGEMENT PROGRAMS: DIAGNOSIS AND ASSESSMENT

Coming together is a beginning; keeping together is progress; working together is success.

—HENRY FORD

Of the fifty-one respondents to the *Talent Management Survey*, we found that a vast majority—forty-two, or over 82 percent—have either a formal or informal talent management program in place (Table C.1). Another four have no plan but intend to create one, while only five reported that they had no plan and did not intend to create one. The overwhelming support for talent management plans indicates that organizations take very seriously their commitment to their people, and they recognize that human capital is not an afterthought but an integral part of a company's success or failure.

Are talent management programs only for the biggest and wealthiest companies? Surprisingly, the answer is no (Table C.2). Of the thirty-one organizations that reported having formal, budgeted talent management plans, eleven respondents were indeed

TABLE C.1. **Companies with and Without Talent Management Plans, Ranked by Response (n=15)**

Type of Talent Management Plan	Percentage	Responses
Formal plan in place	60.8	31
Informal plan in place	21.6	11
No plan, no intention of making a plan	9.8	5
No plan, but intend to create one	7.8	4
TOTAL	100.00	51

TABLE C.2. **Companies with Formal Talent Management Plans, Ranked by Number of Employees in Company (n=31)**

Number of Employees	Percentage	Responses
25,001+	35.5	11
1–100	16.1	5
N/A	12.8	4
5,001–10,000	9.6	3
101–500	6.5	2
501–1,000	6.5	2
1,001–5,000	6.5	2
10,001–25,000	6.5	2
TOTAL	100.00	31

from larger companies with 25,000 employees or more. But the next biggest responding group is small businesses with fewer than one hundred employees. Other responses come from organizations with a variety of staff counts.

Talent management program budgets (Table C.3) vary from under $100,000 to over $20 million. These findings confirm the belief of Best Practice Institute that talent management programs are accepted by, and appropriate for, companies of all sizes.

What spurs a company to initiate a talent management program? Our case studies revealed a wide variety of circumstances. Kaiser Permanente Colorado discovered that too many—65 percent—of its executive hires were coming from outside the company. Ecolab needed qualified executives to meet its aggressive growth projections. McDonald's needed to toughen and define internal promotion metrics because job performance evaluations were unreliable.

The Best Practice Institute's *Talent Management Survey* reveals that the number one catalyst for change was the need to align employee goals with business goals (Table C.4). What does this mean? A colloquial expression is "getting everyone on the same page," or, as Henry Ford said, "Working together is success." Getting internal alignment is critical whether a company has thousands of employees or a dozen: a wagon being pulled in opposite directions isn't going anywhere.

The need for improved productivity ranks high; this is closely related to the need for internal alignment. The number three reason is succession planning, which is a common internal issue and one faced by Southern Company, for example, with dozens of key executives reaching retirement age. Other catalysts for change include

TABLE C.3. Formal Talent Management Plan Budgets, Ranked by Budget Size (n=31; some multiple responses)

Budget	Percentage	Responses
<$100,000	22.9	8
N/A	22.9	8
$100,000–$499,999	17.1	6
$2 million–$5 million	11.4	4
$500,000–$999,999	8.6	3
$5 million–$10 million	5.7	2
$10 million–$20 million	5.7	2
$1 million–$2 million	2.9	1
$20 million–$50 million	2.9	1
> $50 million	0.0	0

TABLE C.4. Factors That Lead the Organization to Implement a Formal or Informal Talent Management Program (n=42; some multiple responses)

Factor	Percentage	Responses
Need for alignment of employee goals with business goals	28.3	26
Need for improved productivity	19.6	18
CEO/top executive succession	16.3	15
Globalization	10.9	10
Other	10.9	10
Turnover rates	8.7	8
Labor cost efficiency	4.3	4
Effects of downturn in economy	1.1	1

globalization, unacceptable employee turnover rates, labor cost efficiency, and the recent downturn in the economy.

DESIGN AND IMPLEMENTATION

Go as far as you can see; when you get there, you'll be able to see farther.

—J.P. MORGAN

Once the challenge has been diagnosed and assessed, what should be the treatment? What goals should be set? What results can reasonably be expected?

The initial stages of program design most often follow from the diagnosis. When Bank of America determined that too many external hires—including executives inherited from acquired banks—were not in tune with the bank's corporate philosophy, the bank created an executive on-boarding program targeted primarily, but not exclusively, at external hires. In Microsoft's SMSG division with its 45,000 employees, there was a high-potential development program in each of its thirteen geographical areas. The programs were not aligned to Microsoft's Leadership Career Model, and there were no consistent criteria for defining high-potentials, making internal movement and promotion cumbersome. Microsoft SMSG focused its efforts internally, on aligning executive capabilities and assessments with one unified set of standards.

One-third of our survey respondents reported that their talent management programs—both formal and informal—are dedicated to developing talent internally (Table C.5). Another third (31.4 percent) target both internal and external hires on a

TABLE C.5. Focus of Both Formal and Informal Programs Designed to Augment Talent Capability of the Organization, Ranked by Responses (n=42)

Program Focus	Percentage	Responses
Develop talent internally	33.3	17
A combination of internal/external driven by case-by-case economic analysis	31.4	16
A combination of internal/external driven by historical practice	11.8	6
Executive mandate	11.8	6
Other	7.8	4
Acquiring external talent	3.9	2

case-by-case economic analysis basis, while 11.8 percent target internal and external hires as dictated by historical practice. The same number cited executive mandate, while only 3.9 percent reported that the talent management program is constructed only for external hires. Clearly, for the companies we surveyed, getting their own house in order is priority number one.

Strategies for internal development can take many forms (Table C.6). Development planning and stretch assignments/projects, neither of which necessarily require dedicated cash budgets, top the list. Formal classroom training follows, along with career planning, mentoring programs, and structured on-the-job training, all of which require some cash outlay. With forty-two respondents providing a total of 347 responses, it is clear that organizations are using multiple approaches, both formal and informal, when designing and implementing talent management programs.

TABLE C.6. Formal and Informal Strategies Designed to Develop Talent Internally, Ranked by Responses (n=42; multiple responses)

Internal Development Program	Percentage	Responses
Development planning	11.5	40
Stretch assignments/projects	11.0	38
Formal classroom training	9.5	33
Career planning	8.6	30
Mentoring programs	8.4	29
Structured on-the-job training	8.1	28
Workforce planning	7.8	27
Competency modeling	7.2	25
Knowledge management/shared methodology	6.6	23
Access to self-paced opt-in training	6.3	22
Job rotations	5.2	18
Proactive redeployment	4.3	15
Access to structured peer learning activities/tools (social networking)	4.3	15
Other	1.2	4

For those companies that are targeting external hires for talent management (Table C.7), the top strategies are internship programs, Internet-based employment marketing, corporate career sites, professional event recruiting, and on-campus college recruiting. In a development that does not bode well for our nation's daily and weekly newspapers, the traditional recruitment tool—print-based employment advertising—ranks dead last.

How do companies define organizational competency (Table C.8)? Perhaps surprisingly, over half (54.8 percent) create organizational competency models wholly in-house. However, only a small percentage (4.8 percent) report that they have no organizational competency model—demonstrating that most companies need a goal to strive for.

TABLE C.7. Formal and Informal Strategies Designed to Acquire External Talent, Ranked by Responses (n=42; multiple responses)

External Acquisition Program	Percentage	Responses
Internship program	8.7	27
Internet-based employment marketing	8.7	27
Corporate career site	8.4	26
Professional event recruiting	8.1	25
On-campus college recruiting	8.1	25
Social networking	7.4	23
Direct sourcing (talent mining)	7.1	22
Employment brand management	6.8	21
Incentives for current employees to recruit contacts	6.8	21
Employee/stakeholder referral programs	6.1	19
Niche job board advertising	5.8	18
Major job board advertising	5.2	16
Remote college recruiting (virtual job fairs, social networking)	4.5	14
Contingent workforce management	4.2	13
Print-based employment advertising	3.9	12
Other	0	0

TABLE C.8. **Method for Development of Organizational Competency Model**

Method	Percentage	Responses
Created it from scratch within organization	54.8	23
Purchased and modified	28.6	12
Other	9.5	4
Do not have an organizational competency model	4.8	2
Purchased off-the-shelf	2.4	1

The identification and grooming of high-potential leaders grows out of the perceived attributes of past and present leaders (Table C.9). Perhaps surprisingly, "technical" abilities including project management, innovation, and sales skills are not at the top of the list of most important competencies, attitudes, and behaviors of organizational leaders. The number one attribute is emotional intelligence, followed by strategic planning, ethics, and customer centricity.

Is software useful to companies that are designing talent management programs (Table C.10)? Apparently not—62 percent report that they don't use it. But of those that do use it or have tried it (Table C.11), over half (56.75 percent) reported that it was "extremely valuable" or "valuable." This may suggest that companies have a bias against talent management software; perhaps they believe that it costs too much or is too complicated, and assume that it won't be worthwhile.

ON-THE-JOB SUPPORT

Always bear in mind that your own resolution to succeed is more important than any other.

—Abraham Lincoln

Talent management is an ongoing process; while there must be measurable goals, these goals are attained over time in an environment that is in flux. For maximum effectiveness, a program must be not just a gateway but also a pipeline, entered by the employee when hired and exited only upon retirement.

Among the organizations with both formal and informal talent management programs, a wide variety of technologies are used to develop and monitor talent management practices (Table C.12). While employee learning management software came in

TABLE C.9. **Most Important Competencies, Attitudes, and Behaviors for the Organization's Leaders (n=42; multiple responses)**

Most Important Competencies, Attitudes, and Behaviors	Percentage	Responses
Emotional intelligence	10.3	29
Strategic planning	9.9	28
Ethics	9.9	28
Customer centricity	8.5	24
Managing people	8.2	23
Innovation	7.4	21
Decision making	7.1	20
Self-aware	6.7	19
Project management	5.3	15
Effective use of communication tools	5.3	15
Consultative skills	4.6	13
Diversity	3.9	11
Negotiation	3.2	9
Other	2.8	8
Sales skills	2.5	7
Crisis management	2.1	6
Consensus building	2.1	6

TABLE C.10. **Use of Software Specifically Designed for Talent Management (n=42)**

Yes/No	Percentage	Responses
No	62	26
Yes	38	16

TABLE C.11. **Value of Software Used in the Talent Management Process. Ranked by Likert Scale: 1 = Not Valuable at All, 4 = Extremely Valuable (n=37)**

Rating	Percentage	Responses
3 = Valuable	43.24	16
2 = Slightly valuable	24.32	9
1 = Not valuable at all	18.92	7
4 = Extremely valuable	13.51	5

TABLE C.12. **Technologies Used to Develop and Monitor the Organization's Talent Management Practices (n=42; multiple responses)**

Technology	Internal/External	Percentage	Score
Employee learning management software	Externally developed	37.00	1.48/4
Asynchronous (on-demand) online learning	Internally developed	35.50	1.42/4
Synchronous web-based training (webinars)	Internally developed	34.00	1.36/4
360-degree feedback program	Internally developed	33.75	1.35/4
Multi-rater feedback tool	Internally developed	32.25	1.29/4
Satellite broadcasts	Externally monitored	22.00	0.88/4
Mobile learning (podcasts, PDA/cell phone)	N/A	20.25	0.81/4
Online communities of practice	Internally developed	19.00	0.76/4

first place with 37 percent response, other strategies were cited nearly as often, including asynchronous and synchronous web-based training, 360-degree feedback programs, and multi-rater feedback tools. Most solutions are internally developed, with the exception of employee learning management software and satellite broadcasts, which are externally developed and/or monitored.

What elements contribute to talent success within an organization (Table C.13)? Perhaps not surprisingly in the current economic and political climate, only two value proposition elements are rated to be of "critical importance": ethics and executive quality. A host of others, including compensation and benefits, are rated highly, while "soft" issues, including workforce diversity, environmental responsibility, and

TABLE C.13. Perceived/Proven Importance of Employment Value Proposition Elements, Formal and Informal Programs, Ranked by Likert Scale: 1 = No Importance, 5 = Critical Importance (n=51)

5 = Critical importance
Ethics
Executive quality
4
Compensation
Health benefits
Retirement benefits
Vacation benefits
Development opportunity
Career advancement opportunity
Organizational stability
Organizational growth
Market position
Product brand awareness
Social responsibility
Innovation methodology/history
Best employer recognition
Work-life balance programs
Co-worker quality
Manager quality
Flexible work schedules/locations
Transparency in executive decision making and communication

3 = Moderate importance
Meritocracy
Workforce diversity
Environmental responsibility
Organization size
Best employee recognition
Work-life balance programs
Work location
Work environment
Education/tuition benefits

There was no responses for 1 or 2; all propositions were rated of moderate importance or above.

education/tuition benefits, are of moderate importance. None of the value proposition elements was rated as having "no importance."

EVALUATION

Leadership is solving problems. The day soldiers stop bringing you their problems is the day you have stopped leading them. They have either lost confidence that you can help or concluded you do not care. Either case is a failure of leadership.

—COLIN POWELL

Not only must individual employees be evaluated, but the talent management program itself must be monitored for effectiveness. If an entire class of schoolchildren fails, it is a good idea to look first at the teacher. An issue that comes both before and after the development of a talent management program is the identification of those forces that impact talent performance (Table C.14). Human resources professionals must populate a universe of possibilities—both negatives and positives. Among our

TABLE C.14. The Impact on Talent Management in the Organization—Selected Factors (n=52; multiple responses)

Factor	Percentage	Average Score
Loyalty and retention of top talent	80.33	2.41/3
Ability to attract and retain top talent	73.33	2.20/3
Impact of stress and multi-tasking on performance	69.33	2.08/3
Motivating and supervising Gen Y employees	65.33	1.96/3
Negative economic effects (downsizing, reduced benefits)	62.67	1.88/3
Differences in technological ability and desire	60.67	1.82/3
Managing mobile/virtual workers	60.67	1.82/3
Workplace conflict due to generational differences	57.67	1.73/3
Employees in workforce after normal retirement age	57.00	1.71/3
New demands of a more diverse workforce	50.33	1.51/3
Trailing spouse/partner issues	47.00	1.41/3
Workers with learning or psychological issues	45.67	1.37/3
Impact of elder care	45.00	1.35/3

survey respondents, "loyalty and a retention of top talent" is the metric most often cited (Table C.14), followed by a related factor, "ability to attract and retain top talent" (80.33 percent and 73.33 percent, respectively). Negative forces or challenges include the number three factor, "impact of stress and multi-tasking on performance" (69.33 percent), and number four, "motivating and supervising Gen Y employees" (65.33 percent). The talent management universe is filled with positive and negative forces that must be managed, much as a spaceship must travel to its rendezvous while avoiding deadly meteorites.

What metrics do we use to measure organizational success? Sometimes it's quantitative. In our case studies, Avon reported a rise in revenue to $11 billion in 2009 from $8 billion in 2005 despite 10 percent fewer Associates. Porter Novelli experienced a decline in turnover of 24 percent from 2005 to 2006. The survey ranks multi-rater feedback as number one (15.4 percent), followed by worker retention, MBO-type performance evaluation, and growth (Table C.15). Net profit and return on investment—shareholder metrics—are lower on the list, suggesting that talent management requires a long-term approach and that success may not manifest itself in a quarterly earnings report.

TABLE C.15. **How the Organization Measures the Performance of Its Top Talent (n=51; multiple responses)**

Measurement Metric	Percentage	Responses
Multi-rater feedback	15.4	26
Worker retention	13.6	23
MBO-type performance evaluation	11.8	20
Growth	11.2	19
Objective measures of productivity	11.2	19
Net profit	8.3	14
Customer retention	7.7	13
Return on investment	6.5	11
Group productivity	5.9	10
Third-party observation	5.3	9
Other	3.0	5

In Table C.14 we saw a few of the negative forces that may impact talent management, including workers with psychological issues and elder care. The survey specifically asked about obstacles that may inhibit a talent management program (Table C.16). Lack of time is number one (19.2 percent), followed by a host of managerial weaknesses: managers ignoring chronic underperformance; managers not committed to developing their employees; managers who fail to separate the talent wheat from the chaff (17.1 percent, 12.3 percent, and 11.0 percent, respectively). These responses serve as a reminder that in a SWOT analysis, sometimes a company's own managers should be placed in the "weaknesses" column!

SUMMARY

Necessity . . . is the mother of invention.

—Plato, *The Republic*

In our journey through the necessities of talent management, we have seen both a commonality of invention and a nearly limitless ability of organizations to create solutions that are uniquely adapted to the crisis at hand. Whether the challenge is external,

TABLE C.16. **Obstacles That Prevent the Organization's Talent Management Program from Delivering Business Value (n=51; multiple responses)**

Obstacle	Percentage	Responses
Lack of time to do everything planned	19.2	28
Managers ignore chronic underperformance	17.1	25
Managers are not committed to developing people	12.3	18
Managers do not differentiate between high, low performers	11.0	16
Senior management does not devote enough time on program	11.0	16
Talent management and business strategies are not aligned	8.9	13
Lack of funds	8.9	13
Resource sharing is discouraged	6.2	9
Other	5.5	8

such as a culture gap with new hires or a cumbersome on-boarding system, or internal, such as employee evaluations that don't work or a wave of impending retirements, successful organizations quickly and confidently forge ahead with the six time-tested phases of talent development:

1. Business diagnosis
2. Assessment
3. Program design
4. Implementation
5. On-the-job support
6. Evaluation

With a clear plan, the fourteen companies in our case studies objectively diagnosed and assessed the challenges before them, designed and implemented effective programs, provided support, and integrated change into the fabric of each organization. In this way organic growth supplanted haphazard acquisitions and/or uncontrolled expansion, and provided a measure of security in a market environment that is unforgiving to those who are not at the peak of efficiency and productivity. Louis Carter, his co-editor Marshall Goldsmith, and the Best Practice Institute look forward to partnering with the world's most dynamic organizations to discover, implement, and promote the very best in organizational and talent development.

Best Practice Institute offers organizations a learning community of leaders dedicated to pioneering and sharing the best practices of all areas of organization development, including talent development. To help companies large and small to meet their goals, Best Practice Institute produces a wide variety of services including online learning sessions, webinars, benchmarking research groups, thought leader and executive case-driven presentations, research publications, and a knowledge portal for its subscribers. Best Practice Institute's subscriber base includes over 50,000 managers, coaches, directors, vice presidents, senior vice presidents, and C-levels of leading Fortune 500/Global 1000 organizations. BPI's faculty includes over two hundred experts and world-renowned thought leaders who are professors or chairs of departments at Ivy League schools, and/or have contributed original research, innovative publications, and practice to the field of management and leadership.

The Best Practice Institute Senior Executive Board is a by-invitation-only group of senior executives who develop actionable plans for their organizations' best practice programs. Executives at the same level come together from various industries to present their plans for designing, implementing, and evaluating their best practice initiatives for the year. Experts interact with these key decision-makers to ensure that they are implementing the best course of action for their practice areas. The objective of the Senior Leadership Lab is to learn from your peers how to plan, organize, and execute in this area.

EPILOGUE

WILLIAM J. ROTHWELL

The chapters in this volume represent truly outstanding examples of talent management programs from diverse economic sectors. They are instructive whether the reader is just starting out to build a program, is trying to enhance an existing program, is a graduate student doing research on talent management programs, or is an old hand with talent management programs. This chapter summarizes what should be regarded as key "take away points" for what is outstanding about these programs. It also lists some thoughts on next generation talent management—that is, what talent management programs of the future should include. This chapter thus emphasizes some thoughts on evaluating talent management programs for what's good—and for what are necessary next steps.

KEY "TAKE-AWAY POINTS"

Each case in this volume deserves special attention for what the company described in the case did particularly well. Each case is briefly summarized below for some, but not necessarily all, of its uniquely strong features.

The Avon Products Case

This case is outstanding for illustrating the practical implications of building the talent practice around "executing on the what" as well as "differentiating on the how." That means "simple, well-executed talent practices dominated at companies that consistently produced great earning and great leaders" but applied Marshall Goldsmith's executive coaching model to practice. Also of special note was Figure 1.2 in the case, which takes the well-known potential and performance grid and makes it more robust.

The Bank of America Case

This case is outstanding for summarizing a truly exceptional executive on-boarding process. The results are impressive: "the Bank of America hired 196 externally hired executives between 2001 and May 2008 and had experienced twenty-four terminations—a new hire turnover rate of approximately 12 percent. This compares to estimates as high as 40 percent turnover in large corporations." Of note is that on-boarding begins in the selection process and includes an entry phase, a mid-point phase (100 to 130 days), and a final phase (one year to one-and-a-half years). On-boarding is thus understood, quite properly, as a socialization process rather than as an orientation program.

The Corning Case

This case is outstanding for basing a talent program on the collective wisdom of internal experts rather than relying solely on external consultants. The goal of the Corning program is to grow "innovation leaders," critical to a business like Corning's. A strategic model (depicted in Figure 3.2 of the case) is of particular note, indicating that a project/program manager is developing around a five-step project process: (1) build knowledge; (2) determine feasibility; (3) test practicality; (4) prove profitability; and (5) manage the life cycle.

The CES Case

This case, about one division of a Fortune 100 company, is outstanding for its application of whole system transformational change theory to talent management. That theory helps organizations overcome the troubling inertia, and lack of necessary commitment and infrastructure, that plagues so many talent management programs. Leaders set the tone by "walking the walk" as well as "talking the talk" of talent management.

The Ecolab Case

This case is outstanding for illustrating how a talent program can be built on, and leverage, the organization's corporate culture and values. Those values include, according to the case: (1) spirit; (2) pride; (3) determination; (4) commitment; (5) passion; and (6) integrity. The talent program was based on internal interviews of company executives.

The General Electric Case

This case is outstanding for describing the application of so-called "lean manufacturing," as pioneered by Toyota®, to address and solve specific talent problems. The process applied a 5S model that consisted of sorting (separating necessary from unnecessary items), setting in order (arranging items in sequence of use), shining (maintaining the work area), standardizing (ensuring consistent application of sorting, setting in order, and standardizing), and sustaining (maintaining and improving the previous four steps). Many HR issues in other organizations lend themselves to the lessons of this case (see Rothwell, Prescott, & Taylor, 2008).

The Internal Revenue Service Case

This case is outstanding for its focus on the public sector. The IRS has developed a robust approach to talent management based on a concrete vision of the organization's future and the leadership competencies essential to make that vision a reality. Competencies are used to define leadership operationally.

The Kaiser Permanente Colorado Region Case

This case is outstanding for its practical approach for addressing a not-uncommon problem of an organization that was too reliant on external hires due to insufficient attention devoted to internal development. The organization uses a systematic leadership development process, as shown in Figure 8.3 of the case. That model integrates diversity, orientation, 360-degree assessment, experience management, peer learning, executive coaching, individual development planning, and recommended participation in external programs. Also of note in this case is the model of potential (see Figure 8.4 of the case).

The McDonald's Case

This case is outstanding for many reasons. They are difficult to reduce to just a few. But here is a quick summary of the best points:

- The program is global in scope and helps to build cross-cultural awareness among participants.

- The talent review template is simple yet profound (see Exhibit 9.4 of the case), focusing on (1) a forecast of corporate leadership talent requirements for the next three years, including positions, people and/or competencies; (2) assessing and developing the current talent pool; (3) meeting replacement needs and diversity gaps; and (4) recommending specific developmental actions.

- The LAMP program is a sophisticated, state-of-the-art program that is designed to build talent through accelerated group experiences (see Exhibit 9.5).

The Microsoft Case

This case is outstanding for its application of research conducted by the Corporate Leadership Council (CLC). Microsoft has chosen to organize its talent management effort around five key areas that, according to CLC research, have the most significant impact on high-potential (HiPo) development. Those are (1) demonstrating senior leadership commitment to developing leaders; (2) the manager's continuing engagement in HiPo development; (3) creating a network of professional contacts that encourages contacts throughout the organization; (4) stretch development plans with clear goals; and (5) targeted on-the-job work experiences designed to build competencies.

The Murray & Roberts Limited Case

This case is outstanding as a representative of how talent management is addressed outside the U.S. context. The company is a leading South African firm. Of note in this case is that the talent program is designed around a simple, although robust, four-step model: (1) destination (building a compelling business goal and clear philosophy); (2) accountability (creating a tailored leadership pipeline and performance standards); (3) foundation (user-friendly performance management and development); and (4) driving mechanism (best practice leadership and development review). The clarity of this model represents a difficult-to-attain elegant simplicity on which to build the talent program.

The Porter Novelli Case

This case is outstanding for its way of relating individual employee engagement to talent management. According to the case author, four fundamental questions must be answered for each employee in any talent program: (1) What *specifically* do you expect of me? (2) How will you define success (and measure me)? (3) What's in it for me if I deliver the results you expect? and (4) Will you provide me the resources I need/eliminate the barriers I face to achieve these results?

The Southern Company Case

This case is outstanding for its differentiation of various levels of leadership—individual contributor, first-line manager, manager of managers, functional manager, multi-functional manager, and CEO—and describing how performance standards were established for each level. The standards were set based on business, management, leadership, relationships, community/external involvement, and customer expectations.

The Whirlpool Corporation Case

This case is outstanding for the clear statement of organizational goals on which the program was based. (A lack of clear, agreed-upon goals is a common source of failure for talent management programs.) The organization defined the purpose of the program as a means to the end of "(1) defining the leadership needed to continue the organization's success; (2) assessing the company's current leadership competencies and defining gaps; (3) developing internal leadership competencies; (4) assessing future leaders against these competencies; (5) providing a consistent set of tools, resources, and a process to manage global talent; and (6) deeply embed the competencies and operationalize the supporting tools and resources."

THOUGHTS ON NEXT-GENERATION TALENT PROGRAMS

While outstanding, these cases are as instructive for what they include as well as what they leave out—so-called "next generation talent management" (Rothwell, 2008a).

Here are a few thoughts on what to look for in the future.

First, organizational leaders must be able to find their talent faster. Speed leads to competitive advantage. How do organizations find their in-house experts (otherwise known as high professionals or HiPros) when the organization faces a crisis? In small organizations the leaders may know everyone. But that is not possible in medium-sized to larger organizations. Hence, one challenge for leaders of the future is to pinpoint their most talented people based on their competencies and special expertise in practical ways so that they can be located quickly when crisis requires that. There is thus a need for competency inventories so that organizational leaders can find people based on their business-specific abilities rather than previous skill inventories based on less useful-to-directly-equate-to-practical-experience degrees, job titles, or language fluency. Such competency inventories may also be extended to an organization's retirees (Rothwell, 2008b).

Second, talent management must go beyond thinking about "potential"—a term that usually equates to "promotability." While potential is important, it is not enough. Additional issues should also be considered. One is that potential can mean more than promotability, but could include capacity to grow in technical ability in a dual career system in which promotion can occur by vertical promotion (up the organization chart) and by horizontal promotion (across a continuum of expertise at the same level) resulting from greater command of technical expertise.

Third, in light of recent scandals on Wall Street in which executives were financially rewarded with lavish bonuses for "performance" by leading their organizations into bankruptcy, ethics must be given more than lip service when considering potential. While many organizations have "codes of conduct" that provide some guidance, those codes are often written by lawyers without regard to more than merely meeting the letter of the law. In public perceptions, and in the popular press, the mere appearance of wrongdoing is as bad as actual wrongdoing. Consequently, talent management programs of the future will have to regard behaviorally based individual assessments of adherence to ethical standards in actual ethical dilemmas encountered by leaders in these organizations. Ethics should be objectively measured first before any potential measurement is done. Ethics should come first before assessments of an individual's ability to do the work at higher levels of responsibility.

Most troubling is that few companies have any objectively measurable ways to compare individuals to the competency and behavioral requirements at the next level up. Talent management programs of the future must separate assessments of performance at the current level of responsibility from assessments of potential to perform at higher levels. If that is not done, organizational leaders are playing to the well-known *Peter Principle*, which takes its name from the 1965 book. According to the Peter Principle, organizational leaders reward individuals with promotion. As long as individuals meet the requirements at higher levels of responsibility, they are promoted. But once they fail, they are plateaued at their current levels. The result: individuals are promoted to one level above their highest level of competence, and thus organizations are filled with people who are actually incompetent to be where they are. To avoid that problem, organizational leaders must realize that performance management is not enough; rather, a separate, objective potential assessment must be conducted to compare individuals to the competency requirements at higher levels of responsibility.

Finally, talent management programs can focus on more than mere promotability. Two other issues could also be a focus of attention.

One is the so-called *knowledge transfer problem* in which experienced workers should be able to transfer some of what they know to their successors. Research suggests that only 40 percent of U.S. firms even attempt to ask workers to transfer some of what they know to others (see Rothwell & Poduch, 2004). The result: many successors have to "reinvent the wheel" by re-learning lessons of experience gained by their predecessors. That problem must be avoided by including practical knowledge transfer strategies in talent management (Rothwell, 2004). That is particularly important for workers whose special technical knowledge may be key to competitive success, which may be true in firms that rely on technical knowledge for competitive advantage.

The second is the so-called *social relationship transfer problem* (Rothwell, 2007). Experienced workers have built vast social networks of important relationships with people who help them obtain results. That may include friendships with people inside key customer organizations, suppliers, distributors, government regulators, and members of the press. When these experienced workers leave the organization, their social relationships are at risk of loss to the organization. That problem must be avoided by including social relationship transfer strategies in talent management. That is particularly important for workers whose social relationships may be key to competitive success—such as in firms that emphasize marketing, sales, public relations, and governmental relations.

CONCLUSION AND SUMMARY

The future is bright for those who devote their time and attention to talent management. People have become key to competitive advantage. It is talent that sets competitive winners apart from the losers. But finding, developing, keeping, and positioning talented people represent challenges of the future for businesses, government agencies, and nonprofit entities.

REFERENCES

Peter, L.J., & Hull, R. (1969). *The Peter principle*. New York: William Morrow.

Rothwell, W. (2004). Knowledge transfer: 12 strategies for succession management. *IPMA-HR News*, pp. 10–12.

Rothwell, W. (2007). Social relationship succession planning: A neglected but important issue? *Asian Quality, 2*(4), 34–36.

Rothwell, W. (2008a). Next generation talent management. *HRM Review, 8*(10), 10–16.

Rothwell, W. (2008b). Tapping the retiree workforce to meet talent needs. *Asian Quality, 3*(3), 66.

Rothwell, W., & Poduch, S. (2004). Introducing technical (not managerial) succession planning. *Public Personnel Management, 33*(4), 405–420.

Rothwell, W., Prescott, R., & Taylor, M. (2008). *Human resource transformation: Demonstrating strategic leadership in the face of future trends*. San Francisco: Davies-Black.

William J. Rothwell, Ph.D., SPHR, is president of Rothwell & Associates, Inc., a full-service consulting firm that specializes in talent management, succession planning, and competency modeling. He is also a professor of workforce education and development on the University Park campus of The Pennsylvania State University, and in that capacity he heads up a top-ranked graduate program in Workplace Learning and Performance. An investigator for the last three ASTD-sponsored international competency studies of the learning and performance field, he is perhaps best known for his many books on talent management, competency modeling, and succession planning. Among his sixty-five books and three hundred articles are *Effective Succession Planning: Ensuring Leadership Continuity and Building Talent from Within* (3rd ed.) (AMACOM, 2005), *Practicing Organization Development: A Guide for Consultants* (2nd ed.) (Pfeiffer, 2005), *Career Planning and Succession Management* (Greenwood/Praeger, 2005), *Next Generation Management Development* (Pfeiffer, 2007), *HR Transformation: Demonstrating Strategic Leadership in the Face of Future Trends* (Davies-Black, 2008), *Working Longer: New Strategies for Managing, Training, and Retaining Older Employees* (AMACOM, 2008), and *Cases in Government Succession Planning: Action-Oriented Strategies for Public-Sector Human Capital Management, Workforce Planning, Succession Planning, and Talent Management* (HRD Press, 2008).

INDEX

Page references followed by *fig* indicate an illustrated figure; followed by *t* indicate a table.

ABOUT BEST PRACTICE INSTITUTE

 Best Practice Institute, Inc. (http://www.bestpracticeinstitute .org) is a leadership association that assists executives in transforming themselves and their organizations. Best Practice Institute produces custom and public research, exclusive research groups, thought leader-led online learning sessions, and an online expert and member system.

Best Practice Institute's subscriber base includes over 50,000 managers, coaches, directors, VPs, SVPs, and C-levels of branded, "household-name" Fortune 500/Global 1000 organizations worldwide. Best Practice Institute's faculty includes over three hundred experts and thought leaders. Many Best Practice Institute faculty members teach as professors or chairs of departments at Ivy League schools and/or have contributed a wide body of original research, innovative publications, and practice to the field of management and leadership.

If you would like to connect with any expert, practitioner, or author in this book, please e-mail through our website us at http://bestpracticeinstitute.org/contact.html. All contributors/authors in this book are listed/known experts within the Best Practice Institute community.

For more information on the Best Practice Institute, visit us online at https://www.bpiworld.com and https://www.bestpracticeinstitute.org or contact us at http://bestpracticeinstitute.org/or contact us at (800) 718-4274.

ABOUT THE EDITORS

Louis Carter (lou@bestpracticeinstitute.org) founded Best Practice Institute on the principles of organization development and positive change. Mr. Carter has written eight books on best practices and organizational leadership, including the *Change Champions* and *Best Practice* book series published by Jossey Bass/John Wiley & Sons. As an expert in the industry, he has been interviewed, profiled, and quoted by such publications as *Business Watch* magazine, *Workforce* magazine, *Investor's Business Daily*, and *CIO* magazine. He founded BPI after obtaining his graduate degree from Columbia University in social/organizational psychology and an undergraduate degree in economics and government from Brown University and Connecticut College. At Columbia, Mr. Carter obtained honors from Kappa Delta Pi, an organization promoting excellence in, and recognizing outstanding contributions to, the field of education. Mr. Carter's books, research, and teaching have been translated into eight languages across Asia, the Middle East, Europe, and North and South America. He has taught at major universities, including Tsinghua School of Business in Beijing, Jackson State University, Seton Hall University, and at Fortune 500 conferences throughout the globe.

He can be reached through http://www.bestpracticeinstitute.org or http://www.bpiworld.com.

Dr. Marshall Goldsmith is a world authority in helping successful leaders become even better—by achieving positive, lasting change in behavior: for themselves, their people, and their teams. His book *What Got You Here Won't Get You There* is a *New York Times* best seller, *Wall Street Journal* number one business book, and winner of the Harold Longman award for Best Business Book of the Year. It has been translated into twenty-three languages and is a listed best seller in six different countries.

The American Management Association named Dr. Goldsmith as one of fifty great thinkers and leaders who have influenced the field of management over the past eighty years. Major business press acknowledgments include: *BusinessWeek*—most influential practitioners in the history of leadership development; *The Times* (UK)—fifty greatest living business thinkers; *The Wall Street Journal*—top ten executive educators; *Forbes*—five most-respected executive coaches; *Leadership Excellence*—top five thinkers on leadership; *Economic Times* (India)—five rajgurus of America; *Economist* (UK)—most credible executive advisors in the new era of business; and *Fast Company*—America's preeminent executive coach.